Empire Girls

This book is available as a free fully-searchable ebook from
www.adelaide.edu.au/press

Empire Girls

the colonial heroine comes of age

Mandy Treagus

Discipline of English and Creative Writing

The University of Adelaide

UNIVERSITY OF
ADELAIDE PRESS

Published in Adelaide by

University of Adelaide Press
The University of Adelaide
Level 1, 254 North Terrace
South Australia 5005
press@adelaide.edu.au
www.adelaide.edu.au/press

The University of Adelaide Press publishes externally refereed scholarly books by staff of the University of Adelaide. It aims to maximise access to the University's best research by publishing works through the internet as free downloads and for sale as high quality printed volumes.

© 2014 Mandy Treagus

This work is licenced under the Creative Commons Attribution-NonCommercial-NoDerivatives 4.0 International (CC BY-NC-ND 4.0) License. To view a copy of this licence, visit http://creativecommons.org/licenses/by-nc-nd/4.0 or send a letter to Creative Commons, 444 Castro Street, Suite 900, Mountain View, California, 94041, USA. This licence allows for the copying, distribution, display and performance of this work for non-commercial purposes providing the work is clearly attributed to the copyright holders. Address all inquiries to the Director at the above address.

For the full Cataloguing-in-Publication data please contact the National Library of Australia: cip@nla.gov.au

ISBN (paperback) 978-1-922064-54-7
ISBN (ebook: pdf) 978-1-922064-55-4
ISBN (ebook: epub) 978-1-922064-69-1
ISBN (ebook: mobi) 978-1-922064-70-7

Editor: Patrick Allington
Book design: Zoë Stokes
Cover design: Emma Spoehr
Cover images: iStockphoto

Contents

Acknowledgements	vii
1 Introduction	
1.1 Ambivalence and the Other: discursive conflicts in white women's writing from the Second World	1
1.2 *Bildungsroman* and the heroine: patriarchy and the conventions of form	13
2 Olive Schreiner *The Story of an African Farm*	
2.1 Introduction	27
2.2 Waldo's tale: work and the deconstruction of the *Bildungsroman* economy	35
2.3 Lyndall's tale: the feminist as romantic	64
2.4 Gendered ends: death and the collapse of meaning in the colonial world	100
3 Sara Jeannette Duncan *A Daughter of Today*	
3.1 Introduction	109
3.2 The heroine as artist: *Künstlerroman* and the New Woman	117
3.3 Death as Denouement: discursive conflict and narrative resolution	158

4　Henry Handel Richardson *The Getting of Wisdom*

    4.1　Introduction   173

    4.2　Child to woman: gender enculturation in the Empire   186

    4.3　Imperialism, the boarding school and the emerging nation   204

    4.4　Narrative possibilities: *Bildungsroman, Künstlerroman* and denouement   217

5　Conclusion: From heroine to hero   243

Works Cited   251

Acknowledgements

I thank Susan Hosking and Phil Butterss, who have been great mentors and friends, and Carolyn Lake, who provided invaluable research assistance in the later stages of this project. Librarians from a number of libraries have been most helpful, especially those from the Australian National Library, Canberra; the Barr Smith Library, University of Adelaide; the State Library of South Australia, Adelaide; Flinders University Library, Adelaide; the Fisher Library, Sydney University; the Mitchell Library, Sydney, and Macquarie University Library. Two anonymous reviewers offered useful comments and appreciated encouragement, while Patrick Allington, and all at the University of Adelaide Press, have been a pleasure to work with. Aileen Treagus has been supportive in ways too numerous to mention. The following cats have put in long hours over the years around the computer: Maz, either at my feet or on my lap; Tohi, who thought she could help with the typing, and Ali'i, who was prepared to sit alongside me in the final stages.

1

Introduction

1.1 Ambivalence and the Other: discursive conflicts in white women's writing from the Second World

This book concerns the *Bildungsroman*, a form of the novel so dominant that it is rarely examined explicitly. The form is generally understood as one that outlines the growth of an individual from youth into maturity, a growth entailing character development culminating in accommodation between the individual and society. Ultimately, such accommodation results in the mature individual finding a place in his or her world. As M.H. Abrams suggests, 'The subject of these novels is the development of the protagonist's mind and character, in the passage from childhood through varied experiences — and often through a spiritual crisis — into maturity, which usually involves recognition of one's identity and role in the world' (193). The examples of the *Bildungsroman* examined here are very particular though: their writers all come from British colonies and feature female protagonists.

Just as 'the novel stands as the central literary form of the nineteenth century', so the *Bildungsroman* became the dominant form of that novel (Sussman 549), with many of the century's most celebrated titles examples of it. *Jane Eyre*, *David Copperfield* and *Middlemarch* are just a few representatives of the form which, in tracing the development of a protagonist from childhood to full productive citizenship, so captured the nineteenth-century imagination. In many ways, this tale of individual development reflected the sense of national development, and showed the form's 'intimate connection ... with the desires, aspirations and anxieties of its readers' (Sussman 549). If the *Bildungsroman* held such appeal to its British readers, how would this novel form fare when taken out of the metropolitan context? In a form that seems to embody the aspirations of the colonising power, how would colonial protagonists fare? And despite the fact that several of the most famous British *Bildungsromane* of the nineteenth century featured female protagonists, what changes might be required in the *Bildungsroman*'s narrative trajectory if its protagonist were a colonial heroine?

In analysing the *Bildungsroman* in its colonial context, it is imperative to consider the role the form itself has had in maintaining the very structures of Empire and patriarchy that I am seeking to critique. I have chosen three novels written by women writers who came from different corners of the British Empire. All three writers are from invader/settler colonies, and all became deeply involved in the literary culture of Europe, spending at least some portion of their lives there. Olive Schreiner lived in Britain in her twenties and thirties during the 1880s and 1890s, returning from South Africa for the duration of the First World War.[1] Her novel, *The Story of an African Farm* (1883), was published in Britain shortly after her arrival. Sara Jeannette Duncan was raised in Ontario, Canada, travelled the world, and lived in Britain briefly before moving to India to marry. Much of her work, including the book under consideration, *A Daughter of Today* (1894), was written in India but after numerous trips back to England she finally settled there in 1915, remaining until her death in

---

[1] The best source of biographical information regarding Olive Schreiner is to be found in Ruth First and Ann Scott, *Olive Schreiner: A Biography*.

1922.[2] Henry Handel Richardson grew up in Victoria, Australia, and left for Germany to study music at Leipzig at the age of 18.[3] She moved to England in her early thirties and was based in London, where she wrote *The Getting of Wisdom* (1910).

Not only do these novels feature non-English heroines, but they are also written for an English audience from an outsider's perspective. All these works were first published in London, and its literary culture and concerns are an important context for all three books. Duncan and Richardson have rarely been seen in terms of the British literary environment.[4] Because they have been absorbed into their national literatures, the national tends to be the dominant context in which they are seen by scholars steeped in those particular literatures. Duncan is written of primarily as a Canadian writer, Richardson as an Australian. In Richardson's case the influence of Continental thought has been fairly thoroughly explored, but not the English literary context. Schreiner was so influential in Britain that she is often thought of *as* English. The relationship of all three to the London literary world remained ambivalent though, and their status as 'colonials' was a major factor in this. All chose to write novels tracing the development of a young non-English girl whose aspirations brought her into conflict with nineteenth-century conventions regarding the heroine. In my discussion of *African Farm*, I outline the fact that the nineteenth-century *Bildungsroman* in English was essentially meritocratic. Most

---

[2] Biographical information regarding Sara Jeannette Duncan can be found in Thomas Tausky, *Sara Jeannette Duncan: Novelist of Empire*, and in Marion Fowler, *Redney: A Life of Sara Jeannette Duncan*.

[3] Biographical information about Henry Handel Richardson can be found in: her autobiography, *Myself When Young*; Axel Clark's *Henry Handel Richardson: Fiction in the Making* and *Finding Herself in Fiction: Henry Handel Richardson 1896-1910*; Dorothy Green's *Henry Handel Richardson and Her Fiction*, and Michael Ackland's *Henry Handel Richardson: a life*.

[4] Though Axel Clark gives an account of the literary reception in England of both *Maurice Guest* and *The Getting of Wisdom* in *Finding Herself in Fiction*.

narratives demonstrate a denouement in which the worthy are rewarded for their pains and honest aspirations, and the unworthy are disappointed, or even severely punished, for theirs.

The meritocratic drive of the *Bildungsroman*, endlessly repeated throughout the nineteenth century, seemed to be predicated on the existence of Empire, and grounded in England's sense of power and wellbeing due to its position in the world and the prosperity which flowed from that empire. The very fact that such reiteration continued to be compelling and indeed necessary, appears to express a level of doubt in the national consciousness about its actual ability to deliver just outcomes to its populace. On the whole, from the mid-century, the novel was written by, and for, the middle classes, whose livelihoods often depended on the successful functioning of the Empire. That the *Bildungsroman* flourished during this time, becoming the dominant form of the nineteenth century, could be seen to be contingent on colonial expansion. That the rise of both occurred simultaneously may suggest a symbiotic relationship which is not at first apparent. The novel itself rose concurrently with the Empire as a whole, its first expressions occurring when England was just beginning its assault on the globe. Perhaps the novel is *the* high cultural artefact of the Empire, and the *Bildungsroman* the product of late-colonial expansion, expressing both its confidence and its underlying insecurity at the same time.

Though the links between Empire and *Bildungsroman* may seem circumstantial, the presence of Empire is an enabling narrative factor in many of the examples of the genre from the nineteenth century. Gayatri Spivak has demonstrated, famously, how economic benefits from the Empire make possible the self-realisation of *Jane Eyre*, showing that Jane's feminist individuation is predicated on the domination of other women (and men) who are exploited and enslaved in that empire.[5] While

---

5 See Gayatri Spivak, 'Three Women's Texts and a Critique of Imperialism'.

all three novels under examination here demonstrate a level of resistance to Empire, they are complicit, also, in its maintenance. All three authors benefit to some degree from what I call the imperial dividend.[6] They gain a range of benefits which are unavailable to those outside of the Empire, and to those who are more subordinate *within* the Empire, with race underpinning a series of privileges. At the same time this benefit is limited because these writers are 'colonials', and are thereby not seen to exercise the full subjectivity possessed by those from the centre. This is also true of their protagonists, who receive some of the imperial dividend, while also experiencing its exclusions. Gender is a chief factor in these exclusions, as I shall demonstrate. As these writers function both within and outside of discourses of gender and Empire, they always express ambivalence in their work. Indeed, implication in oppressive structures may be a condition of all representation, as Edward Said has suggested: 'representation itself has been characterized as keeping the subordinate subordinate, the inferior inferior' (Said, *Culture and Imperialism* 95).

The white woman writer from a British or ex-British invader/settler colony provides a site at which various and often conflicting discourses meet, creating an ambivalence of voice. While I do not wish to diminish the specificity of this voice, I do want to argue that the condition it reflects — that of ambivalence — is a condition of all postcolonial fiction.[7] My other qualification is that in asserting a common ambivalence for all postcolonial fiction, I do not wish to imply that the experiences of

---

[6] I borrow this term in part from R.W. Connell, whose use of the term 'patriarchal dividend' to describe the benefits for all men living in a patriarchy is both highly apt and very succinct. See her *Masculinities* for examples of its use. I use the term to refer to those benefits which are to be gained just by being part of the British Empire, benefits which come whether one is actively involved in maintaining that empire or not.

[7] While I am aware of the debates around the term 'postcolonial', I have chosen to use it because it is still meaningful in the academy and because another and less problematic term has not come into common usage. For one view of these problematics, see Aijaz Ahmad, *In Theory: Classes, Nations, Literatures*.

different colonised groups can be conflated. The colonialism experienced, for instance, by Duncan as a white woman in an invader/settler colony cannot be compared with the colonisation that an indigenous woman from Canada has experienced and is experiencing.[8] What I am suggesting is that they do share a common element, and this is an ambivalence of voice which is a direct consequence of colonisation. Such ambivalence breaks down the binary oppositions inherent in the colonised/coloniser opposition and avoids the essentialism implied by a critical practice which looks for the postcolonial only in the literatures of the Third and Fourth Worlds and among the indigenous peoples of the Second World. While this ambivalence has always been apparent in Second World literature, it is also the condition of postcolonial fiction in English from the Third and Fourth Worlds. One does not have to go further than the very fact that such fiction is in English, the language of the coloniser, to see this. The assumption that it is possible to find some pure postcolonial space in the Third and Fourth Worlds, or in the literature of indigenous people of the Second World, is an expression of naïve desire which flies in the face of human activity vis-à-vis colonialism in all areas of the world.

As a Tunisian, Albert Memmi critiqued the process of colonisation in his work *The Colonizer and the Colonized* (1956). Looking back on this analysis in the 1960s, Memmi acknowledges, 'Here is a confession I have never made before: I know the colonizer from the inside almost as well as I know the colonized' (xiii). Colonising impulses are not confined to those whose nationality identifies them with colonial powers. When

---

[8] Arun Mukherjee argues passionately against the conflation of 'the experience of white and non-white post-colonials' and I take note of her resistance to 'totalizations of both the post-colonialists and the postmodernists that end up assimilating and homogenizing non-Western texts within a Eurocentric cultural economy' (Mukherjee 2, 1). I am attempting to posit the usefulness of placing Second World fiction within the postcolonial field, without wishing to deny the specificity of different literatures within such a field.

Memmi writes of those French in Tunisia who were 'the model for the portrait of the coloniser of good will', he acknowledges that 'their inevitable ambiguity ... was a part of my own fate' (xv). Through such admissions, Memmi begins to collapse the binary opposition of coloniser/ colonised. Such an opposition leads to the positing of what must be seen as an essentialist position of postcolonial purity, a position which cannot be sustained. In light of this, Stephen Slemon explains why Second World fiction is important in the postcolonial field:

> [T]he *illusion* of a stable self/other, here/there binary division has *never* been available to Second-World writers, and that as a result the sites of figural contestation between oppressor and oppressed, colonizer and colonized, have been taken *inward* and *internalized* in Second-World post-colonial textual practice. By this I mean that the *ambivalence* of literary resistance itself is the 'always already' condition of Second-World settler and post-colonial literary writing, for in the white literatures of Australia, or New Zealand, or Canada, or southern Africa, anti-colonialist resistance has *never* been directed at an object or a discursive structure which can be seen as purely external to the self. (38, emphases in original)

This ambivalence is apparent in the fictions of Schreiner, Duncan and Richardson as white women writers, in relation to the discourses of both colonialism and femininity. While they resist their own conditions as those colonised through both gender and nationality, they also participate in colonisation through their nationality and race and because of their partial investment in discourses of femininity. Ambivalence is apparent in their negotiations of the *Bildungsroman* form, for while it is employed, part of the purpose in this appears to be to examine its efficacy as a means of conveying stories of the colonial girl and her growth. The form is interrogated at every turn. This is done most strongly in the fiction of Schreiner who appears ultimately to abandon it, but also by Duncan who resolves the narrative dilemmas it raises in the death of her heroine. Richardson negotiates the form by blowing open the usual denouement in order to give her heroine the space in which to keep developing.

One of the mechanisms which makes possible both colonialism and patriarchy is the practice of Othering. Theory about this mechanism has at least a sixty-year history and has its roots in the philosophical writings of Emmanuel Levinas. Though the concept of the Other might seem to have had more application in the area of race and colonial discourse analyses, its origins are in theorising gender difference. When Levinas wanted to create a picture of the Other, he turned to the feminine, because, as he asserts, 'alterity is accomplished in the feminine' (50). In his 1947 work *Time and the Other*, Levinas proposes that it is the mystery of the feminine that gives it this quality: 'Alterity makes for all its power. Its mystery constitutes its alterity' (49). Levinas had an immediate response from Simone de Beauvoir, who wrote in her introduction to *The Second Sex* in 1949 that one of her intentions was to explore 'why woman has been defined as the Other' (28). She saw the differences between men and woman as socially constructed, and complained that Levinas' description of the feminine, 'which is intended to be objective, is in fact an assertion of masculine privilege' (de Beauvoir 16).

It is easy to see how the term 'the Other' can be applied to any person or group that seems to embody qualities which are not immediately accessible to the viewing subject and which also seem mysterious. Of greater consequence than the application of the term is the psychological mechanism which denies full subjectivity to those who appear to embody difference. This is, at heart, the process of Othering. Levinas assumes that this is an ontological given, or at the very least a consistently occurring phenomenon: 'It can be said that intersubjective space is not symmetrical' (48). In other words, relationships tend to fall into hierarchies. However, this is not usually a benign phenomenon. Othering encompasses any practice of ascribing difference with the view to creating or fixing unequal power relations. In the creation and maintenance of the systems of patriarchy and Empire the tendency of individual subjects to Other is one of the chief mechanisms by which full subjectivity is denied to women, children and those of other races, classes, customs and nationalities. Obviously many of these categories can intersect, resulting in multiple Otherings, and multiple exclusions and oppressions. In what has become known as Intersectionality (since Kimberlé Crenshaw's germinal piece in 1991), multiple Otherings create their own dynamics of oppression above and beyond individual factors like gender or race (Crenshaw 1241-1299). The practice of Othering functions as a basic technology of racism, misogyny and colonialism. Some of the effects of this technology are outlined in the texts under examination, which reflect the particular colonial and patriarchal moments from which they emerged. The 'differences' on which these practices of Othering are built are maintained rigorously by the hegemonic power, because they are crucial strategies in the continuance of that hegemony. Homi Bhabha outlines how the stereotype has functioned to sustain a belief in the difference of the Other, and also how such stereotypes have had a subversive potential.[9] In this way, imperialism and patriarchy are imbricated, not only because they occur together but also because the technologies by which they are maintained have a common base.

The most obvious example of the application of theories of Othering to the field of postcolonial studies has been seen in Edward Said's concept of Orientalism. However, this is not its only application. Sara Mills discusses the various ways in which the tendencies outlined by Said have been uncovered in many and varied colonial writings, not merely those which deal with the 'Orient' (87). While Mills expands

---

9 See his 'Difference, Discrimination and the Discourse of Colonialism' and 'The Other Question ... Homi Bhabha Reconsiders the Stereotype and Colonial Discourse'.

Said's definition of Othering, she confines her use of the term to issues pertaining to colonialism. I wish to broaden it to encompass any practice which concentrates on or creates alterity for the purposes of negative discrimination. Such practices can be found in the rhetoric of the oppressed, as well as in those of the oppressor. Accordingly, Memmi notes how those resisting colonialism used similar strategies to colonialism itself, practices which, on reflection, he found disturbing: 'While I was virtuously busy debunking the myths of colonization, could I complacently approve of the counter-myths fabricated by the colonized?' (xv). Beginning with de Beauvoir, feminists have described the process by which patriarchy has constructed 'woman' as Other. These same mechanisms are at work in issues of class and nationality, as well as gender, race and Empire. Is this a given of human life, as Levinas appears to suggest? Mills reads Said in this way:

> Said implies that 'Othering' is an inbuilt psychological mechanism which is simply part of human nature. Every nation attempts to construct other nations with which it is in conflict as the Other, but for Lévi-Strauss, the concept of the Other is something which comes to the fore especially at certain historical moments, particularly in colonial expansion. (88)

As a practice, Othering has been a consistent part of dominant modes of western knowledge:

> [T]he disqualification of the woman is a structural need of the phallogocentric system of knowledge, which is read in the light of the 'metaphysical cannibalism' that consumes the many 'others' of theoretical reason, in order to legitimate itself. (Braidotti 211)

However, while such a practice underpins dominant constructions of western subjectivity, the system is not so closed that resistance is impossible. Though it may be a recurring practice, it is one which has been, and continues to be, contested. An examination of the practice of Othering as a strategy of both Empire and patriarchy is part of an ongoing feminist and postcolonial political process which seeks to unmask the technologies that make such hegemonies possible. A tactic deeply imbricated in Othering as colonial practice is the strategy by which whiteness is maintained as racially dominant, at the same time as rendering invisible the technologies employed to facilitate such privileging.

Naturalising whiteness serves to support the Othering of those who are regarded as non-white, and who are thereby viewed inherently as racially inferior in this dominant system of race relations. The colonial novel of female fictional development is always implicated in a system of race relations, which adhere to its progressive aims while miring such fiction in its own set of exclusions. I reiterate Vron Ware's insistence on 'first, the need to perceive white femininity as a historically constructed concept and, secondly, the urgency of understanding how feminism has developed as a political movement in a racist society' (xii-xiii). White women's writing, and the gestures toward broader narrative ends for the heroines I examine here, have arisen out of deeply racist literary cultures that are inexorably tied to the imperial project. In the writing of Duncan and Richardson especially, Aileen Moreton-Robinson's assertion that 'Colonial processes have shaped white feminists' oblivion to their race privilege and their indifference to the history of their relations with Indigenous women' is very much to the point (182).

Whiteness was not an entirely elided and unstated category in the late nineteenth century and early twentieth century, when racial typographies were at their height. Within Schreiner's *African Farm*, especially, whiteness itself is seen to have degrees of acceptability, as a range of ethnic and racial groups are formed into distinct and hierarchised categories. Schreiner's depiction of varieties of whiteness de-essentialises the whiteness that is often represented, even within contemporary anti-racism studies, as 'a static, ahistorical, aspatial, "thing": something set outside social change, something central and permanent, something that defines "the other" but is not itself subject to others' definitions' (Bonnett 121). The complex racially and ethnically mixed society of *African Farm* cannot be reduced to any simple monolithic representation of naturalised whiteness. Schreiner shows that this world is hierarchical, and that its hierarchies are contingent on changing power relations, rather than fixed ones.

In analysing the particularities of these three novels, I am concerned to reveal the technologies which maintain both the Empire and the patriarchal system in which they were generated. The heroines of these texts are both the object of Othering practices, and subject others to further Othering practices, reflecting their ambivalent position in relation to the discourses of patriarchy, imperialism and racism. Their forms of resistance are partial and the conflicts that arise from this are similar to those found by Mills in British women's travel writing: 'By attempting to locate the discourses of femininity and colonialism, it is possible to view these texts by British women in the colonial period as the site for many discursive conflicts' (106). Another element of discursive conflict is added because these texts have a colonial origin, and are Second World products, rather than British. While these stories are set in different institutions of the Empire, the experiences of all three heroines have great similarities. All spend much of their time as lonely, misunderstood figures, isolated by their perception of the inequities around them and by the aspirations which drive them. The restrictions experienced by these heroines on a remote farm, amongst the artistic world of the metropolis and in a colonial boarding school are different, but all ultimately serve to maintain the dominance of patriarchal and imperialistic hegemonies. Narrative conflicts which arise from resisting such hegemonies result in the death of two of the heroines, and cause the third text to eschew narrative closure altogether in order to liberate its heroine from these restrictions.

1.2 *Bildungsroman* and the heroine: patriarchy and the conventions of form

Before considering the specificity of Olive Schreiner's *The Story of an African Farm*, Sara Jeannette Duncan's *A Daughter of Today* and Henry Handel Richardson's *The Getting of Wisdom* as *Bildungsromane*, it is useful to consider the status of the *Bildungsroman* in their era, especially in light of the fact that the protagonists of all these fictions are heroines. If the *Bildungsroman* is an expression of a patriarchal and imperialistic system, can it be used by a woman writer to give voice to a narrative of a woman's development, or is it so implicated in this system that it undermines the very project that has been embarked upon? The term *Bildungsroman* has been used to describe a type of novel which traces its descent from Goethe's *Wilhelm Meisters Lehrjahre*. It can be used in a narrow sense, such as the 'classic *Bildungsroman*' as described by Franco Moretti's *The Way of the World*, or more generally as any novel which focuses on the progress of one protagonist and his or her interaction with the world while passing from youth to maturity. Most broadly, Jerome Buckley describes the English *Bildungsroman* as 'a convenient synonym for the novel of youth or apprenticeship' (13). He goes on to discuss certain key elements that are worth repeating here, if only as a guide to the way in which the plots of women's *Bildungsromane* cannot fully comply but are forced into their own different narrative denouements. This is Buckley's 'broad outline of a typical *Bildungsroman*':

> A child of some sensibility grows up in the country or in a provincial town, where he finds constraints, social and intellectual, placed upon the free imagination. His family, especially his father, proves doggedly hostile to his ambitions, and quite impervious to the new ideas he has gained from unprescribed reading. His first schooling, even if not totally inadequate, may be frustrating insofar as it may suggest options not available to him in his present setting.

He therefore, sometimes at a quite early age, leaves the repressive atmosphere of home (and also the relative innocence), to make his way independently in the city (in the English novels, usually London). There his real 'education' begins, not only his preparation for a career but also — and often more importantly — his direct experience of urban life. The latter involves at least two love affairs or sexual encounters, one debasing, one exalting, and demands that in this respect and others the hero reappraise his values. By the time he has decided, after painful soul-searching, the sort of accommodation to the modern world he can honestly make, he has left his adolescence behind and entered upon his maturity. His initiation complete, he may then visit his old home, to demonstrate by his presence the degree of his success or the wisdom of his choice. (18)

The conventions regarding heroines in nineteenth-century fiction make many of these elements of plot impossible in the experience of the female protagonist. She cannot just leave her home; in fact, she can rarely go anywhere by herself. If she engaged in a sexual encounter, it could only ever be considered 'debasing'. Such an act would make her a fallen woman with little chance of coming to any kind of satisfactory terms with the world. Fictionally her fate would rarely be anything but death, thus curtailing the whole *Bildungsroman* narrative. Curtailment is certainly the fate of many fictions of female development. Buckley criticises George Eliot's *The Mill on the Floss*, claiming that 'George Eliot has identified herself too closely, too emotionally, with Maggie to know precisely what to do with her' and that the novel 'describes the beginning of a life necessarily still incomplete' (115).

It is notable that when fictions of female development fail to conform to those of male development, the author is considered to be at fault (a fact that will be reiterated in critical responses to all three of these novels), yet it is clear that plots with female protagonists cannot follow the complete pattern outlined by Buckley. Can they then still be described as *Bildungsromane*? Franco Moretti's definition is probably narrower than Buckley's, yet he includes fictions of female development in his understanding of the genre, as he takes as his definitive texts both Goethe's *Wilhelm Meisters Lehrjahre* and Jane Austen's *Pride and Prejudice*. Both texts end with the 'perfect' marriage, yet marriage is an ambivalent element in women's texts, signalling, as it often does, the end of fictional life for heroines. However, marriage denotes a particular economy in Moretti's view of the novel: to him it encapsulates the compromise between individual freedom and the restrictions of society: 'marriage becomes the model for a new type of *social contract*: one no longer sealed by forces located outside the individual (such as status), but founded on a sense of "individual obligation"' (22, emphasis in original). Thus, for Moretti, 'the classic *Bildungsroman* "must" always conclude with marriages' (22).

The issue of individual freedom versus the restrictions of society is key to Moretti's understanding of what the *Bildungsroman* is all about. He sees the genre arising from the trauma of modern society, in which youth comes to stand for modernity and change. In examining growth from youth to maturity, the *Bildungsroman* narrative is able to bring an order to this turbulence, and the apparent synthesis of the potentially opposing ideals of personal freedom and the order of society would be expected to be reassuring for the bourgeois reader.

After the period of Austen and Goethe, which Moretti terms that of the classic *Bildungsroman*, the impact of Napoleon and resulting changes in Europe cause diversions in the path of the *Bildungsroman* as it develops concurrently in England and in mainland Europe. The European *Bildungsroman* is thereafter characterised by something of an abandonment of the previous desire for synthesis: 'With Stendhal, though, dialectic synthesis falls apart, and his first major works — the *Life of Napoleon* and *On Love* — explore the opposite poles of a wholly public existence and a strictly private passion' (Moretti 79). The unhappy ending becomes more of an expectation for these works. Moretti's view of the function of this ending is that it once again reassured readers that the values espoused by the main protagonist had indeed survived into the modern era. The fact that they are untenable in this new world is demonstrated by the fact that the narrative virtually expels the protagonist from its pages. However, the reader is reassured because

> [t]he unhappy ending lets the reader continue *believing* in the professed principles of legitimacy, since no 'higher' values have been offered in their stead: they can be 'kept alive' — simultaneously, they can be 'kept from becoming alive', because the story's unchangeable 'reality' shows that they cannot be realized, as the threat of destiny hangs over them. (Moretti 127, emphasis in original)

While Europe underwent considerable turmoil, English society maintained a stability, particularly of values, which is reflected in the English *Bildungsroman*. Moretti sees its chief preoccupations as being an interest in moral certainties, in judgements, and the confirmation of the values of childhood. He describes its structures as those of the courtroom trial, or the fairy tale:

> Since the prescriptive vocation of the fairy-tale novel is already totally entrusted to its structure — in the clearcut opposition between 'good' and 'bad' characters, and in the ending that deals out rewards and punishments — there is really not much left for the protagonist of the English *Bildungsroman* to do. (187)

Needless to say, Moretti finds this less than satisfying in comparison with the issues being examined in the European novel. Yet he finds two outstanding exceptions: 'Together with Jane Austen, [George Eliot] was the only novelist to dismiss the judicial-fairy-tale model and deal with the issues characteristic of the continental *Bildungsroman*' (214).

What was it about these women novelists which forced them beyond the English tradition? Gender is certainly not an issue that is raised by Moretti, but it would seem to have an obvious bearing on this question. Where the novel examines, as *Middlemarch* does, the conflict between 'abstract vocation and everyday viscosity' (Moretti 220), the presence of an intelligent woman as protagonist heightens the conflict between these poles. Social reality, let alone literary convention, made any satisfying synthesis between individual ambition and the development of society impossible in the character of a woman. This kept Eliot from the 'fairy-tale-judicial framework' that Moretti sees in most other nineteenth-century English fiction (215). For female protagonists of nineteenth-century realist fiction, there is always something suppressed or contained by the text. Heroines' aspirations seem to be in conflict with the realist novel.

Leo Bersani sees conflict between the protagonist (not necessarily female) and the form of the novel as a factor in all realist fiction. This is particularly so in the French novel, and demonstrates the link between Eliot's work and the European novel: the protagonists hold desires that cannot be fulfilled in the text, and that the form itself appears to punish. Bersani claims that 'Desire is a threat to the form of realistic fiction', and that the 'nineteenth-century novel is haunted by the possibility' of the expression of such desire (66). As previously suggested by Moretti, all kinds of values and desires can be held by the protagonist, as long as they are ultimately contained by the text. These can be the value-systems of the pre-modern world, or the barely acknowledged and generally unnamed aspirations of heroines. Either way, the text cannot endorse such disruptive forces: 'Realistic fiction admits heroes of desire in order to submit them to ceremonies of expulsion' (Bersani 67). While this is obvious in relation to European realism, in English fiction it also applies to many women's texts. Bersani could well be describing Maggie Tulliver when he states that: 'The figures of nineteenth-century novels who refuse to cooperate with social definitions of the self and of the nature and range of the self's desires are the literary scapegoats of nineteenth-century fiction' (68-69).

I would suggest that female protagonists are always in conflict with realism in some measure. There is inevitably something the text has been unable to contain, an element of desire which Penny Boumelha defines as 'a longing for something (quite probably unformulated) which is different, other, more, than what is available' (Boumelha, *Charlotte Brontë* 19). This can result in narrative closure in which female desire remains unfulfilled or, more overtly, actually punished. The desiring heroines of the nineteenth century are like George Eliot's unknown Saint Theresas: 'Their ardour alternated between a vague ideal and the common yearning of womanhood, so that the one was disapproved as extravagance and the other condemned as a lapse' (Eliot, *Middlemarch* 8). However, it is often the yearning of the protagonist that provides the impetus for narrative.

Nancy K. Miller, extrapolating from Freud's 'The Relation of the Poet to Daydreaming', seeks the suppressed plots in women's fiction. Freud's suggestion is that while young men's fantasies are both ambitious and erotic, young women's are 'generally comprised in their erotic longings' (Miller 32). Miller challenges this, with another suggestion that she sees borne out in women's writing:

> The repressed content, I think, would be not erotic impulses but an impulse to power: a fantasy of power that would revise the social grammar in which women are never defined as subjects; a fantasy of power that disdains a sexual exchange in which women can participate only as objects of circulation. (35)

Being the expression of those largely without power, such an aspect of plot would be to some extent hidden, and in need of decipherment. While it may be intimated in the plot, it may necessarily be repressed in its denouement. Peter Brooks also discusses the relationship between ambition and women's plots:

> The female plot is not unrelated, but it takes a more complex stance toward ambition, the formation of an inner drive toward the assertion of selfhood in resistance to the overt and violating plots of ambition, a counter-dynamic which, from the prototype *Clarissa* on to *Jane Eyre* and *To The Lighthouse*, is only superficially passive, and in fact a reinterpretation of the vectors of plot. (39)

That 'inner drive toward the assertion of selfhood' is what fuels the plot of female development: it is the dynamic driving the narrative, the desire which propels both reader and plot toward an end which will not be able to contain it. This has resulted in what has been described as the incongruities and implausibilities in women's plots,[10] but I hope to show that these elements are but necessary irruptions of desire in the textual landscape, expressions of the conflict between that drive for selfhood, and English nineteenth-century realist plots.

What are these women's plots, and has a novel of female development even been possible when Buckley's description is taken into account? In her study of female *Bildungsromane*, *The Myth of the Heroine: The Female Bildungsroman in the Twentieth Century*, Esther Labovitz is emphatic in her assertion that no nineteenth-century texts could actually be described as a *Bildungsroman*. Sticking to a narrow understanding of the genre, she insists that '*Bildung* belonged to the male hero' and that the characteristics of the typical hero 'were hardly the possession of female fictional heroines' (Labovitz 2, 3). It is changes in material circumstances which differentiate the twentieth from the nineteenth century. Labovitz finds the actual restrictions women experienced in life to be the decisive difference:

> [T]his new genre was made possible only when *Bildung* became a reality for women, in general, and for the fictional heroine, in

---

10 See for example Bird on Richardson, and Cross, Walpole and Krige on Schreiner.

particular. When cultural and social structures appeared to support women's struggle for independence, to go out into the world, engage in careers, in self-discovery and fulfilment, the heroine in fiction began to reflect these changes. (7)

For Labovitz, the female *Bildungsroman* is purely a twentieth-century phenomenon. This view is shared by few others writing about this genre, though: even Moretti, who could hardly be said to be consciously supporting a feminist line, begins his discussion of the English *Bildungsroman* with the character of Elizabeth Bennet and insists that it reaches its peak in *Middlemarch*.

Elizabeth Abel, Marianne Hirsch and Elizabeth Langland suggest that novels of female development *were* written in the nineteenth century, but that the course such development took differed markedly from that of the male protagonist. They question, in fact, whether female protagonists could be said to desire such patterns of development: 'The fully realized and individuated self who caps the journey of the *Bildungsroman* may not represent the developmental goals of women, or of women characters' (10-11). Drawing on the work of psychoanalytic theorists such as Chodorow, Dinnerstein and Gilligan, they suggest a developmental paradigm which is more concerned with connecting and relationship than with individuation and personal achievement. Maggie Tulliver's return to Tom and the River Floss could be viewed then as a positive fulfilment rather than the curtailment of, to use Buckley's words, 'a life necessarily still incomplete' (115). Though I have some reservations about this model — while it recuperates Maggie's death, she still dies — it does highlight the notion that women's developmental goals may well differ from those of men, and that a study of female *Bildungsromane* should take women's stories of growth on their own terms, rather than continually judging them from the perspective of a male model.

Abel and her co-authors suggest two predominant patterns of narrative for such novels of growth. The first, like that of the male protagonist, is linear, tracing a chronological growth from childhood to maturity. *Jane Eyre*, *Villette*, and *The Mill on the Floss* are examples of texts that conform to this pattern. Another pattern is that in which development is somewhat delayed until adulthood and then occurs in a single moment of awakening or in 'brief epiphanic moments', such as in *Mrs Dalloway* or *The Awakening* (Abel et al. 12).

While the linear plot may result in a conventional ending, it can, by way of emphasis, give credence to an end it never reaches. As Boumelha suggests, 'the sequence of the plot need not abolish the range of narrative possibilities intimated in the course of the text' (Boumelha, *Charlotte Brontë* 74). In this way a sub-text of dissent can be written within a conforming frame, suggesting undefined narrative ends which nevertheless leave an impact on the reader. While the linear plot moves toward closure, 'there still resides a core of utopian desire, a critique of the very plots that make closure possible' (Boumelha, *Charlotte Brontë* 37).

Another aspect of the female plot of development is the degree to which the protagonists *do* interact with the world in the traditional manner of the *Bildungsroman*. Hirsch sees the precursor of future narratives of development in Goethe's paradigmatic text, *Wilhelm Meisters Lehrjahre*. As well as the plot of Meister's growth (and he is the archetypal *Bildungsroman* hero), there is also that of The Beautiful Soul, the apparently unrelated female character whose narrative is inserted into Book Six of the novel. The fact that her development is characterised by an almost excessive interiority is not entirely the result of her choices. Just as is the case for future heroines, her choices are very limited, and the opportunities Meister has for interaction with the world are not available to his female counterpart. Interiority is one journey that can be made by a heroine, even if the chance to explore herself by interacting with society is restricted. Where no other path is possible, the interior journey can be the only 'assertion of selfhood' available. As Hirsch says of Antigone: 'Her affirmation of her "inner" self, of the past and her childhood, is both a form of rebellion and a form of extinction' (Hirsch, 'Spiritual *Bildung*' 24). As it is for Antigone, Maggie Tulliver and countless others, death is often the result of this type of self-assertion.

Hirsch recognises that interiority is not the sole possession of heroines, but suggests that for heroes its outcome is quite different. She points out that such interiority in males generally results in the sub-genre *Künstlerroman*:

> Similarly dissatisfied and led to withdraw into the inner life, its male heroes find a solution that saves them from the heroines' death, the solution of art which is virtually unavailable to the young woman in the nineteenth-century novel. The story of female spiritual *Bildung* is the story of the potential artist who fails to make it. (Hirsch, 'Spiritual *Bildung*' 28)

Rather than finding an expression and therefore becoming the story of the artist's interaction with the world, the heroine's interiority leads either to excessive accommodation or death. For the strongly impassioned heroine, death is the simplest way of dealing with her desire in narrative terms.

Susan J. Rosowski suggests that the plot of awakening in the heroine is triggered when 'an inner, imaginative sense of personal value conflicts with her public role: an awakening occurs when she confronts the disparity between her two lives' (68). Such an awakening can result in acquiescence, or the heroine can refuse to be restrained in such a way and find some kind of outlet in death, either by her own action, as in Chopin's *The Awakening*, or as the result of the type of 'rescue' staged by Eliot in *The Mill on the Floss*. As Rosowski points out, 'Each represents an awakening to limitations. Each presents a resolution only at great cost to the protagonist. She must deny one element of herself' (68). Even in late nineteenth-century and early twentieth-century fiction, where the *Künstlerroman* becomes a fictional possibility for heroines, some element of self-denial is still integral to the denouement of plot.

Kathleen Blake describes this phenomenon as 'feminine self-postponement' (Blake viii). Generally such postponement involves the dominance of love plots over those of *Bildung*, as heroines are constrained by their sexual roles and succumb to the romance plot. Blake suggests that 'For all its value within Victorian literature, love is shown to be a condition that defines the limits of a woman's world and invites acceptance of limits, tantamount to self-limiting or self-postponement' (224). Blake also discusses at length the theoretical difficulties experienced by late Victorian feminists as they tried to grapple with questions of career versus marriage, and celibacy versus erotic freedom. The deep ambivalences expressed, particularly with regard to sexual issues, reflect the problems that women had even envisaging a world where they could pursue personal and intellectual expression *and* erotic fulfilment. In fiction, Rachel Blau Du Plessis discusses this in terms of two kinds of plot:

> This contradiction between love and quest in plots dealing with women as a narrated group, acutely visible in nineteenth-century fiction, has, in my view, one main mode of resolution: an ending in which one part of that contradiction, usually quest or *Bildung*, is set aside or repressed, whether by marriage or by death. (3-4)

Plots that begin as potential *Künstlerromane* are sabotaged by the sex of the protagonist. Ultimately heroines are almost exclusively defined by their gender, rather than any other characteristic: they never escape the plot of woman.

By the *fin-de-siècle* period, during which most of the fiction I wish to consider was written (albeit in the Empire rather than the metropolitan centre), the strictures of nineteenth-century fiction were beginning to loosen. Fictional possibilities for heroines remained limited, though the somewhat submerged rebellion of certain nineteenth-century women's plots becomes more overt in some texts, leading to severe disruption of narratives and refusal of closure. The cynicism regarding plotting noted by Boumelha in Eliot and Brontë is more inclined to draw attention to itself by flippant manoeuvres in this later period (15), and heroines are less inclined to suppress their own *Bildung* in favour of the romance plot. The strictures are looser: they have not gone. The choice generally has still to be made between romance and *Bildung*. Interiority remains the safest area for female development, yet more and more the heroine interacts with the world and attempts to find a place for herself in it. This place has been mapped out for her in the romance plot, yet she is far more resistant to taking it on terms which are not her own. The 'assertion of selfhood', which Brooks finds to be a prime element of the female plot, becomes more overt, and narrative, 'one of the large categories in which we think', begins to demonstrate that thinking about women and plot can change (39, 323).

In my reading of *The Story of an African Farm*, I will explore what use Schreiner makes of the male/female double *Bildungsroman*, especially in light of the fact that this form already has a tradition of commenting strongly on the process of gender enculturation, as exemplified by texts such as *The Mill on the Floss*. I will also be concerned to trace the influence of Goethe and the German *Bildungsroman* tradition, and how Schreiner's rendering of the genre comments on the values of the societies from which it sprang. This will concentrate on Christianity, the notion of vocation and on the conditions which gave rise to the meritocratic drive of previous *Bildungsromane*. Lyndall's plot raises questions about the conflict between feminist rhetoric and the romance plot, and about the possibilities for women on the colonial frontier.

Duncan's *A Daughter of Today* is very much a product of the 'New Woman' era of fiction, and as such it comments on many of the same issues as other texts from the period. One of its most radical features is the depiction of an egotistical ambitious heroine, and I will look at the way in which this contravenes nineteenth-century codes of femininity and narrative conventions. Because this text is that specific type of *Bildungsroman*, the *Künstlerroman*, it raises questions about women as artists. I will examine the way in which conflict arising from this issue is negotiated, and also what impact the romance plot has on the *Bildung* project. Discursive conflicts arising from Elfrida's Orientalism and her pursuit of feminine self-realisation also have an impact on the resolution of her narrative.

Richardson's *The Getting of Wisdom* takes us out of the nineteenth century, and presents new narrative possibilities. In its parody of earlier fictional forms, especially those written with the young woman in mind, the text comments on the politics of those earlier works and the value systems they endorse. I will also focus on how its setting, in a boarding school of the British Empire, allows two oppressive systems, patriarchy and imperialism, to come under critical scrutiny. The strategies by which these systems are maintained will be examined and compared. Richardson brings a fresh approach to her negotiation of the romance plot, and she responds to the usual curtailment of female development in closure by bypassing it altogether, thereby opening up possibilities for the heroine's *Bildung*.

2

Olive Schreiner

The Story of an African Farm

2.1 Introduction

'This of course is not a justification of my method but touches what seems to me a weakness and shallowness in your mode of criticism' (Cronwright-Schreiner, *The Letters of Olive Schreiner* 99). When Olive Schreiner wrote these words to her lifelong friend and correspondent Havelock Ellis, she might well have addressed them to the numerous critics of later years who have found fault with her method, especially with her approach to narrative and plot. Like Ellis, many of these critics have viewed her as a talented but incomplete writer, 'one half of a great writer; a diamond marred by a flaw', as Virginia Woolf observed (103). An early anonymous review mentions 'the vagueness and indeterminate convolutions of the plot' (*Young Man* 71); G.W. Cross said in 1897, 'Plot has never been the author's strong point' (86); Hugh Walpole repeated the assumption in 1927 when he wrote 'construction was never Olive Schreiner's strong suit' (91); and Uys Krige in 1955 asserted that 'the young poet ... is at loggerheads with the incipient novelist to the detriment of the unity or balance of her work' (77). In all of these responses, the passion of the writing is seen to be the factor which undermines its structure. Certainly it is true that for readers trained in the traditions of the English realist *Bildungsroman*, *The Story of an African Farm* (*African Farm*) seemed an affront to polite agreements regarding form which had been maintained by authors and their readers for most of the nineteenth century. However, more recent readings of this novel have suggested that rather than letting her passion run away with her to the detriment of the novel form, Olive Schreiner very knowingly usurped the traditions of the English *Bildungsroman*, and intentionally shaped the structure of her text.

Both Rachel Blau Du Plessis and Gerd Bjørhovde have proposed that Schreiner's rejection of nineteenth-century realism was precipitated by the form's imbrication with nineteenth-century ideologies of gender. Du Plessis also demonstrates how the critique of Christianity (and the authority and reliability of its Scriptures) which is embodied in *African Farm* unsettles all teleological narratives, including that of the realist novel.

In addition to the issues of gender and faith, there are two other elements which have not been given due consideration with regard to their impact on the form of *African Farm*. These are firstly the fact that Schreiner had been impressed deeply by the German *Bildungsroman* tradition, in particular by Goethe's *Wilhelm Meisters Lehrjahre*, and secondly that her colonial position placed her in an ambiguous relation to Britain's high cultural artefacts and the ideologies which they embodied. Jed Esty is one of the few to make the connection that the narrative is more explicable when read with both Goethe's literary heritage in mind, and its colonial setting (407-430). It was not only the ideologies of gender which affected Schreiner's treatment of the *Bildungsroman*, it was also her situation on the edges of Empire. Looking backwards through the lens of imperialism from the colonies, beyond the experience of affluence which the Empire brought to many at its centre and to some at its outposts, Schreiner was not able to endorse the meritocratic drive which had been so integral to the Victorian *Bildungsroman*. Instead, in the world of her text, the oppressor and the materialist prosper, while the morally brave and spiritually inclined pass away. On the underside of Empire, the naïvety of the Victorian *Bildungsroman* cannot be maintained. Its cultural particularity is revealed as its universality is exploded; its wilful blindness is stripped away. Such a view need not have been confined to the outposts of Empire; obviously a similar questioning of meritocracy could conceivably have emerged from those classes in Britain which also failed to draw the imperial dividend. In his study of the *Bildungsroman* in European culture, Franco Moretti has claimed that from Fielding to Dickens, the English *Bildungsroman* demonstrates

> a tradition that has absorbed and propagated one of the most basic expectations of liberal-democratic civilization: the desire that the realm of the law be certain, universalistic, and provided with mechanisms for correction and control. (213)

As a consequence, 'these novels do not simply state that everyone "has a right" to justice; they maintain instead that everyone, in fact, *receives* justice' (Moretti 213, emphasis in original). These narratives reflect a world in which there is order, meaning and justice for all, as the denouements of the *Bildungsroman* from this period are characterised by the distribution of rewards and punishments. This concern with moral certainties and judgements precludes the ambivalences and ambiguities involved in the spiritual quest which is more typical of the German *Bildungsroman*. In contrast with the German tradition (which is the object of his study), Martin Swales has said that in the English *Bildungsroman* 'There is not ... the same concern with the definition and validation of human wholeness as mediated through the person of the protagonist' (164). Instead we have an English tradition which is singularly lacking in ontological *angst*. The difference, for Moretti, is summed up in the fact that while children do not read *Wilhelm Meister*, many children have read

Jane Eyre and *Great Expectations*, suggesting that the English novel was not really prepared to deal with adult themes. The 'sense of the sheer elusiveness (and unrealisability) of the self in all its complexity' in the German *Bildungsroman* has certainly had an impact on the structure and preoccupations of *African Farm* (Swales 164). However, though Schreiner has drawn on the German tradition she has critiqued it just as comprehensively as the English one. In many ways, the development of the individual in the African Karroo in a world without God is shown to fulfil the early but discarded motto for the book: 'Life is a series of abortions' (Ellis, 'Notes on Olive Schreiner' 41).

The term *Bildungsroman* was coined in the early 1820s by Karl Morgenstern, who regarded Goethe's *Wilhelm Meisters Lehrjahre* not only as the prototypical *Bildungsroman*, but also as 'the work which inaugurated the modern novel in all its resonance' (Swales 12). Schreiner's view of *Wilhelm Meister*, expressed to Havelock Ellis, was that it was 'one of the most immortal deathless productions of the greatest of the world's artists', typifying what she referred to as 'organic art', in which the craft of the artist is invisible (Rive 79). According to Ellis, Schreiner 'read *Wilhelm Meister* many times, each time with growing pleasure. She thinks Goethe is the writer who best expresses all that she aimed at before leaving the Cape' (Ellis, 'Notes on Olive Schreiner' 41).

Certainly 'the discursiveness, the intellectual debate which is so much a feature of the [German] *Bildungsroman*' is an obvious element of *African Farm*, and one of the factors which led to criticism of its structure (Swales 147). As the reviewer from the *Church Quarterly Review* complained with obvious exasperation: 'Whole chapters are devoted to soliloquy and dissertation, during which the tale does not advance one inch' ('Three Controversial Novels' 75). The readiness with which the characters in *Wilhelm Meister* embark on discussions regarding such issues as the function of theatre in the national psyche, the purpose of vocation and art, or the marriage of persons of equal spirituality, is obviously reflected in the dialogue in *African Farm*. *Meister* also appears to allow more ambiguity than the Victorian *Bildungsroman*, which also links it to Schreiner's work. At one point Wilhelm states that 'it is the property of crime to extend its mischief over innocence, as it is of virtue to extend its blessings over many that deserve them not; while frequently the author of the one or the other is not punished or rewarded at all' (Goethe I, 224). However, while such sentiments appear to be at variance with the outcomes of nineteenth-century English fiction, the actual narrative ends of *Meister* are remarkably similar to them. In fact, rewards and punishments are distributed just as clearly at the end of *Meister* as at the end of *Great Expectations*, the chief difference being that a greater complexity of plot in the German text creates more opportunities for repentant female death scenes. *African Farm* is a departure from and critique of both models. The appearance of influential strangers is also a feature of both *Meister* and *African Farm*, though their overall purpose in the lives of the protagonists is ultimately shown to be radically different. While Wilhelm's strangers are linked by their connection to his positive 'destiny', the strangers in *African Farm* reinforce the arbitrary nature of existence for Waldo and Lyndall. Wilhelm's strangers appear because they are the watchful members of the Guild to which he is finally initiated, evidence of the benign nature of the universe in which his *Bildung* occurs. The appearances of the strangers in *African Farm* are never shown to be part of a plan: they are isolated occurrences which reinforce the arbitrary nature of life without God on the fringe of the Empire. *African Farm* is an examination and critique of the two dominant patterns of European narrative in Schreiner's experience. Both are found wanting, and in their place, Schreiner has fashioned a narrative which has dominated the consciousness of southern

African writers for well over a century.[11]

Though I have quoted critiques of Schreiner's plot structures that have become the truisms of Schreiner criticism through most of the twentieth century, this note of reproach was not the dominant one in early reviews of *African Farm*. Reviewers consistently responded strongly to those areas which touched the preoccupations of London intellectual life at the time. The most obvious of these areas is 'The Woman Question', but also significant, if not quite so current, is the issue of free-thinking and religion. The ways in which the book questions the Eurocentric and imperialist notions at the heart of Empire is either not seen, or misunderstood. These reviews tend to reveal more about the attitudes of their authors than about the content of *African Farm*. For instance, the self-satisfied smugness and superiority of the anonymous essayist in *The Westminster Review* is barely concealed in the description of the setting as 'A Dutch farm-house in a vast flat plain of south Africa, with its scarcely civilised inhabitants and their squalid surroundings' ('Modern English Novels' 143, 149). In his 1887 discussion of the novels of the previous five years, H. Rider Haggard states that only two 'have excited his profound interest', but he responds only to the intensity of *African Farm* and not to its setting and its inherent criticism of his own style: 'both convey the impression of being the outward and visible result of inward personal suffering on the part of the writer, for in each the keynote is a note of pain' (180). This is despite the fact that in Schreiner's preface to the second edition of the novel (also published in 1883), she ironically mocks the genre in which Haggard was to become so successful:

> It has been suggested by a kind critic that he would have liked the little book if it had been a history of wild adventure; of cattle

---

[11] Robyn Visel traces the influence of *African Farm* which has had a continuing relationship to later southern African works by white writers, particularly that of Isak Dinesen, Doris Lessing, Nadine Gordimer and J.M. Coetzee. The work of black writer Bessie Head is also related to this tradition (Visel 1990).

driven into inaccessible 'kranzes' by Bushmen; 'of encounters with ravening lions, and hair-breadth escapes'. This could not be. Such works are best written in Piccadilly or in the Strand: there the gifts of the creative imagination untrammelled by contact with any fact, may spread their wings. (*AF* 27-28)

Perhaps Haggard felt that he was immune from this comment, for though his highly successful *King Solomon's Mines* had made its mark well before he wrote on *African Farm*, and would seem to fit Schreiner's description well, he could assure himself that he, at least, had been to Africa. However, his role in the colonial administration and in the annexation of Transvaal meant that his belief in 'the white man's burden' would inform all of his writing about Africa, romantic or otherwise.

What is noteworthy about Haggard's response is that its biographical emphasis was to be so typical of all subsequent Schreiner criticism. The division between woman and work seems to blur and the woman herself becomes the object of scrutiny. This has been a common fate of women writers. Their work has been seen to be autobiographical to a much greater degree than that of male writers. Perhaps this has been a way of accounting for the otherwise puzzling facility women writers have shown in the area of creative imagination.

Since the publication in 1924 of S.C. Cronwright-Schreiner's *The Life of Olive Schreiner*, his account has dominated such biographical readings of Schreiner's work. Whether any spouse can ever write a balanced biography is highly questionable. The answer to whether a separated and disappointed spouse can do so seems obvious: he or she cannot. Cronwright-Schreiner asserts in his preface, not once but twice, as if to forestall criticism, 'that I am the only person who can be said to have known her, the only person who ever had adequate opportunity of knowing her fully (not excluding even her own family)' (Cronwright-

Schreiner, *The Life of Olive Schreiner* ix). In the preface to *The Letters* he insists that

> I complete my contribution to a study of genius by one who loved, and lived in long, close and continuous contact with, a woman of genius, having thus had the rare opportunity of watching, not only with loving interest and tender devotion, but also with reverential scientific ardour, a quality of mind strange and wonderful in its manifestations and in some of its physical reactions. (Cronwright-Schreiner, *The Life of Olive Schreiner* vii)

Nevertheless he presents an account in which he is the hero, and Schreiner the neurotic and tiresome disappointment to whom he was selflessly devoted. He evokes the twin icons of 'genius' and 'science' to validate his choice of subject and his treatment of it.

While his accounts might be understandable in light of his relation to Schreiner, it is harder to see why they have been so influential. It is disappointing that the only other full biography, that by Ruth First and Ann Scott, is so informed by Cronwright-Schreiner's interpretations and accounts of his wife's behaviour. In what is purportedly a study informed by feminism and socialism one might have expected more distance from the Cronwright-Schreiner version. Added to this limitation is the projection of a Freudian interpretation onto Schreiner's asthmatic condition. Admitting that '[p]erhaps this gives an overly "psychogenic" basis to Olive's asthma; unfortunately we have no information at all about the state of her respiratory system in childhood', they still assert that 'her symptoms — which were frequent and acute — might then be interpreted as an unconscious attempt to free herself from the sinfulness of her sexuality' (First and Scott 68). Could not Schreiner have been allergic to dust mites or grass seed like other asthma sufferers? But perhaps, as this biography is now over 30 years old, its overly psychological reading is more reflective of its historic moment than of Schreiner's life.

Because the strongest response of early reviews was to elements seen to relate to 'The Woman Question', far more attention was paid to the character of Lyndall and to her fate than to Waldo and his. For example, *The Englishwoman's Review* quoted a large section of Lyndall's speech likening the marriage contract to prostitution, a concept which became widespread in late-nineteenth-century feminism and which was enlarged upon in Schreiner's essay 'The Woman Question' and later in *Woman and Labour* as 'sex-parasitism' (Schreiner, 'The Woman Question' 85).[12] This review merely prefaced its large quotation with a comment relating to the education of women in both Britain and South Africa:

> We have been more especially attracted, however, by some remarks on the narrow education of women, which, if they be genuine expressions of Cape life, tend to show that the colony has quite as necessary lessons to learn as the mother country. ('Reviews', *Englishwoman's Review* 362)

The political application of Lyndall's statements seemed to bring her to prominence in the eyes of most readers, but, in terms of the construction of the novel, Waldo's story is actually given more space and attention, and both beginning and end have him as their focus.

2.2 Waldo's tale: work and the deconstruction of the *Bildungsroman* economy

African Farm is structured as a male-female double *Bildungsroman*, immediately evoking Emily Brontë's *Wuthering Heights* and George Eliot's *The Mill on the Floss*. To some extent this structure cannot help being

---

[12] This idea had been described by Mary Wollstonecraft as 'legal prostitution' in *A Vindication of the Rights of Men* (a, 23), and *A Vindication of the Rights of Woman* (b, 129, 218). The phrase 'legal prostitution' had previously been used by Defoe in *Conjugal Lewdness; or, Matrimonial Whoredom* (1727) (Wollstonecraft b, 129). It was a common enough concept by the 1890s to be rephrased as 'monogamic prostitution' by W.T. Stead ('The Novel of the Modern Woman' 65).

subversive of hegemonic gender systems, as the inequities of patriarchal society are clearly revealed in its description of the different paths open to both protagonists. The reader is drawn into the frustrations of the female character and vicariously experiences her restrictions. Charlotte Goodman suggests that both Eliot and Brontë felt

> [t]he imperative need ... to dramatize in their respective novels the tragic fragmentation which growing up entails, particularly for creative, energetic girls whose education perforce trains them to subdue their aggressive instincts and to conform to the narrowly defined female roles assigned to them by a patriarchal society, while their male counterparts are free to journey into the larger world. (33)

Schreiner's critique goes further than this, however. By interrogating the *Bildungsroman* genre itself, she questions its assumptions that individuals 'find themselves' in meaningful work and in the marriage partnership. Waldo finds neither of these things, yet still comes to the kind of accommodation to his world which could be said to characterise the *Bildungsroman*. Waldo's story is a radical rewriting of the genre which rejects its Eurocentric assumptions and its teleological worldview.

Waldo has been variously read as non-male — 'the nominally masculine, but essentially sexless character of Waldo' (Visel, *White Eve* 42) — and even more incredibly as a black African: 'Waldo "is" the black African' (Du Plessis 203). However well intentioned, these attempts by feminist critics to explain Waldo's marginalisation by denying his gender or race are distorted readings, which detract from the radical potential of his story. While she gives reasons for her reading, Rachel Blau Du Plessis's assertion is also an attempt to gloss over the racism obvious in Schreiner's writing from this period. It is an attempt to create a meaningful black African character when the novel does not contain one. Surely it is more useful to examine how Schreiner negotiates the discourse of racism and how her position moves in later writings with her greater grasp of the workings of capital and Empire. Rewriting Schreiner teaches us nothing about her and her available discourses, or about ourselves and the probable limitations of ours. It is because Waldo is a white male protagonist that his plot is so challenging to the teleological Judeo-Christian view of the world, and to Eurocentricity itself.

Though not concerned with the implications of the colonial origin of *African Farm*, Du Plessis does demonstrate the way in which the text 'exposes the critical collapse of several related narrative paradigms', which she outlines as follows:

> The Christian Story and the teleological melodrama on which it depends features a battle between good and evil, which conventionally ends with the triumph, or at least the martyred justification, of right. This story about the revealed ruling purpose of the cosmos is run aground in the first part of *African Farm*. The second story, a *Bildungs* plot, centers in *African Farm* on Waldo Farber, who searches vainly for purpose, but stops and simply dies. The third story, centering here on Lyndall, combines various romantic thraldom and marriage plots in which the fictional heroes and heroines have traditionally acted. Taken as a whole, the book marks the 'end' of the consoling stories of the Christian, quest, and romance varieties. (21)

Du Plessis claims that Schreiner gives the reader 'promissory notes' regarding these plots, which she never honours (25). The effect is to undermine the power of these dominant narratives, and to question the ideology which is encapsulated in them.

That Waldo's story will deal with issues of religion and philosophy is signalled to the reader in the first chapter, before we have even learnt his name. The first section, 'The Watch', introduces Waldo as the only wakeful person on the farm, 'a great head of silky black curls and the two black eyes', who is grappling with the concept of eternal damnation and a Calvinistic understanding of God's will 'that never changes or alters, you may do what you please' (*AF* 36, 37). In 'The Sacrifice', he seeks to recreate the incident on Mount Carmel when Elijah the prophet called down fire from heaven to consume his sacrifice and confound the prophets of Baal. Instead of offering a bull, Waldo makes do with a chop, and interprets the lack of heavenly fire as God's displeasure and rejection of himself. In the final part of this chapter, 'The Confession', Waldo's inability to reconcile the judgemental Old Testament God with the more loving New Testament God as seen in Jesus is summed up in his fearful admission, 'I love Jesus Christ, but I hate God' (*AF* 42). When we do learn his name from Em, the connections between his name and that of the narrator, Ralph Iron, become obvious. Schreiner's tribute to Ralph Waldo Emerson does not end with these names, however: the religious intensity of Waldo's childhood finally emerges as a complete Emersonian sensibility by the end of the book.

Part One of *African Farm* is overwhelmingly concerned with religious questions. Most of these are raised by Waldo, but Lyndall is also involved in the questioning of accepted wisdom. There is a concern with truth, which later becomes the goal of the Hunter in the Stranger's allegory. Part of this concern is expressed in an examination of the veracity of the Bible and whether it can be relied upon as a source of truth. This critique of Christianity is significant in *African Farm* not only because it allows Schreiner to range through the current 'Freethinker' debates but also because the Christian worldview is one of the European master narratives which allowed a form such as the *Bildungsroman* to develop. Through much of the nineteenth century the English *Bildungsroman* was meritocratic in its narrative denouements, linking it intrinsically with Du Plessis's description of the Christian teleology as 'a battle between good and evil, which conventionally ends with the triumph, or at least the martyred justification, of right' (21). Schreiner not only overturns this narrative pattern: she also undermines the worldview on which it depends. The critique of Christianity which occurs in Part One and in the first two chapters of Part Two is important, then, not only because it describes Waldo's *Bildung* but because at the same time it questions the whole concept of *Bildung*. There is, however, an ambivalence in the narrative voice toward the discourses of Christianity. While its central tenets are apparently rejected, some of its values, as expressed in nineteenth-century missionary culture, are retained and indeed endorsed, without being examined.

The critique of Christianity progresses on two levels. One is through the various crises of faith which beset Waldo, the other through the irony of the narrative voice and the way in which this ironic voice structures events on the farm. Carolyn Burdett notes that Waldo's loss of faith had wider relevance as it reflects 'a stage which Victorian bourgeois culture in general has to pass through in its accession to the modern spirit' (20). In an early review, and one which Schreiner apparently liked, Canon MacColl claims that Schreiner 'has been driven from her religious and moral moorings' by two factors, the first of which is 'the ghastly theology of Calvinism' (73). The reader's initial glimpse into Waldo's consciousness is through his anxiety about the injustice of hell, and his conviction that he himself is unworthy of God. His confession that he loves Jesus Christ but hates God indicates the two theological poles between which Waldo oscillates. One is primarily Calvinistic, emphasising an inflexible God's concern with justice and hence punishment. The other could be described as Wesleyan, concentrating on a predominantly New Testament view of a loving God with whom humans can commune. It is a theology of grace rather than law.

The differences between the two theologies are best exemplified by their stances on the question of predestination and freewill. The Calvinist view is that certain individuals are predestined for salvation by God. Such an understanding leads to a rather static social understanding due to its inherent fatalism. The church of the South African Boers, the Dutch Reformed Church, was Calvinist in orientation. Arminius had rejected the theology of predestination, and had a profound influence on 'John Wesley (1703-1791), so that all streams of English theology are imbued with Arminianism' (Richardson and Bowden 43). Gottlob Schreiner, Olive's father, had been an evangelical Lutheran, and Rebecca, her mother, had come from a dissenting group of Wesleyans who had adhered to predestination. Sometime into his not very successful missionary career, Gottlob read Wesley's sermons and wrote to the Wesleyan Mission Society that 'I found that I had been all along a Wesleyan in doctrine and principle as far as I know it' (First and Scott 40). Otto's spirituality and life typify the Wesleyan understanding. He gives virtually all that he has to Blenkins, cares for the farm servants, who are native Africans, and experiences a spiritual reality which can sustain him in a state of ecstatic joy throughout the night. Waldo has his own moments of Otto's 'heaven on earth'. He experiences

> that delightful consciousness of something bending over him and loving him. It would not have been better in one of the courts of heaven, where the walls are set with rows of the King of Glory's amethysts and milk-white pearls, than there, eating his supper in that little room. (*AF* 78)

However, Waldo's sense of communion is shattered by the betrayal and death of his father, Otto, and he is forced to admit to Lyndall that 'There is no God! ... no God; not anywhere!' (*AF* 102).

Both the Calvinist and Wesleyan approaches to religion are represented in the novel as literalist and intolerant of examination. Otto's faith is based on the uncritical acceptance of all that he is told, biblical or otherwise, and when Lyndall questions Blenkins' lies, he responds with a rejection of all questioning:

> How do you know that anything is true? Because you are told so. If we have to question everything — proof, proof, proof, what will we have to believe left? How do you know the angel opened the prison door for Peter, except that Peter said so? How do you know that God talked to Moses, except that Moses wrote it? That is what I hate! (*AF* 62)

As Waldo examines the scriptures, he finds obvious discrepancies in literalist readings of them. His internal question — '*Why did the women in Mark see only one angel and the women in Luke two*' — is the beginning of a long list of these inconsistencies, some of which are minor like this one, and some of which involve more significant issues such as the moral nature of God (*AF* 67). In the narrow world of the Karroo, there are no other models for reading the scriptures, and his questions themselves are seen as evil. In order to have faith in this environment, he must divorce his mind from his spirituality, a requirement which, together with the injustices he suffers, ultimately obliges him to give up his faith. The adults around him have made a conscious decision not to admit any knowledge which could possibly challenge their received view of the universe. As Tant' Sannie states when rejecting Waldo's book unexamined, "'Didn't the minister tell me when I was confirmed not to read any book except my Bible and hymn-book, that the Devil was in all the rest? And I never have read any other book", said Tant' Sannie with virtuous energy, "and I never will!"' (*AF* 113). Because there is one dominant 'interpretive community' (to use Stanley Fish's term) functioning in Tant' Sannie's environment, she is not only closed to sources outside the Bible but she is closed to alternative meanings from *within* the Bible (485). As Margaret Daymond suggests, 'What hems Waldo in so cruelly is not, of course, the Bible itself but the bigotry of his immediate society where ignorance is the chief source of its pieties' (173).

When Part Two begins Waldo is lying 'on his stomach on the sand' and the narrator informs us that 'The soul's life has seasons of its own'

(*AF* 137). What follows is in the voice of the narrator, but is clearly also a retelling of Waldo's spiritual journey, his soul's seasons. The narrative voice shifts to first person plural, creating a very strong identification between Waldo and the narrator. The journey is shown to have been something of a torment. As the child's intelligent and inquiring mind questions the justice and orthodoxy handed to it, the process is experienced as the intervening voice of the Devil. This results in a torturous obsession which terrifies the young child:

> It is nothing to him [the Devil] if we go quite mad with fear at our own wickedness. He asks on, the questioning Devil; he cares nothing what he says. We long to tell someone, that they may share our pain. We do not yet know that the cup of affliction is made with such a narrow mouth that only one lip can drink at a time, and that each man's cup is made to match his lip. (*AF* 141)

Once again the narrowness of the Calvinist understanding of the nature of God is shown in the sermon described by the narrator, in which the death of an atheist is interpreted as God's judgement. The fact that he has been struck down by lightning is ample proof for the preacher, who is sure the man's soul 'has fled to the everlasting shade' (*AF* 146). The narrator cannot reconcile the preacher's message with scriptural verses regarding God's forgiving love, and is forced to run from the building. The other theological emphasis, the Wesleyan one, is briefly referred to when, in the voice of the narrator, Waldo is described as having discovered the fifth chapter of Matthew at the age of seven: 'It is a new gold-mine. Then we tuck the Bible under our arm and rush home ... we tell them we have discovered a chapter they never heard of' (*AF* 139). However, even this chapter, with its message of mercy for the downtrodden, is represented through the lens of the interpretive community. The child chooses to see only the sacrificial emphasis, concluding, 'We will deny ourself' (*AF* 139). There is no reinforcement of a different kind of Christianity in the environment of the Boer-dominated Karroo. Links between the narrator and Waldo are further strengthened by the mention of instances from Waldo's life which have already been recounted, such as 'In the dark night in the fuel-room we cry to our Beautiful dream-God … But He is not there', recalling the night he was whipped by Blenkins (*AF* 148-149). Like the earlier account, this one ends with a loss of faith: 'Now we have no God' (*AF* 149).

In both accounts of the spiritual journey Waldo has moments of devotion that seem analogous to sexual experiences. In the first account, Waldo is so taken with his closeness to God that he no longer wishes to live:

> I want to die — to see Him. I will die any death. Oh, let me come!'
> Weeping he bowed himself, and quivered from head to foot. After a long while he lifted his head.
> 'Yes; I will wait, I will wait. But not long, do not let it be very long, Jesus King. I want you; oh, I want you, — soon, soon!' (*AF* 68-69)

In the second account in 'Times and Seasons', a different experience is described, in which the fear of judgement leads to ecstasy:

> After hours and nights of frenzied fear of the supernatural desire to appease the power above, a fierce quivering excitement in every inch of nerve and blood-vessel, there comes a time when nature cannot endure longer, and the spring long bent recoils. We sink down emasculated. Up creeps the deadly delicious calm.
> 'I have blotted out as a cloud thy sins, and as a thick cloud thy trespasses, and will remember them no more for ever'. We weep with soft transporting joy. (*AF* 143-144)

It appears that the usual sexual drive of the *Bildungsroman* hero has been subsumed by spiritual striving. Waldo seems unaware of his sexuality until the very end of his tale, when he realises his connection with Lyndall, and even this is spoken of more in spiritual terms than sexual. In contrast, at the start of *Wilhelm Meister*, Wilhelm is in the first stages of a blissful sexual relationship, and it is represented as an important stage in his development. His partner, being female, must die to achieve any virtuous end, but Wilhelm is enabled to go on and meet his ideal partner for life, who is not only virginal and strong but also of the right class. The usual English hero may not have been portrayed as experiencing a *sexual* relationship but he was definitely drawn to find a partner from a young age. Even Pip, who exceptionally does not marry at the end of *Great Expectations* (though this is open to question), is at least emotionally educated by his relationship with Estella, who has proven to be an unsuitable partner for the young man. In *African Farm*, while Waldo's sexuality is apparently absorbed by his spirituality, the opposite is true of Lyndall. She also questions the received dogma, and seems to relate to Waldo's growing Emersonian understanding of life. However, her response to the knowledge that she is now in a world without God is expressed sexually. She longs for something to worship but chooses to tie herself to a union which will only satisfy her physically and temporarily.

The critique of Christianity which occurs throughout *African Farm* is significant for a number of reasons. It not only unsettles teleological narratives, but in particular it undermines the worldview which produced the *Bildungsroman*. Wilhelm Meister's benign and intentional universe is replaced with the unjust and seemingly random events of the Karroo. The contrast between these two worlds reveals how Eurocentric the Christianity of Waldo's world is. Its tenets are not vindicated in colonial society, nor do they account for Waldo's overwhelming experience of the African landscape, which in part leads him into his final Emersonian understanding. Christianity is, in fact, shown to be one of the straightjackets that restrict human development in Waldo's world. In terms of Waldo's own *Bildung*, his alienation from the Christian understanding of God is crucial for his ultimate abandonment of quest, work, romance and, finally, desire.

Apart from the direct recounting of Waldo's spiritual disillusionment, the other way in which Christianity is undermined as a source of truth is by the ironic use of scriptures. Riccardo Duranti, who translated *African Farm* into Italian, suggests that 'the rapport Olive Schreiner establishes with the Scriptures had a highly conflictual edge to it' (76). This is demonstrated through continual misquotations, some obviously intentional, others possibly accidental. However, whether by accident or design, Schreiner undermines the Bible's position in Karroo society as the ultimate source of truth. One instance is quoted above, when Waldo has the rather sexually-charged experience of forgiveness. Schreiner records the verse as concluding 'and will remember them no more for ever', when it actually ends with 'return unto me; for I have redeemed thee' (*AF* 144, KJV Is. 44.22). While there is nothing particularly subversive about Schreiner's rewriting (it replicates sentiments found elsewhere in Scripture), it does add to an air of unreliability and untrustworthiness about the Bible and its uses. This is reinforced by the uses made of it by Bonaparte Blenkins, who is repeatedly proven to be a liar who misuses the Bible. In Blenkins's case, his misquotations are part of the comic construction of his villainous character and seem intentional on the part of the narrator, referring as they do to well-known passages.

The best example of this is the bogus sermon preached by Blenkins. He uses this occasion to create a smokescreen about his own practices, having inveigled from Otto not only his best clothes but also his cherished opportunity to preach. Though his biblical knowledge is limited, he uses what he has to create an aura of authority. He begins with a misquotation designed to suggest that his sermon has divine backing: 'a very few words are all I shall address to you, and may they be as a rod of iron dividing the bones from the marrow, and the marrow from the bones' (*AF* 70). While this mention of bones fits in well with his gruesome story about the somehow miraculously still vocal skeleton of the suicide floating in 'the seething sea' within Mount Etna (*AF* 71), the actual biblical verse he half remembers reads, 'For the word of God is quick, and powerful, and sharper than any twoedged sword, piercing even to the dividing asunder of soul and spirit, and of the joints and marrow, and is a discerner of the thoughts and intentions of the heart' (KJV Heb. 4.12). His versions of scripture always reflect an element of fancy. While this verse from Hebrews is potentially a dangerous one for Blenkins, with its concentration on 'the thoughts and intentions of the heart', he forestalls questioning of his own hidden purposes. Blenkins's opening question is designed to avert suspicion: 'What is a liar?' (*AF* 70). In an anecdote which anticipates the sermon heard by the narrator in Part Two, Blenkins tells the story of a boy who choked to death immediately upon lying. To illustrate the boy's eternal judgement, Blenkins then tells the fantastic story about the suicide in the volcano of Etna. In the telling of this tale, he also misquotes a verse from the Psalms, a verse which is repeated in the gospels during the temptation of Jesus in the wilderness. Instead of 'They shall bear thee up in their hands, lest thou dash thy foot against a stone' (KJV Ps. 91.12), Blenkins refashions the verse to read 'And in their hands shall they bear thee up, lest at any time thou fall into a volcano' (*AF* 71). His misquotations are not without their humour. Just as they are intended, by him, to add to Blenkins's authority and to make him credible, so it is with this story about Mount Etna. In it he rewrites a parable from Luke chapter 16, casting himself as the righteous Lazarus to the skeleton's rich man. With this identification, endorsed by the comments of the tortured skeleton, Blenkins shows himself to be one of the elect, already in Abraham's bosom, just as Lazarus is. He finishes his sermon by attacking the notion of being 'in love', asking 'Was Jeremiah ever in love, or Ezekiel, or Hosea … ? No. Then why should we be?' (*AF* 72). The whole point of the story of Hosea was that he *was* 'in love', and tragically, at the command of God, in love with a prostitute who continued to be unfaithful. This was so that he could experience the pain God was feeling at the unfaithfulness of his people. Hosea's living parable, which Blenkins effectively denies, reflects a different God from the one who vindictively chokes a small boy for lying and who torments a suicide victim forever. The picture of God in 'Hosea' is one who feels emotions in a human way, the kind of God Waldo is searching for but who cannot be seen in the theology found in his interpretive community.

By putting the Bible in the hands of such an unreliable figure as Blenkins, who only uses it to manipulate and oppress others, its authority as a source of truth is undermined. In fact, it is shown to be powerfully dangerous, especially when evoked in an environment of ignorance. In *African Farm* the Bible is an external prop, one of many employed by Blenkins to deceive others. As the narrator ironically comments with regard to the effect of this sermon on Tant' Sannie and 'the coloured girl': 'They did not understand the discourse, which made it the more affecting' (*AF* 73). The ironic stance of the narrator regarding the Bible is confirmed by the use of Biblical quotations as chapter headings, such as 'I Was A Stranger, And Ye Took Me In'. This heading undermines the position of scripture in the life of Otto, who although he is sincere, is completely duped by evil. Blenkins and Otto seem to sit at opposite poles in their approach to others, evoking the biblical injunction to the disciples to 'be ye therefore wise as serpents, and harmless as doves' (KJV Matt. 10.16). With Blenkins functioning as a serpent, and Otto as a dove, neither can present a balanced view of Christianity, thus discrediting it and its scriptures utterly in the eyes of the developing Waldo.

Despite this, the narrator's relationship to the scriptures is an ambivalent one. Like Blenkins, Ralph Iron is not above invoking the authority of scripture to achieve his ends, while at the same time undermining it. One of the ways in which this occurs is that Waldo, even as he loses his faith, is increasingly portrayed as a Christ-like figure. This is signalled in the episode in which Tant' Sannie is told by Blenkins that Waldo has an evil book. Though neither of them has any idea what the book is about, or possibly *because* they have no idea, they decide it should be burnt. Before the burning though, Tant' Sannie throws it at Waldo, hitting his head. J.S. Mill's *The Principles of Political Economy* is then thrown into the oven, 'gone out of existence, like many another poor heretic of flesh and blood' (*AF* 114). Waldo's passivity evokes Christ: likening a book to a martyr reinforces the imagery of religious persecution. This is further developed in the whipping incident. Though questioned and accused of a theft he has not committed, Waldo remains silent. He continues to be silent throughout his ordeal, though Blenkins whips him severely. Both Waldo's passive silence and his experience of being whipped link him to Christ prior to the crucifixion. This link is reinforced by Waldo's prayer in the fuel-house after the whipping; 'When he clasped his hands frantically and prayed: "O God, my beautiful God, my sweet God, once, only once, let me feel you near me tonight!" he could not feel him' (*AF* 125). This recalls Jesus's prayer on the cross: 'My God my God, why hast thou forsaken me?' (KJV Matt. 27.46). Both prayers express an overwhelming sense of abandonment in the face of injustice. The final image of Waldo in this guise comes when Tant' Sannie realises at least some of Blenkins's duplicity and turns on him. Waldo gives up his supper, his bed, his hat and his few coins when Blenkins asks for them, and shows no interest in taking any form of revenge on his persecutor. He is the living if somewhat sullen embodiment of Matthew chapter five that the narrator finds so compelling in 'Times and Seasons': 'whosoever shall smite thee on thy right cheek, turn to him the other also'; 'And if any man will sue thee at the law, and take away thy coat, let him have thy cloak also'; 'Give to him that asketh thee, and from him that would borrow of thee turn not thou away'; 'Love your enemies, bless them that curse you, do good to them that hate you' (KJV Matt. 5.39, 40, 42, 44).

While the Calvinist theology of much of her early interpretive community is rejected by Schreiner, she retains and indeed endorses aspects of the nineteenth-century missionary ethos without subjecting them to the rigorous attention she gave to the theology. Part of this ethos is a belief in the unquestioned value of suffering and self-denial, which gives the whole novel a mood of grim puritanism. This is apparent in Waldo's persecution, Lyndall's choices and death, and is especially encapsulated in the allegory of the Hunter, with its hopeless message of total striving and sacrifice for little or no reward. Joyce Avrech Berkman, in her first study of Olive Schreiner and her work, concludes that 'though she jettisoned Christian theology, she retained much of the ethics of a Christian missionary family throughout her life' (49). Despite her attempts to throw off the constrictions of her parents' brand of Christianity, Schreiner still demonstrates how strongly she has been constructed by it and how powerfully its discourses work in her. The heritage of Christianity is not easily dismissed. Edward Aveling, the *de facto* husband of Eleanor Marx, assumed in his 1883 review that it could be, to be replaced immediately and naïvely with a new god: 'Religion here, as everywhere, has failed men. Science has solved the problem of the hereafter' (68). Schreiner's ambivalence shows that the move away from the old belief system was not so easily accomplished.

Schreiner marks the shift from Christianity with the allegorical tale in the chapter 'Waldo's Stranger'. She evidently thought enough of this piece to include it as 'The Hunter' in *Dreams*, a collection of short fictional allegories first published in 1890 and republished many times over the next forty years. Schreiner was maligned throughout the twentieth century for 'wasting' her talents on these allegories instead of producing more novels, but Schreiner's allegories were very popular, which is some justification of her choice of the genre. It may show once again the dissatisfactions with the form of the realist novel that are seen in *African Farm*. As Bjørhovde suggests, 'It seems more fruitful to regard Schreiner's short pieces in light of her reaction against the conventional novel form' (55). They also provided inspiration to activists, especially to the suffragettes in the first part of the twentieth century. Constance Lytton, who was jailed four times for activism in the cause of suffrage, records how in the prison hospital ward, Mrs Pethick Lawrence retold Schreiner's 'Three Dreams in a Desert' from *Dreams*, which

> seemed scarcely an allegory. The words hit out a bare literal description of the pilgrimage of women. It fell on our ears more like an A B C railway guide to our journey than a figurative parable, though its poetic strength was all the greater for that. (157)

She goes on to record that after this story, the women went to bed 'content': 'As I laid my head on the rattling pillow I surrendered my normal attitude towards literature, and thought "There is some point, some purpose in it after all"' (158). The spirit in which this story was received reflects the spirit in which all of these allegories were written: they are full of self-sacrificial missionary zeal. Though 'The Hunter' from *African Farm* is ostensibly an outline of the abandonment of a Christian belief system, its ascetic puritanism is as extreme as any grim version of Calvinism, and possibly more so, as it leaves no room for any comfort or fulfilment. At least the Calvinist has the joys of heaven to look forward to. The Hunter has only the thought of others who will attain what he has sought, and the assertion that somehow all people are connected:

> Where I lie down worn out other men will stand, young and fresh. By the steps that I have cut they will climb; by the stairs that I have built they will mount. They will never know the name of the man who made them. At the clumsy work they will laugh; when the stones roll they will curse me. But they will mount, and on *my* work;

they will climb, and by *my* stair! They will find her, and through me! And no man liveth to himself, and no man dieth to himself. (*AF* 168, emphasis in original)

The sacrifice of the one for the many has strong Christian overtones, as does the language used.

Schreiner's ambivalence towards the Christian scriptures is also strongly evident in the style of language she employs. While undermining the authority of Scripture in the ways I have discussed, the narrator still exploits its power in 'The Hunter'. By using language reminiscent of the *King James Version*, the narrator seeks to give this story the force of sacred text. Schreiner does more than adopt a genre: she exploits the fact that certain biblical phrases, words and sentence structures carry the sense of scriptural authority even when they are used in another setting. In her later allegories, the biblical links are even more obvious, with God as a character and heaven as a setting. In 'I Thought I Stood', it is God who tells two women to 'take the message' down to 'Man', presumably a message about the oppression of women, though this is only implied (Schreiner, *Dreams* 128-129). Schreiner, in the *Dreams* collection and in 'The Hunter', clearly draws on the authority of the Bible to empower and authorise her own writing, further demonstrating her ambivalence toward the Christian heritage.

Though the presence of this allegory in *African Farm* came as something of a surprise to many of her readers, Schreiner did have a clear precedent in *Wilhelm Meister*. It was also an effective enough narrative strategy to be followed by Pater. In *Marius the Epicurean* (1885), published only two years after *African Farm*, he used a similar technique, interjecting a translation of Apuleius's story of Cupid and Psyche into the main story. In Goethe's novel, Wilhelm's story is interrupted by the lengthy 'Confessions of a Fair Saint', which, although providing remote background information about Wilhelm's future bride's family, nevertheless is non-essential with regard to the plot of *Meister* as a whole. Like 'The Hunter', it describes a spiritual *Bildung*. Both protagonists renounce the pleasures of the world to seek after higher things, and both believe they are on the path to truth. In *Meister*, the story is read by Wilhelm to the fallen woman Aurelia, bringing her contentment and peace as she dies after being abandoned by her lover. Its effect is to cause her to forgive the lover (who is painted throughout the book as an excellent man, despite the fact that he seduces a succession of women) and to induce quiet acquiescence in the face of death. The story of the saint herself is a mixture of feminine subservience and spiritual independence, the overall effect of which is to affirm the spiritual realm over any other. Importantly, it is concerned with the dynamics of Christian conversion and discipleship, and with questions of living the spiritual life in the material world. In contrast, 'The Hunter' is concerned with the abandonment of Christian belief. It even goes beyond issues of living in the material world, as the world the Hunter occupies can only be thought of in mythic terms. Just as Schreiner overturns the model of *Bildung* at work in the whole of *Wilhelm Meister*, so she overturns the basic intent of this encapsulated story. It is another way of asserting that the narrative models of Europe are insufficient for the outposts of Empire, where the narrative certainties of Western realism cannot be maintained.

In his description of the English *Bildungsroman*, Moretti has identified it as a form which reflects 'a truly *widespread* culture of justice' (213, emphasis in original). Such a culture 'must necessarily cherish certainties, prohibitions, punishments and rewards; it must necessarily see things in black and white, as the never-ending story of innocents and criminals' (Moretti 213). These innocents have tended to be children, at least at the beginning of their tales. Jane Eyre and Pip, David Copperfield and Heathcliff, have all found themselves at some stage as innocent and vulnerable children at the mercy of oppressive adults. It is unsurprising then that at the start of *African Farm*, Lyndall and Em are already orphans and Waldo becomes one during Part One. So Waldo and Lyndall begin as many an English protagonist begins: both are orphaned and treated cruelly by the adults around them. In the English *Bildungsroman*, they could be expected to come into their own by the end of the novel, having found their place in the world and been rewarded for their innocence. The cruel adults would have been punished in some way, and the world would seem an ordered place. Such a scenario is expected by the reader, and the narrator gives enough hints about its likely fulfilment to make the abandonment of this plot a disturbing experience for readers. Blenkins's treatment of Waldo, especially the whipping, is the type of behaviour which brought down narratorial punishment on its perpetrators in earlier *Bildungsromane*. Characters like Pip's sister Mrs Joe in *Great Expectations* typify what Moretti means by 'criminals'. When we first encounter her, she is the persecutor not only of Pip but also of her husband Joe, and one of her chief instruments of abuse, her cane, is given the benign designation 'Tickler'. The progress of the narrative is not forgiving of Mrs Joe: she is bashed and incapacitated, finally dying in a completely powerless state. Similarly, all those who cross Jane in *Jane Eyre* are burned or removed. Nothing is allowed to stand in the way of Moretti's 'innocents' coming up in the world. The self-realisation of the protagonist is the axis on which all the action revolves. Many of these plots involve substitute parents like Mrs Joe who are not only unsatisfactory but also cruel and unjust. They throw the powerless state of the young protagonist into strong relief against the backdrop of their own criminality. The rise of the hero/heroine is predicated on their fall: the innocents cannot find their place in the world unless the criminals are punished, and generally up until this stage in the English novel, they are.

It should not be surprising, then, that just as both Lyndall and Waldo are unwilling or unable to find vocation or marriage, the symbols of successful growth in the *Bildungsroman* economy, so the 'criminals' go unpunished. At first it appears that Blenkins has been run out of the farm and thwarted in his object of marrying a wealthy farm-owning widow. It is only in the last few pages that the narrator lets us in on the news that Blenkins has succeeded in his aims by marrying an old woman with dropsy and cancer, who is expected to die within months. Tant' Sannie, the other adult who has a persecuting role (though she is not confined to this), also succeeds in getting another husband she can control, having a child, and consolidating her wealth: in short, all she has ever wanted. Though these outcomes are presented in a comic manner, this does not detract from the fact that they are a reversal of the earlier form. If Moretti is right, and the English *Bildungsroman* from Fielding to Dickens is the expression of a culture preoccupied with 'the realm of the law', then *African Farm* can be read as the expression of a culture in which injustice is the only certainty (213).

The society depicted in *African Farm* is multilingual, multiracial and multicultural, but nowhere does this lead to equality. Wherever there is difference, there is hierarchy. This is implicit throughout the text, beginning with the very first scene. Margaret Lenta has said, 'The opening scene of *The African Farm* is evidence that the humblest domestic structures manifested, as they continue to do today, that determination to maintain separation' between races (Lenta, 'Racism, Sexism and Olive Schreiner's Fiction' 18). The narrator describes the layout of the farm: 'First, the stone-walled "sheep-kraals" and Kaffir huts; beyond them the dwelling-house' (*AF* 35). As Itala Vivan notes, there are 'Two separate worlds: the one for animals, the other for men [sic]' (97), and the black Africans are clearly with the animals. This is the reality of the world of *African Farm*. Racism is endemic in the society; the narrator does not escape the power of this discourse and it is not difficult to find comments which express a racist attitude. References to 'an ill-looking Kaffir', 'a sullen, ill-looking woman, with lips hideously protruding' and to 'a small naked nigger' as 'the little animal' suggest that the narratorial voice is fully implicated in this racist discourse which sees non-whites as intrinsically inferior and allied with the animals (*AF* 41, 87, 292). However, at other times there is a knowingness in this voice which suggests a far greater distance from the simple racism such comments might seem to imply.

When Waldo discusses the Bushmen, in one of his more voluble moments, he uses similarly pejorative comments. The Bushmen (the San) were 'so small and ugly', and they created images 'that make us laugh' (*AF* 49). However, Waldo is aware of his affinity with the San artist. Deborah Schapple has suggested that there is a connection

> between the novelist, her male protagonist, and the displaced San ... Interpretations of the crucial role that these paintings play in the novel, therefore, have largely corresponded both with Schreiner's degree of empathy (no matter how conflicted) toward the San and with her growing anticolonial sentiments. (79)

Waldo imagines the thoughts and actions of the painter, who 'worked hard, very hard, to find the juice to make the paint' and who 'used to kneel here naked, painting, painting, painting; and he wondered at the things he made himself' (*AF* 49, 50). As art remains one of the few activities not stripped of meaning in *African Farm*, this is a strong endorsement of the humanity of the San painter. And Waldo is aware of the fate of the San: 'Now the Boers have shot them all, so that we never see a yellow face peeping out among the stones' (*AF* 50). The narrator makes explicit the rationale for this kind of violent behaviour when 'a small Kaffir' is described as a 'son of Ham' (*AF* 52). By viewing the black Africans as descendants of the biblical figure Ham, the biblical exegetes of the Dutch Reformed Church and the Boer invader/settlers sought to justify their domination and exploitation of these groups. Ham was associated with Egypt, and his son Cush with Ethiopia. While there are some prophecies against both nations in the book of Ezekiel, it is difficult to see how these, or any other biblical injunctions, justified this perception of black Africans as less than human. However, with this reference to Ham, the narrator makes it clear that he is aware of the apparatus used to condone the violent racism of the Boers. He is not so completely interpellated by the discourse of racism that he cannot stand back from it. The ironic distance of the narrator from the racism of the characters is also shown in relation to Tant' Sannie and the Sunday service: 'The Kaffir servants were not there, because Tant' Sannie held that they were descended from the apes, and needed no salvation' (*AF* 69). By taking just enough from Darwin to justify dehumanising black Africans, but not so much that she dehumanises herself, Tant' Sannie is living demonstration of the emptiness of any justification of racism. Neither Tant' Sannie's nor the 'biblical' rationale are based on knowledge, but are driven by expediency. Likewise, Blenkins sprouts egalitarian sentiments about the availability of God's grace which he knows will meet with Otto's favour: 'Do we know distinctions of race, or of sex, or of colour? *No!*' (*AF* 84). However, his preceding comment shows that such a thought would not affect his actual exploitative behaviour: 'Do we not love the very worm we tread upon, and as we tread upon it?' (*AF* 84). Whatever characters say, racism (and sexism) are a way of life in the Karroo.

The impact this has on the form of the novel is unmistakable. The English *Bildungsroman* plot which encapsulates a culture's belief in the certainty of justice is meaningless in this new environment. Instead, this new approach to the form tracks the effect of injustice on the protagonists, who are not rescued by strangers, vocation, romance or inheritance. The certainty of injustice is established in 'Times and Seasons', when the narrator records:

> And, we say it slowly, but without sighing, 'Yes, we see it now: there is no God.'
> And, we add, growing a little colder yet, 'There is no justice.

> The ox dies in the yoke, beneath its master's whip; it turns its anguish-filled eyes on the sunlight, but there is no sign of recompense to be made it. The black man is shot like a dog, and it goes well with the shooter. The innocent are accused, and the accuser triumphs. If you will take the trouble to scratch the surface anywhere, you will see under the skin a sentient being writhing in impotent anguish.' (*AF* 149)

Providence has departed, and the form produced by those living in its shadow must undergo a transformation.

While Waldo's *Bildung* is so dominated by his disillusionment with Calvinistic Christianity, his development does encompass other areas. He is at least launched on plots involving the usual preoccupations of the *Bildungsroman* hero, even if he does not arrive at the same destinations. Work, quest, romance, the interventions of benign others; all of these are at least gestured toward in *African Farm*, although they all begin in the form of ways of filling the hole left by God.

When Waldo begins to study, it is in reaction to this gap:

> What should we think of now? All is emptiness. So we take the old arithmetic; and the multiplication table, which with so much pains we learnt long ago and forgot directly, we learn now in a few hours and never forget again... We save money for a Latin Grammar and an Algebra, and carry them about in our pockets, poring over them as over our Bible of old. (*AF* 151)

Initially a substitute for God, education comes to be valued for its own sake. Fresh attention is also turned to Nature: 'All these years we have lived beside her, and we have never seen her; now we open our eyes and look at her' the narrator tells us (*AF* 151). This activity is begun as coldly as the book learning. When observations are made about the development of chickens in the egg, the narrator records, 'We are not excited or enthusiastic about it; but a man is not to lay his throat open, he must think of something' (*AF* 152). If the universe is merely a chance occurrence, then life is without meaning. The realisation of this is completely deadening to Waldo for a time:

> Whether a man believes in a human-like God or no is a small thing. Whether he looks into the mental and physical world and sees no relation between cause and effect, no order, but a blind chance sporting, this is the mightiest fact that can be recorded in any spiritual existence. It were almost a mercy to cut his throat, if indeed he does not do it for himself.
>
> We, however, do not cut our throats. To do so would imply some desire and feeling, and we have no desire and no feeling. (*AF* 150)

However, through the methodical dissection of ducks and lambs, connections between living things begin to emerge for Waldo. The similarities between networks of blood-vessels, the outline of thorn trees and the antlers of the horned beetle gradually suggest a link within Nature, which grows into a sense of the unity — and meaning — of all things: 'Nothing is despicable — all is meaningfull [sic]; nothing is small — all is part of a whole, whose beginning and end we know not' (*AF* 154). It is this which keeps Waldo from utter despair, and develops into a much more complete Emersonian view of life by the end of the book.

The gesture this text makes towards the idea of vocation for Waldo is twofold. It records his experiences of work, in the conventional sense, and his self-expressions such as his carvings, which can be described as art. Waldo is working virtually from the time we meet him. At the time he offers his sacrifice of a mutton chop, he is herding the sheep, and all of his time on the farm is spent in various forms of farm labour. The text offers one of the 'promissory notes' referred to by Du Plessis with regard to Waldo's working life. We see him sharing with the distressed Em his great secret of the invention he has made. On his way back from his trip to the mill, unaware that his father is dead, he not only draws great comfort from 'the hand in his breast resting on the sheep-shearing machine' but also from dreaming about its worldwide success (*AF* 97). He makes plans for what he will do with the money he earns, plans which include the purchase of 'A box full, full of books. They shall tell me all, all, all' (*AF* 97). The scenario he imagines, of instant success and comparative wealth, can be dismissed as the naïve dream of the adolescent, which education in life will modify and make more realistic. However, Victorian readers would have been unlikely to anticipate the complete abandonment of the project and indeed of all ambition in the inventive area. Waldo's dreams can be read as promissory notes which evoke in the reader an expectation of eventual positive outcomes in his vocation. Not only does Blenkins shatter these expectations, but Waldo lets them dissolve with his utter passivity. The narrator completely undermines any readerly expectations about the likelihood of Waldo's success with the picture of Waldo's dog Doss, who, following Blenkins's destruction of the machine,

> walked off to play with a black-beetle. The beetle was hard at work trying to roll home a great ball of dung it had been collecting all the morning; but Doss broke the ball, and ate the beetle's hind legs, and then bit off its head. And it was all play, and no one could tell what it had lived and worked for. A striving, and a striving, and an ending in nothing. (*AF* 107)

The natural world reflects human society, with the narrator implying that no effort, work or vocation has any purpose or outcome. In terms of the European *Bildungsroman*, this is a severe shift in values. Waldo's further experiences of work do nothing to alleviate this extreme rejection of the central tenets of the form.

With the approaching marriage of Em and Gregory, Waldo decides to leave the farm before Gregory will become master. His dreams have not been entirely destroyed. When he discusses his plans with Lyndall, he says he wants to 'See — see everything' (*AF* 197). Though Lyndall assures him that he will be disappointed, he leaves the farm with some sense of exhilaration. Once again, very late in the novel, we embark on the journey which has, in the history of the *Bildungsroman*, been so vital in the hero's development. The sense of throwing off the restrictions of provincial society and domestic duty which is such a feature of fictions such as *Wilhelm Meister* and *Great Expectations* when the hero leaves home is suggested here. As Waldo considers his possible return, he thinks, 'To come back some day! Would the bird ever return to its cage?' (*AF* 221). His view of the other farm-dwellers changes as well: 'He was leaving them all to that old life, and from his height he looked down on them pityingly. So they would keep on crowing, and coming to light fires, when for him that old colourless existence was but a dream' (*AF* 223).

We hear no more about Waldo's journey until his return. This return itself shatters any illusions the reader may still hold about the success, in conventional terms, of Waldo's journey. He does not return unrecognisable, or dressed as a gentleman like Heathcliff: rather he arrives with a small bundle and the admission that even his horse has died. His clothes are patched and his hat worn, and as he begins to write an account of his journey for Lyndall, his thoughts confirm what his appearance has suggested: 'He would tell her all he had seen, all he had done, though it were nothing worth relating' (*AF* 252). He has not found his fortune or vocation. He has not even learnt anything other than the fact that he longs for Lyndall. Though his reading has continued (*Elementary Physiology* and Spencer's *First Principles*), Waldo does not pursue education in any institutionalised way. Instead he works, first as a salesman in a shop, where the falseness of the sales staff repulses him, and then as a wagon driver. Everywhere he goes, he encounters hypocrisy and brutality.

Though Waldo plans to continue his reading while the oxen rest, tiredness becomes his dominant feeling, and all he can do is eat, sleep and work. The other side of meaningful work is meaning*less* work, as Waldo discovers: 'You may work, and work, and work, till you are only a body, not a soul' (*AF* 256). Drunkenness, the habitual condition of the wagon master, becomes the habit for Waldo also. It is only the thought of Lyndall, who increasingly occupies his mind, that provokes him to abandon drinking. Work, for Waldo, has been completely discredited. However, while he abandons the pursuit of work for himself, he does not abandon the whole idea of work as such. At the conclusion of his letter to Lyndall, he commits himself to the support of *her* work: 'I am very helpless, I shall never do anything; but you will work, and I will take your work for mine' (*AF* 263). Unable to give up all hope, he projects whatever aspirations he may have had onto Lyndall, and is thus able to acquiesce with regard to his own. While this is revolutionary with regard to gender roles, it does not come to pass because Lyndall has employed just the same strategy, disclaiming her own capacity to achieve: 'I will do nothing good for myself, nothing for the world, till someone wakes me … To see the good and the beautiful … and to have no strength to live it, is only to be Moses on the mountain of Nebo, with the land at your feet and no power to enter. It would be better not to see it' (*AF* 196). Yet she continues to assume that Waldo will achieve something, telling Gregory that Waldo is 'like a thorn-tree, which grows up very quietly, without anyone's caring for it, and one day suddenly breaks out into yellow blossoms' (*AF* 231). Both find it necessary to disqualify themselves from the pursuit of active vocation, while projecting their hopes onto the other.

Up until this point, I have not referred in detail to the other dominant writer of the mid-nineteenth century: George Eliot. This could be seen as somewhat disingenuous, as Eliot's interpretation of the *Bildungsroman* was radically different from that of Dickens. In noting the differences, Moretti, with obvious relief, states that 'The first thing to change is the protagonist's intellectual physiognomy, in that now, thank God, they have one' (214). He recognises the contribution made by Eliot's knowledge of *Wilhelm Meister* and German culture, especially its impact on the idea of work. It is Eliot who really pursues the concept of 'vocation', and in doing so she moves away from the meritocratic world of Dickens. In addition, and significantly for *African Farm*, Moretti asserts that 'Besides being by far the finest nineteenth-century English novel, *Middlemarch* is also the only one which dares to deal with the major theme of the European *Bildungsroman*: failure' (216). However, Waldo and Lyndall do more than fail: they give up the quest before they reach their adulthood. Casaubon is without sufficient talent for his life's work; Lydgate chooses a poor marriage partner, and sabotages his scientific yearnings; Dorothea also makes a poor marriage choice, and is inhibited by her gender from having the impact on her world that she desired, though she is finally romantically fulfilled. All experience vocational failure, as do minor characters such as Bulstrode and Brooke, but never is the actual idea of vocation questioned. For Waldo and Lyndall, vocation becomes impossible, and irrelevant. Growing up as the orphans of Empire in the Karroo, inheriting from their European parents only enough to alienate them from both Boer and native societies, Waldo and Lyndall are unable to take up this integral expression of nineteenth-century capitalist values. It is a European goal that both they, and Schreiner, shed, with most of the other ideological values which constituted the *Bildungsroman* form. Their only vestige of attachment to this goal is that though Waldo and Lyndall abandon it individually, they hang onto some ambition for the other. Like the Christian tradition, it proves difficult to throw off.

Because the quest aspect of the *Bildungsroman* is so intertwined with the idea of vocation, it must also be discredited. This is probably best achieved when Waldo, having abandoned wagon driving and become a storeman, encounters his Stranger in the Grahamstown Botanic Gardens. When they had parted, the Stranger had uttered the classic anticipator of plot, 'Well, I trust we shall meet again some day, sooner or later' (*AF* 173). Once again, this is one of the 'promissory notes' Du Plessis refers to, designed to assure the reader that this meeting will indeed occur, and be significant once again for Waldo and his development. The first meeting has been important for Waldo, because it has provided him with an articulation of his spiritual journey, which he was unable to express verbally. It also gave him a sense of affinity with another person, the knowledge that he was not alone in his thoughts, and the awareness that the emptiness he was experiencing was unavoidable. As the Stranger assures him, 'We of this generation are not destined to eat and be satisfied as our fathers were; we must be content to go hungry' (*AF* 172-173). In his account of his journey, Waldo reveals that the thought of finding his Stranger was continually on his mind as he journeyed: 'wherever I have travelled I have looked for him — in hotels, in streets, in passenger wagons as they rushed in, through the open windows of houses I have looked for him, but I have not found him — never heard a voice like his' (*AF* 260). When Waldo finally sees him, he is spoken of as a love object, 'still as beautiful', with brown eyes 'more beautiful than any one's, except yours' (*AF* 261). However, this sighting does not fulfil the promise expected of it. The Stranger is with two beautifully dressed women, and is looking elegant, carrying a little cane and followed by an Italian greyhound. Everything about him announces his class, a factor which had not impinged on their meeting in the Karroo. Instead of greeting Waldo with enthusiasm, he pays him no attention whatsoever, and the ladies treat Waldo as some kind of lower species. The promised meeting does not even occur, thereby demolishing any dependence the reader might have on such plot devices. There is no benevolent God/author to guide Waldo in his quest. In fact, this (non)meeting has the effect of leading him to abandon the journey. It awakes loneliness in Waldo. Made aware of his class, and its inadequacies in the eyes of the Stranger and his companions, Waldo gives up his search for the communication he had had with the Stranger: 'I wanted clothes, and to be fashionable and fine. I felt that my hands were coarse, and that I was vulgar. I never tried to see him again' (*AF* 261). While awareness of class prompts a character like Pip in *Great Expectations* to strive to change his manners, education and dress, in Waldo this awareness only induces withdrawal. It also centres his longings on Lyndall.

2.3 Lyndall's tale: the feminist as romantic[13]

When Canon MacColl wrote his 1887 review of *African Farm*, he cited Calvinism as one of two factors which drove Schreiner 'from her religious and moral moorings' (73). The other factor was 'the difficulty which she finds in reconciling the facts of the world around her, and especially the injustice done to her own sex, with the doctrine of a God who is omnipotent, compassionate and just' (73). It is significant that MacColl links Schreiner's apprehension of gender issues to her crisis of faith, because the technique of using joint protagonists who are male and female would seem to allow for the neat separation of the issues of spirituality and gender. Marcia Gordon reads the text thus:

> In her pairing of central characters (Lyndall and Waldo) and parallel narrative development, Schreiner emphasizes the ideological similarities between religious and sexual oppression. Yet she painstakingly avoids any overlapping or seepage between these gender-differentiated Victorian cultural crises. Men explore the spiritual realm while women define themselves within the material-social realm. (157)

However, this reading ignores the explicit connection made by the narrator and Lyndall herself between the vacuum left by the absence of God and Lyndall's pursuit of self-destruction through romance. Lyndall's embroilment in the romance plot follows her clear rejection of Christianity and the resultant grief this rejection brings. She is portrayed

---

13 An earlier version of this section appeared as 'The Feminist as Romantic'.

as being in a state of loss, unreconciled to the psychic isolation of post-Christian life: 'I want to love! I want something great and pure to lift me to itself! ... I am so cold, so hard, so hard; will no one help me?' (*AF* 242). The Christian God may have been left behind, but Lyndall is still seeking salvation. While Waldo's *Bildung* may contain the more complete account of loss of faith, this journey has been Lyndall's also, and her subsequent battering at the hands of the romance plot is predicated upon her having made it. (The first person plural of 'Times and Seasons' also implies the inclusion of Lyndall with Waldo in the journey away from faith.) She begins as hero but finishes as heroine, ultimately choosing the role that the romance plot thrusts upon her. Du Plessis sees her as caught between the two: 'To be split between the hero, doing something for the world, and the heroine, waiting to be awakened, to be split between delivered and deliverer, is Lyndall's stalemate between romance and vocation' (27). But in terms of narrative denouement, she cannot remain there. Whatever the start of her journey promises, it finishes with Lyndall as nineteenth-century heroine, however subversively she may play the role. Implicit in this progression from potential hero to heroine is the spiritual crisis of losing God, and finding nothing to fill the void.

Like Waldo, Lyndall is an orphan whose father 'leaves no legacy, except his consumptive constitution' (Gordon 160). We know nothing at all of her mother. Through Em's father, she has the provision of a boarding school education, which she forces the otherwise inadequate mother-substitute Tant' Sannie to provide. Her ability to dominate others is the most notable and precocious feature of the young Lyndall, and seems to illustrate a 'hierarchy of souls' set up by the narrator. For while Bonaparte Blenkins is able to manipulate others through power and deceit, Lyndall uses only the force of her spirit, and this is shown to be stronger than Blenkins. When Tant' Sannie beats Em, Lyndall overcomes the woman's vastly superior strength using her personal force:

> For one instant Lyndall looked on, then she laid her small fingers on the Boer-woman's arm. With the exertion of half its strength Tant' Sannie might have flung the girl back upon the stones. It was not the power of the slight fingers, tightly though they clenched her broad wrist — so tightly that at bed-time the marks were still there; but the Boer-woman looked into the clear eyes and at the quivering white lips, and with a half-surprised curse relaxed her hold. The girl drew Em's arm through her own.
>
> 'Move!' she said to Bonaparte, who stood in the door; and he, Bonaparte the invincible, in the hour of his triumph, moved to give her place. (*AF* 91)

Lyndall appears to be an illustration of Ralph Waldo Emerson's assertion in 'Self-Reliance' that some spirits will dominate others: 'Who has more obedience than I masters me, though he should not raise his finger. Round him I must revolve by the gravitation of spirits' (Emerson, *Complete Works* 29). Later, when she takes the key to the fuel-room in order to release Waldo, neither Blenkins nor Tant' Sannie is prepared to stop her. This personal power, though obviously limited, promises much for her later life, and sets up clear readerly expectations about Lyndall's *Bildung*. Her own comments reinforce these, when she says, 'When that day comes, and I am strong, I will hate everything that has power, and help everything that is weak' (*AF* 93). This expectation that Lyndall will fight for justice is strengthened when she asserts to Waldo upon his release, 'we will not be children always; we shall have the power too, some day' (*AF* 127).

Lyndall's admiration for Napoleon Bonaparte is based on the recognition that he, too, was a dominating spirit of the type described by Emerson. While a child, Lyndall asserts that 'He was the greatest man who ever lived … the man I liked best' (*AF* 47). Her description of his life hints at great things for her own: 'Once he was only a little child, then he was a lieutenant, then he was a general, then he was an emperor. When he said a thing to himself he never forgot it. He waited, and waited, and waited, and it came at last' (*AF* 47). Her childish statements regarding the future take on the aspect of never-to-be-forgotten promises in light of Napoleon's life. When she returns from school with a fully articulated feminist analysis we wait for her to turn these promises into action and use 'the gravitation of spirits' to the advantage of the cause. However, Lyndall's time away has not just revealed to her the workings of patriarchy; something has occurred in her personal growth which will undermine the expectations held by reader and Lyndall alike. Once again, 'promissory notes' have been given to the reader, but the rest of the narrative will go about tearing them up.

At the age of 12, when Em sees only marriage ahead, Lyndall articulates her plans to force Tant' Sannie to send her away to school. Her aim is knowledge, for as she tells Em, 'There is nothing helps in this world … but to be very wise, and to know everything — to be clever' (*AF* 45). Her motivation is in part economic. Em will inherit the farm when she turns seventeen but as Lyndall says, 'I … will have nothing. I must learn' (*AF* 46). Her boast is that 'When I am grown up … there will be nothing that I do not know' (*AF* 46). However, when Waldo quizzes her about what she has learnt at school, it has clearly been a disappointment. This account of her time away, though brief, parallels his letter to her after her death, detailing *his* journey. Neither finds what they are seeking, though both gain some measure of self-knowledge. Lyndall's account consists principally of a critique of the English-speaking boarding school, and its impact on girls. It was not the fount of knowledge which she had sought: 'I have discovered that of all the cursed places under the sun, where the hungriest soul can hardly pick up a few grains of knowledge, a girls' boarding-school is the worst' (*AF* 185). Lyndall describes the school as a 'nicely adapted machine for experimenting on the question, "Into how little space a human soul can be crushed?"' (*AF* 185) In it, girls only develop 'imbecility and weakness' (*AF* 185). Describing those who submitted to this treatment as 'the drove', Lyndall survives conformity by separating herself from all 'those things that were having their brains slowly diluted and squeezed out of them' (*AF* 186). Refusing to learn sewing or music, Lyndall continues her own self-education through newspapers and books in a bedroom of her own, which she gained through the force of her will. In light of her analysis of the gendering process which follows this account, her separation from, and condemnation of other females, may seem extremely unsympathetic. As she comments, 'Women bore me' (*AF* 199). But it may also be true that in order to resist the totalising power of the construction of gender in a British boarding school, strong measures were needed, including separation from submitting females. Taken with the oppressive early life on the farm, and Waldo's disappointing forays into the workforce, the boarding school can be seen as another example of the restrictive nature of South African life. Annalisa Oboe suggests that 'Schreiner experienced South Africa as a fundamental threat to the individual', and that in this environment, no individual dreams could prosper (84).

Out of the school Lyndall's education continues more quickly: 'In the holidays I learnt a great deal more. I made acquaintances, saw a few places, and many people, and some different ways of living, which is more than any books can show one' (*AF* 186). Lyndall also touches on another possible outcome of her *Bildung*: she airs the possibility of her development as a female artist. The brief mention that she 'found time to write some plays, and find out how hard it is to make your thoughts look anything but imbecile fools when you paint them with ink on paper', fills out the school account as the beginnings of a *Künstlerroman* plot (*AF* 186). There have already been other promises about the power of Lyndall's personality, or 'spirit'. She has even evoked the prophet Jeremiah when explaining to Waldo why she speaks well about women's issues: '"Speak! speak!" she said; "the difficulty is not to speak; the difficulty is to keep silence'" (*AF* 195).[14] The suggestion is that Lyndall is exceptionally gifted and, like a prophet, endowed with special insight. Indeed, prior to this Lyndall 'is presented from the very beginning of the novel as potential creator, threading beads with determined accuracy and transforming ice-plant leaves and blades of grass into a lovely ornament' (Wilkinson 110). Also apparent is her stated need and desire for economic independence, and a life as a female artist could potentially provide this. Talking to Waldo later, Lyndall appears to have a much clearer idea of where she might go. Describing her qualities, she concludes that these equip her to act: 'The actor, who absorbs and then reflects from himself other human lives, needs them all, but needs not much more. This is her end; but how to reach it?' (*AF* 216). She then recounts to Waldo how she was able to overcome seemingly insurmountable obstacles in order to go to school. We are presented with a heroine who has talents and determination enough to find success in her art. She also has a strategy for achieving it, one that seems rather ironic in light of Schreiner's subsequent life: 'They talk of genius — it is nothing but this, that a man knows what he can do best, and does it, and nothing else … the secret of success is concentration; wherever there has been a great life, or a great work, that has gone before' (*AF* 215). The *Künstlerroman* plot has not just been hinted at: it is the stated aim of this protagonist. However, this promise is never realised. Even as she says these words Lyndall is already pregnant, though the reader only discovers this later. She will go on to make a series of choices which will preclude her from gaining any artistic objective. Ultimately, the *Künstlerroman* is demolished by Lyndall's submission to aspects of the romance plot.

---

14 This is a direct reference to the prophet Jeremiah's experience of trying not to prophesy, thereby aligning Lyndall with a prophetic role: 'Then I said, I will not make mention of him, nor speak any more in his name. But his word was in mine heart as a burning fire shut up in my bones, and I was weary with forbearing, and I could not stay' (KJV Jer. 20.9).

Despite her partial capitulation, though, Lyndall's critique of the construction of gender remains a masterly piece of analysis, which in some ways draws force from the fact that she was unable to transcend it by demonstrating any alternative to its restrictions. Ann Ardis sees this as a limitation — 'Notwithstanding her damning characterization of the Victorian sexual economy, Lyndall never establishes a different kind of exchange between men and women' (66-67) — but in many ways Lyndall's inability to do this confirms her own analysis. Whatever the heroine's outcome, her words certainly had an impact in their day. That they were seen as subversive is illustrated by the recollections of Mrs Huth Jackson, a student of Cheltenham Ladies College, in Cruse (363): 'Girls smuggled in *African Farm*, then just out. The whole sky seemed aflame and many of us became violent feminists. (I was one already.)'. The main focus of Lyndall's feminist analysis is the way society constructs men to be active, and to '*Work!*', while women are constructed to '*Seem!*' by being pleasing to men (*AF* 188). Accordingly, the knowledge Lyndall has sought so earnestly is seen as being less valuable than 'this little chin' because the only way a woman can gain anything is through attracting a man, and her cute chin is a major asset in this endeavour (*AF* 188). The type of womanhood described here is somewhat at odds with the femininity of Tant' Sannie and the girls' upbringing on the farm. It is very much a picture of a cultured English woman of the city rather than the Boer woman of the farm, and seems to owe more to the picture in Tant' Sannie's bedroom than any living woman so far present in the text. As a child Lyndall is not only full of admiration for this picture of womanhood, but she aspires to be like her. Although her first aim is intellectual — 'there is nothing I will not know' — it is followed by 'I shall be rich, very rich; and I shall wear not only for best, but every day, a pure white silk, and little rosebuds, like the lady in Tant' Sannie's bedroom, and my petticoats will be embroidered, not only at the bottom, but all through' (*AF* 46). Though she has come to recognise the artificiality of this, it has its appeal.

Lyndall traces the restrictions placed on women through childhood to the point where women accept their confined state, fitting their 'sphere as a Chinese woman's foot fits her shoe, exactly, as though God had made both — and yet He knows nothing of either' (*AF* 189).

The picture Lyndall paints of the restrained child kneeling 'with one little cheek wistfully pressed against the pane' recalls the passage in 'Times and Seasons' in which the narrator, speaking in first person plural as Lyndall does here, describes a similar scene with a child standing at the window: 'We, standing in a window to look, feel the cool, unspeakably sweet wind blowing in on us, and a feeling of longing comes over us — unutterable longing, we cannot tell for what' (*AF* 189, 138). Specific scenes from this section have linked the narrator to Waldo: this scene makes the connection to Lyndall also. It also recalls earlier English heroines, and places Lyndall in a specific lineage. The first of these concerns the famous passage from *Jane Eyre* in which Jane looks out from the top of Thornfield-Hall to the horizon. Jane 'longed for a power of vision which might overpass that limit' and goes on to anticipate some of the thoughts which Schreiner expands upon in the chapter 'Lyndall' (Brontë 110). Jane's thoughts, that 'women feel just as men feel; they need exercise for their faculties, and a field for their efforts just as much as their brothers do' (Brontë 110), have developed into Lyndall's assertion that 'when each woman's life is filled with earnest, independent labour, then love will come to her' (*AF* 195). The kind of labour Lyndall is thinking of is quite specific, as she mentions 'doctors, lawyers, law-makers, anything but ill-paid drudges', making her agenda explicitly the entry of women into the paid professions (*AF* 190). While Lyndall has specific social goals, Jane is more prepared to recognise the universality of her feelings, as she acknowledges that 'Millions are condemned to a stiller doom than mine, and millions are in silent revolt against their lot' (Brontë 110). However, Lyndall keeps herself free from 'the drove' and never makes an intellectual connection with other women. (Waldo is also linked to Jane, when Tant' Sannie throws the book at him. The narrator quite self-consciously draws attention to this, when he writes, 'Books have been thrown at other heads before and since that summer afternoon, by hands more white and delicate than those of the Boer-woman' (*AF* 114)).

The other heroines evoked by Lyndall's image of the longing girl at the window are those of George Eliot, women described in the Prelude to *Middlemarch* as 'the offspring of a certain spiritual grandeur ill-matched with the meanness of opportunity' whose 'ardour alternated between a vague ideal and the common yearning of womanhood', and who come to be exemplified by Dorothea Brook (Eliot 7, 8). While Eliot provides the information by which the reader can conclude that gender is a major inhibiting factor for her heroines, she never actually spells out that their 'meanness of opportunity' is due to it. Schreiner, on the other hand, makes this quite explicit. With the force of all this feminine longing behind her, Lyndall, who has articulated what the other heroines have only hinted at, is no more able to escape nineteenth-century plots for women than they were. In fact, they may be viewed as doing rather better than her. She does, however, exercise a degree of volition in her end which sets her apart, if tragically.

In Goethe's *Wilhelm Meister*, the account of Wilhelm's *Bildung* comes to an end when he is about to marry Natalia, the perfect marriage being the sign of his adaptation to society and his guarantee of happiness. In *African Farm*, the marriage of those with spiritual affinity would be expected to occur between Lyndall and Waldo, and yet their cultural growth does not occur at the same rate. While it appears that Lyndall is capable of holding her own in sophisticated South African English society, as exemplified by her Stranger, Waldo's brush with this world at the Botanic Gardens leaves him aware of his inadequacy. Yet it is to Waldo that Lyndall opens her heart, and it is Lyndall who becomes Waldo's focus. The narrative appears to offer 'promissory notes' that set up a possible romantic conclusion between Waldo and Lyndall. Their parallel developments at least offer spiritual unity. At the Boer wedding, Lyndall tells him:

> 'I like you so much, I love you.' She rested her cheek softly against his shoulder. 'When I am with you I never know that I am a woman and you are a man; I only know that we are both things that think. Other men when I am with them, whether I love them or not, they are mere bodies to me; but you are a spirit; I like you. (*AF* 210)

When Waldo writes his letter to Lyndall on his return to the farm, he has come to realise the place she has in his psyche. However, when he writes 'The back thought in my mind is always you', the reader is dubious about any romantic conclusion (*AF* 254). Though we are not yet privy to the fact that Lyndall is dead, we know she has gone off with her Stranger, breaking the romantic codes and placing herself in the position of fallen woman. It is through this episode that Schreiner concertedly examines the contradictions of the romance plot for heroines. There is no marriage to cap this tale of development. The endorsement of society which marriage brings to the end of the *Bildungsroman* is not to be offered here; rather, the opposite will be true. The discourses of power which operate in this society are examined and found to be ultimately destructive to the individual.

As Lyndall makes clear in her statement to Waldo above, she has spent time with other men and they have been 'mere bodies' to her (*AF* 210). By the time her Stranger actually appears on the farm, the reader has been given enough information to realise that Lyndall is pregnant to one of these men. She has discussed the origins of children born out of wedlock with Waldo, and after repeating the saying that 'God sends the little babies', she asks 'who sends the little children then? The Devil, perhaps!' (*AF* 209, 10). She has also pondered the responsibility of becoming a parent: 'it must be a terrible thing to bring a human being into the world' (*AF* 209). To clarify her condition, when Gregory offers to serve her, asking nothing in return, she responds by asking him to marry her, saying 'I want nothing more than your name' (*AF* 232). However, the arrival of the Stranger forestalls this arrangement, and she leaves the farm with him instead, despite having refused *his* offer of marriage.

Lyndall's reasons for these actions are an expression of her highly ambivalent position regarding romance and sexuality, and have elicited plenty of critical interest, from the time of the novel's release until now. D.F. Hannigan, writing on 'The Artificiality of English Novels' in *The Westminster Review* of 1890, notes that

> [h]er refusal to marry the man she loves is in apparent contradiction to all our preconceived ideas concerning the sex. But this is a superficial view of the matter. Lyndall has never met a man whom she could love with all her soul. Therefore, though she is ready to surrender herself she refuses to sacrifice her moral freedom. (263-264)

This view is reiterated by the somewhat suspiciously named Thomas F. Husband, who in a highly feminist 1894 review of *African Farm* wrote:

> Marry him she will not, for she knows that marriage, where there is not love as well as passion, is not marriage. He is naught but her instrument, which she discards when she has used it — we are more familiar with the opposite case in the relation between the man and the woman. (633)

Crucial to these sympathetic responses to Lyndall's actions is the impact of the contemporary critique of the institution of marriage. *African Farm* had helped to bring this debate into popular circulation and by the 1890s it was difficult to pick up a journal which did not refer to it in some way. Lyndall's picture of marriage as a form of prostitution highlights its reduction to an economic exchange in which sex and full personhood are surrendered for keep and respectability. She contrasts the higher possibilities of marriage with its common practice: 'Marriage for love is the beautifullest external symbol of the union of souls; marriage without it is the uncleanliest traffic that defiles the world' (*AF* 190). While Lyndall does claim a love for her Stranger, she suggests that it is the wrong sort of love for marriage. His appeal is immediate, and physical, and as she informs him, 'You call into activity one part of my nature; there is a higher part that you know nothing of, that you never touch. If I married you, afterwards it would arise and assert itself, and I should hate you always, as I do now sometimes' (*AF* 237). However, while some early reviewers seemed quite sympathetic to Lyndall's distinctions (though just as many were shocked), more recent critics have generally been appalled at her choices.[15] What is the appeal of the Stranger, and why is she relatively powerless in his presence?

The dynamics of their interaction in the cabin on the farm reflect a different Lyndall to the one we have seen up until this time. He begins by complaining about the fact that he is being hidden to disguise the realities of their relationship, insulting her in the process: 'Your conscience is growing to have a certain virgin tenderness', he tells her (*AF* 235). Both seem to accept the double sexual standard of the day, assuming that she is somehow less worthy than he as a consequence of their sexual relationship. She describes herself through his eyes as one who has 'put herself into my power, and who has lost the right of meeting me on equal terms', as though this is a fact (*AF* 238). When he asks why she loved him,

---

15 For instance MacColl notes, 'We have heard the book described as "immoral" and "blasphemous"', and in another review a certain Anon asked, 'Are the details of such rottenness fit for commendation in a high-class English newspaper "for all and sundry to read"?' (MacColl 73; Anon. qtd in Clayton 75). Second-wave feminist disapproval is probably best summarised by Elaine Showalter's dismissal of all of Schreiner's heroines: 'Like Schreiner, they give up too easily and too soon' (203). Laurence Lerner questions the whole book's feminist reputation, and is particularly puzzled by Lyndall's rejection of her Stranger, finally asking in exasperation, 'Why will she not marry?', thereby completely missing the point of her critique of marriage (Lerner 185).

she foregrounds the most disturbing aspects of the relationship in terms of her power of self-determination: 'Because you are strong. You are the first man I ever was afraid of' (*AF* 238). Only her last reason seems to empower her: 'because I like to experience, I like to try' (*AF* 238). If his strength and her subsequent fear are the main source of attraction, there is a masochistic drive in Lyndall which we have not seen until now. This is where Lyndall's position with regards to the romance plot is revealed in all its destructive ambivalence.

The partial resistance she puts up is treated by him as a kind of amusement, a new erotic entertainment. When she tells him why she cannot marry him, he refuses to respond to the content of what she says, choosing to continue to view her as a sexual object rather than as a person, with his comments, 'I like you when you grow metaphysical and analytical' and 'I like you when you get philosophical' (*AF* 237). These are the statements of one supremely confident of his power. He can say what he likes knowing that he will still be able to enthral her. Though she is able to analyse his motivations just as clearly as she has outlined the processes involved in the construction of gender, she still seems unable to analyse her own, and what they will mean for her life. She recognises what drives him:

> I have seen enough to tell me that you love me because you cannot bear to be resisted, and want to master me. You liked me at first because I treated you and all men with indifference. You resolved to have me because I seemed unattainable. That is all your love means. (*AF* 238)

In spite of her perception of his motivations, she is largely under his control. The narration bears out his confidence of this, recording that 'It was certainly not in her power to resist him' (*AF* 240). Lyndall's decision to keep something back by not marrying him is her only real point of resistance. Both of them regard marriage as some form of higher submission, as is shown when he finally pleads with her, 'my darling … why will you not give yourself entirely to me?' (*AF* 239). Though she is caught up in what she acknowledges as 'madness', she is analytical enough to realise that it will pass and that she will not want to find herself permanently in his power: 'if I had been married to you for a year, I should have come to my senses, and seen that your hands and your voice are like the hands and the voice of any other man. I cannot quite see that now. But it is all madness' (*AF* 237). That marriage is seen as an irreversible loss of freedom is made clear by Lyndall when she tells him, 'if once you have me you would hold me fast. I shall never be free again' (*AF* 236).

Why this clearly unequal relationship has power over her at all is a question which has engrossed critics, especially those concerned with issues of gender. Du Plessis has said that Lyndall's 'death is provoked by a conflict between her identity as a "new woman" … and her already constituted psychic needs', claiming that 'She is split between her sensual needs and her feminist ideals' (27). Kathleen Blake expresses her dismay by stating, 'What is terrible is that Lyndall wants the kind of love that she distrusts' (Blake, *Love and the Woman Question* 214). Lenta again suggests a sort of self-division: 'The absolute separation which she makes between sexual satisfaction and love is causing a split in her own personality' (Lenta, 'Independence as the Creative Choice' 43). One can see Lyndall's dilemma as an expression of her own individual personality. However, I believe Lyndall's choices and fictional ends are not just specific to herself, as a fictional heroine, but reveal much about the power of the romance script, especially for the woman of the nineteenth-century world.

Blake has noted that 'The sexual energy of dominance and submission charges their scene together' (Blake, *Love and the Woman Question* 214). It should not be surprising that a nineteenth-century text figures the erotic in such terms. In a society such as that described by Lyndall, in which women are constructed to be sexual objects pleasing to men, the pattern of dominance and submission is being played out between genders in every sphere of life. Heterosexual relationships are virtually impossible outside of these patterns. Therefore, the dynamic of dominance and submission is built into all heterosexual contact. Lyndall is right to conclude:

> [W]hen love is no more bought and sold, when it is not a means of making bread, when each woman's life is filled with earnest, independent labour, then love will come to her, a strange sudden sweetness breaking in upon her earnest work; not sought for, but found. Then, but not now. (*AF* 195)

It is only outside of this inequality that heterosexuality will be free of the dynamics of dominance and submission. While women are not without power, as Lyndall admits, it is of the covert, manipulative kind, legitimate power being denied them. The relationship between Waldo and Lyndall is spiritual, almost genderless, but it is not surprising that it remains unfulfilled. It is the alternative which cannot be realised in a society of institutionalised gender inequality. Instead, we are presented with the obviously flawed liaison between Lyndall and her Stranger in which the inequality itself has become a source of the erotic. The hunter and hunted game they play is just a sexualised version of all gendered interaction around them. With no extant examples of equal heterosexual relationships, there are no other models. Power is sexy because sex always involves power.

The other function of this pattern is that it provides a way of negotiating Victorian codes regarding the sexual desires of women, which, in the middle-classes at least, were assumed to be negligible. If a woman is dominated, losing her power of volition, then she is no longer responsible for the desires evoked in the process. There is a fine line in this. If a woman allows a man to 'have his way with her', she is responsible, as Lyndall and her Stranger agree. However, having got to that point, if she then finds this to be sexually stimulating or fulfilling, she can be free of the assumption that she has inappropriate desires, because she has not done the initiating. The pattern of dominance and submission is thus a way of authorising a woman's sexuality, because her responses remain just that: responses. It should not be surprising, then, that Schreiner has created a scenario in which Lyndall's sexual desires are expressed in a relationship of obvious inequality, in which fear and strength are the main source of erotic appeal. It is a means of negotiating the denial of women's sexuality, and a reflection, if extreme, of all heterosexual relationships of the time, at least legally and socially. It is the expression of a narration which is both caught in the romance discourse, and critical of it. Just as Schreiner is deeply critical of Christianity, yet still keen to draw on the power of its discourse when it suits her purposes, so she is shown to be equivocal about romance. That the romance script still has a deep appeal to women is evident today in the huge sales of genre fiction connected with it.[16] It is not just Lyndall who is attracted by the fearful, powerful man. Her dilemmas are not only the private agonies of a particularly damaged psyche, as Du Plessis, Blake and Lenta seem to suggest. They are widely displayed conflicts which are experienced by large numbers of women today. When inequality becomes eroticised in a seemingly legitimised way, it is appealing. But despite its appeal, because of this inequality the romance plot always contains some element of the sadomasochistic. The romance plot is another clear area of ambivalence in the narrative voice of this text.

Where Lyndall really departs from the script of her times is in rejecting the marriage contract, and it is this which is both her downfall

---

16 For an overview of the popular romance genre and Harlequin Publishers which produces much of it, see Ann Barr Snitow's 'Mass Market Romance: Pornography for Women is Different', in which she discusses the erotic appeal of contemporary romance genres. The current appeal of SM erotica, most notably in the writings of E.L. James, is an example of the contemporary eroticisation of power difference.

and her gesture at independence. In this she anticipates the New Woman novelists of the 1890s, for whom marriage became a major preoccupation. Schreiner differs from many of these in that she does not feel the need to portray the potential husband as a monster in order to question the notion of marriage.[17] Lyndall's critique of marriage has been constant, beginning with her comments to Em: 'I am not in so great a hurry to put my neck beneath any man's foot; and I do not greatly admire the crying of babies' (*AF* 184). In terms of plots for heroines, once she rejects marriage there tends to be only one other scenario. Susan Sheridan, in what must be one of the earliest second-wave feminist responses to *African Farm*, points out that 'Having refused to submit to the subservient good-woman role, Lyndall is virtually forced into acting out the equally degrading bad-woman opposite' (22), the end of which is death. While in most nineteenth-century fiction the death of the fallen woman is punitive, Lyndall's death is both lovingly depicted and illustrative of Victorian gender codes. It further demonstrates the way in which this plot is both resistive of, and conforming to, nineteenth-century narrative patterns.

Daymond claims that Lyndall 'finds her options concentrated in just one combat: that with her stranger over the question of a woman's freedom in a relationship' (178). This is also the understanding of the Stranger himself, when, after the death of the baby, he again proposes marriage: 'I have learnt to love you more wisely, more tenderly than of old; you shall have perfect freedom. Lyndall, grand little woman, for your own sake be my wife!' (*AF* 278). However, once again Lyndall rejects the offer, despite the promise of freedom. She foregrounds two other factors, the first of which is the quality of love she has for him: 'I cannot be bound to one whom I love as I love you' (*AF* 279). The second is related to her

---

17 Two of the earlier overviews of this fiction, and the way it deals with the subject of marriage, can be found in Chapter Four of Boumelha, *Thomas Hardy and Women*, and in Bland, *Love and the Woman Question*.

quest for vocation, but seems more metaphysical or religious in nature, as she writes to him of her dream:

> One day — perhaps it may be far off — I shall find what I have wanted all my life; something nobler, stronger than I, before which I can kneel down. You lose nothing by not having me now; I am a weak, selfish, erring woman. One day I shall find something to worship, and then I shall be — (*AF* 279)

Though she has succumbed to his other attractions, the Stranger does not offer the possibility of spiritual union so she will not attach herself to him permanently. When they originally left for the Transvaal, she proposed a free union and she maintains her expectation of this, though he obviously finds this unsuitable in the end. The free union as an alternative to marriage was both being discussed and sometimes practised in late nineteenth-century intellectual society, though as a social practice it was one with a high cost to women. Social ostracism was the usual outcome as such a union immediately invoked the double sexual standard. Lyndall is aware enough to know that this will be the case, so she suggests the Transvaal as a destination, rather than Europe or 'down country', for it 'is out of the world' (*AF* 239). Once she has rejected her lover and had the baby, her status as fallen woman is assured, and it is this which the Stranger seeks to protect her from when he proposes marriage for the second time, offering to 'guard [her] from the world' (*AF* 278). Her final rejection of him as husband includes her determination to fight her fallen status, as she writes, 'I am not afraid of the world — I will fight the world' (*AF* 279).

In this she embodies the spirit of Ralph Waldo Emerson's essay 'Self-Reliance', with its emphasis on pursuing the individual path through life. Emerson exhorts his reader to 'Trust thyself: every heart vibrates to that iron string' and asserts that 'Whoso would be a man must be a non-conformist' (Emerson, *Complete Works* 19, 20). This 'iron' quality is presented as Lyndall's force. Her step into non-conformity is her chance to show her qualities, rather than her mistake. What Lyndall perhaps does not assess adequately is the power of society's enforcement of gender codes. In her discussion of 'free love', Emily Toth suggests that Schreiner uses Lyndall 'to dramatize society's limits' (647). Despite this, her decisions can be viewed as signs of moral courage rather than fallenness, following Emerson's claim that 'truly it demands something god-like in him who has cast off the common motives of humanity, and has ventured to trust himself for a taskmaster' (Emerson, *Complete Works* 31). Accordingly, Lyndall attracts worship wherever she goes, and Gregory, as her last devotee, is able obsessively to observe some of the consequences of her choices, including her death. Society may have limits, but she has bravely pushed them. That this same 'iron' quality is claimed in the narrator's name suggests some point of identification between them.

While romance would seem to stall Lyndall, her overriding thought is not romantic. While others worship her, she seeks her own object of devotion. Her quest for something higher to worship is an expression of her dissatisfaction with herself, a quest for self-transformation by some external means. Having abandoned hope of Christian salvation, Lyndall is unable to find new mechanisms for achieving this. Her lack of satisfaction with herself has been apparent throughout Part Two. When Waldo calls on her to pursue woman's rights, she rejects the role: 'I will do nothing good for myself, nothing for the world, till someone wakes me. I am asleep, swathed, shut up in self; till I have been delivered I will deliver no one' (*AF* 196). She tells Gregory that Em's 'little finger has more goodness in it than my whole body' (*AF* 231). This self-hatred reaches the peak of its expression immediately after Lyndall has arranged to depart with her Stranger. At the grave of Otto, she says, 'I am so weary of myself! It is eating my soul to its core — self, self, self! I cannot bear this life! I cannot breathe, I cannot live! Will nothing free me from myself? ... I want to love! I want something great and pure to lift me to itself!' (*AF* 241). Clearly, the

Stranger does nothing to fill the void left by God. Lyndall finds some peace on this occasion in gazing into her own eyes in the mirror, a habit she has maintained since childhood. Sheridan explains this apparent narcissism as a response to the feminine gendering process described by Lyndall: 'the little girl's physical energy is repressed and takes the sublimated form of narcissistic self-love as a compensation for her loss of physical freedom' (22). However, in this narcissistic space, Lyndall finds a source of strength, which goes some way toward appeasing her longing to be saved externally: 'We shall never be quite alone, you and I … We are not afraid; we will help ourselves!' (*AF* 243). Having neither sought nor found any collective female support, she makes do with herself. When she goes out into the countryside to die, she does not go out in despair: 'The old strong soul gathered itself together for the last time; it knew where it stood' (*AF* 283). Once again, strength comes from gazing into her own eyes. She remembers her connection to her image, and the lack of fear which self-knowledge brings. Sheridan suggests that 'Schreiner seems to imply that the narcissism of the female slave-mentality may be turned inside out and become a source of strength, the authentic self-love necessary for independence', so that when Lyndall dies gazing at herself in the mirror, 'the implication is that she has reached the point of total self-acceptance' (27). She has moved from the desire for an external saviour, to peace with herself.

Though this is an achievement, in terms of her *Bildung* it is somewhat limited. Whatever possibilities have been hinted at in Lyndall — political activist, playwright, actress — her death puts a stop to them. In a world which required self-abnegation of its women, any attempt by Lyndall to pursue vocation could be interpreted as egoism. R.D. Haynes has read Lyndall's life as basically egotistical, and the text as a critique of such egoism. She suggests that 'even Lyndall herself seems to recognise the limitations of egoism' (Haynes 71). Gerald Monsman also describes her death with mirror in hand as indicative of 'an entrapment within the idolatry of self' (Monsman, 'Patterns of Narration' 266). While I find this a less helpful reading than that offered by Sheridan, some of Lyndall's self-loathing could be said to have come from a distorted sense of self, of which egoism can be an expression. Both egoism, and its polar opposite, self-abnegation, are expressions of a twisted view of self, but they seem dominant among the limited options available to women in Victorian times. Lyndall's move to self-acceptance is therefore a rejection of these gender codes. However, it does seem a small gesture in light of what she promised both the reader and herself, especially when the choices that lead to her death seem to be so clearly her own.

A large proportion of Goethe's *Wilhelm Meister* is taken up with questions concerning the staging and interpretation of Shakespeare's *Hamlet*. At one point Wilhelm says of the play, 'the perpetrator seems as if he would evade the abyss which is made ready for him; yet he plunges in, at the very point by which he thinks he shall escape and happily complete his course' (Goethe I, 224). This is reminiscent of Lyndall. Her crime is against literary convention and morality. She has expressed her sexuality, and she has done so outside of marriage. According to literary expectation of her era she will die, and she does. However, it seems at one point as though she will not have to, because she has rejected the punitive and restrictive view which traditionally has bound the heroine's sexuality. It is at this point of possible escape that she seems to engineer her own death, and her literary fall is complete. The reasons for this are complex, but show that while Lyndall rejects some patriarchal assumptions about gender, she is still deeply caught in the power of their discourse. The final expression of this is that in her sickness and death she almost seems to punish herself.

Monsman has said that Lyndall 'embraces death rather than compromise' when it comes to refusing marriage (Monsman, 'Olive

Schreiner' 595). However, this is not strictly true. Would marriage have somehow protected her from the perils of childbirth? In the end, though, it is not only childbirth which kills her. While she is greatly weakened by the birth, and very nearly dies during it, the narrator suggests that it is not this which brings about her end. In a paraphrase of the landlady's account, the narrator tells us that following the birth, 'After a while she was better' (*AF* 269). Moretti points out that George Eliot's characters 'always choose freely those characters who will most harm them' (215). The fully functioning adults of Eliot's work demonstrate that a clear transition has been made from the childish innocents of earlier fiction. Lyndall freely chooses her Stranger, but Schreiner shows the powerful workings of the discourses in which she is caught, discourses which affect her choices. She also freely chooses the actions which bring about her death, but her tragedy is that she is not yet an adult, and therefore really not able to make such choices wisely. While the orphan might rise to success in the English *Bildungsroman*, the orphan of the African Karroo has no theoretically just society by which to be nurtured.

Lyndall's death has its literary precedent in Goethe also. In *Wilhelm Meister*, Aurelia, the young woman who is comforted before death by reading 'Confessions of a Fair Saint' also brings about her own death. She goes out poorly clad into the cold and rain, and returns to die rather more quickly than Lyndall. Like Aurelia, Lyndall is driven by passion to endanger her life deliberately by unwise actions. She too goes out into the rain and wind, becoming sick in the process. Lyndall does this sitting at her baby's grave in poor weather, resisting those who would shift her. When she returns it is to illness and death. This unspecified illness, though it comes after convalescence, appears to suggest that there is something inherently fragile and unwell about women, in that they can succumb so easily. Laurence Lerner is generally disgusted with Schreiner for not finishing the novel *From Man to Man*. His reason is that Rebekah 'is exactly the kind of woman the feminist novel needed', but that 'the feminists had to make do with Lyndall' (191). Lyndall is a great disappointment to him, and her death is a large reason for this:

> Like so many other Victorian heroines, Lyndall goes into a decline, that mysterious complaint, unaccompanied by any precise diagnosis, which is somehow quintessentially female, and suggests that the functioning of the female body is both secret and unreliable, surrounding illness with the same hush of frightened modesty that, for the woman, surrounds sex ... It is a most unfeminist way to die. (Lerner 187)

In fact, such a belief about the female body was commonplace, as many studies of nineteenth-century medical approaches to women have shown. Barbara Ehrenreich and Deidre English claim that 'The medical view of women's health not only acknowledged the specific risks associated with reproductivity, it went much further: it identified *all* female functions as *inherently* sick' (20, emphasis in original). Lorna Duffin agrees, stating that 'Generally female disorders were traced to one of two sources: first, women were ill because they were women; and secondly, women became ill if they tried to do anything outside the female role clearly defined for them' (31). However, this belief about women was not extended to the working-classes, whose bodies were required for labour. It was only relatively affluent women who could indulge in the practice of 'female invalidism' (Ehrenreich and English 17). Ehrenreich and English claim that 'The boredom and confinement of affluent women fostered a morbid cult of hypochondria' (17), in which sickness became a substitute occupation. Alongside this cultivation of sickness was the actual prevalence of tuberculosis, which in the mid-nineteenth century 'raged at epidemic proportions' (Ehrenreich and English 19). The incidence of this disease was much higher among young women than among the rest of the population, apparently due to hormonal factors. The description of

Lyndall's decline, and the graveside vigil which stirred it up, would seem to suggest that Schreiner could be describing a consumptive death. This possible scenario is made more likely by the connection of the disease with 'desirable' feminine qualities. Lyndall is presented to the reader through the narrator's eyes as an object on which to gaze right up until her death. Ehrenreich and English make this connection between femininity and the disease quite explicit:

> The association of TB with innate feminine weakness was strengthened by the fact that TB is accompanied by an erratic emotional pattern in which a person may behave sometimes frenetically, sometimes morbidly. The behaviour characteristic for the disease fit [sic] expectations about woman's personality, and the look of the disease suited — and perhaps helped to create — the prevailing standards of female beauty. The female consumptive did not lose her feminine identity, she embodied it: the bright eyes, translucent skin, and red lips were only an extreme form of traditional female beauty. (21)

Lyndall's death, therefore, becomes not only an opportunity to look at her, but seems to reinscribe conventional nineteenth-century notions regarding connections between femininity, sickness and tuberculosis. It can also be seen as a source of reading pleasure for other reasons.

Regina Barreca has observed that, 'The pleasures of death, in contrast to the pleasures of sex, have long been the focus for all forms of Victorian literature' (2). She notes:

> Death involved high passion, and permitted an abandonment to feeling. Affliction, not affection, was the Victorian construct of passion. The passions of desire were shifted on to the passions of death through a metaphysical and metaphorical sleight of hand. Approaching death, a character could be described in detailed physical terms, could achieve a heightened bodily, even

> sensual, awareness, experience an ecstatic, profound and epiphanic transformation which, under other more favourable circumstances, would certainly appear orgasmic in nature. (7)

While Lyndall does not experience physical ecstasy, she does achieve mental and spiritual clarity, and Gregory is allowed to touch and gaze upon the body which would otherwise be forbidden him. He is satisfied with this closeness, for, as the narrator notes, 'Passion has *one* cry, one only — "Oh, to touch thee, Beloved!"' (*AF* 273, emphasis in original).

The presence of Gregory, the hopelessly besotted lover, means that Lyndall will remain sexualised even in sickness. Not only is this the deferred sexuality described by Barreca, in which illness justified an otherwise improper concentration on the body of the dying one. As well, there is a more overtly sexual aspect to Lyndall's illness which is created by the reader's knowledge that Gregory is a desiring potential lover. Whenever the narrator describes Lyndall being dressed or tended in any way by Gregory, the disguised nurse, the reader, and especially the Victorian reader, is conscious of the fact that the barely clad, and at times presumably unclad, Lyndall, is alone in her room with a man. This brings a sexual tinge to the description of Lyndall's last days, which tends to position not only Gregory, but also the reader, as a voyeur. The most pathetic scene is surely that which follows Lyndall's worst night of pain, during which she vocalises the abandonment of all her aspirations in favour of 'a little freedom from pain' (*AF* 274). However, even this is eroticised for Gregory and the reader, as Lyndall requests that Gregory 'turn open the bosom of her night-dress that the dog might put his black muzzle between her breasts' (*AF* 274). She then 'crossed her arms over him' and the dog lay like a lover in Lyndall's arms, watched by Gregory and the reader alike (*AF* 274). The narrator seems determined that whatever might occur, Lyndall will at the same time remain a sexualised and beautiful object.

Aesthetically, this could be said to fulfil the vision of Edgar Allan Poe, who, after a rather idiosyncratic argument came to the conclusion that 'the death, then, of a beautiful woman is, unquestionably, the most poetical topic in the world' (19). The role of Gregory could be seen to concur also with Poe's suggestion that 'the lips best suited for such a topic are those of a bereaved lover' (19), for while Lyndall's end is not recounted by Gregory himself, it is largely presented through his consciousness, and it is this which adds so strongly to the sexualisation of her sickness. In this Schreiner concurs with Victorian literary conventions regarding death. In other ways she flouted them. The function of Lyndall's death in *African Farm* is both within and outside of the Victorian discourse of literary death. The degree to which the Victorian reader could view a literary death as a pleasure was determined by particular factors, as Amy Cruse points out:

> The Victorians were willing to accept death, if it came in heroic, beautiful fashion, as a suitable and happy ending; the tears they shed for Little Nell were not tears of revolt. But they did demand that virtue and innocence should be rewarded either by happiness in this world or by an assured passing to the joys to come, and undeniably they preferred the former. (414)

While Lyndall's choices can be seen as heroic, she cannot be seen to have repented and been assured of the 'joys to come'. Therefore the reader either has to see her death as completely tragic, or to concur with Lyndall's rejection of Christianity and the consequences this brings. It is a disturbing, uncomfortable death. Either way, its overriding message is that there is no room in the world of this text for a heroine such as Lyndall, and this in itself seems intended to be experienced as tragic. By engaging the reader's sympathies with a heroine who bucks feminine restrictions and conventions, the text forces the reader into experiencing some of these same binds. Our engagement in Lyndall's *Bildung* and its possible conclusions mean that its abandonment is a profound disappointment to the reader as well as to Lyndall. Using the conventional 'feminine decline' to achieve this can be seen as another way of overturning literary expectations.

As I have pointed out, many critics, especially second-wave feminists, have been highly disappointed with Lyndall's end. Sandra M. Gilbert and Susan Gubar have seen Lyndall's death as unsatisfactory, claiming that *African Farm* 'meditates on the inexorability of female victimization in patriarchal culture, more explicitly identifying femininity with martyrdom' (82). Certainly in Schreiner's short fiction, martyrdom is a constant theme. Rebecca West, writing in *The Freewoman* in 1912, sees it in *African Farm*, and was highly critical of Schreiner's emphasis on suffering, finding no redemptive qualities in it at all:

> Just as the kind-hearted outside broker, on his way home from the bucket shop, tries to save his soul by giving his spare pennies to any drunken beggar he passes, so women try to earn salvation quickly and simply by giving their souls up to pain. It may only be a further development of the sin of woman, the surrender of personality. (590)

However, others see the rebellion inherent in a death such as Lyndall's. While she is ultimately destroyed, she has made the choices which induce this destruction. Some power of volition is maintained. This kind of power is evident in the heroines described by Patricia Waugh: 'Female protest can only be through the body itself, for, like Freud's hysterics, the central women characters of romantic fiction "speak out" through psychosomatic illnesses, fevers, "wasting" diseases or sexual transgression' (180). While this *is* a form of rebellion, as a long-term strategy for feminist action is it obviously limited. As Monsman has said of Lyndall, 'she dies unfulfilled, seeking a reconciliation between her aspirations and society's norms' (Monsman, 'Patterns of Narration' 266).

Schreiner indulges in the Victorian displacement of sensuality from sex to death, yet at the same time she upsets the comfortableness of this arrangement by presenting us with a heroine who foregoes repentance in favour of self-reliance. This reflects her practice with regard to both Christianity and romance. The text functions within and outside of these discourses, both resisting and complying. Teresa De Lauretis has stated that 'the movement in and out of gender as ideological representation ... characterizes the subject of feminism' (26). Envisaging the representation of gender as a topographical space, De Lauretis has argued that there is a space within the 'male-centered frame of reference', and a space outside of it, and that these two kinds of spaces 'exist concurrently and in contradiction' (26). *African Farm*, then, rather than being unusual in being caught within and outside of various discourses, typifies the state of feminism: 'to inhabit both kinds of spaces at once is to live the contradiction which ... is the condition of feminism' (De Lauretis 26).

This is also observable in the stance of the narrator toward Lyndall. There are three chapters in which Lyndall's size is mentioned to the point of obsession. In 'Lyndall', 'Lyndall's Stranger' and 'Gregory's Womanhood', the narrator uses diminutive adjectives constantly, with 'little' being by far the most frequently used. In the space of a few pages in 'Lyndall', we hear of 'little feet', 'little one', 'little cheek', 'little chin', 'little finger', 'little arms', 'little quivering face', 'little silvery laugh', 'little teeth', 'little hand', 'little neck' and even 'little eternal self' (*AF* 187-198). Not only does the narrator use these terms, Lyndall also speaks of herself in this way. What makes this more curious is that it occurs as part of the chapter in which the gendering process is described as one in which the growing female is methodically squashed into as small a space as possible, just 'as a Chinese women's foot fits her shoe' by being bound and broken (*AF* 189). As Blake has observed, this passage 'offers a critique of the diminutive as a requirement of feminine desirability, while the diminutive is, at the same time, rampant in Lyndall's, and Schreiner's own language about women' (Blake, 'Olive Schreiner' 85). In 'Lyndall's Stranger' the same thing occurs. Both Lyndall's resistance and her submission are expressed through her 'little lips', 'little figure', 'little hand' and 'little brown head', and she is described as 'a little child' (*AF* 238-242). In 'Gregory's Womanhood', there is more variation, but the intent is the same. Once again we are presented with 'little hands', 'little lips', a 'queenly little figure', a 'little trembling body', a 'shrunken little body', 'little swollen feet' and finally the impersonal 'little crushed heap'. She is also described as a 'small child' and twice compared to a doll (*AF* 272-282). What all of these scenes have in common is that they occur between Lyndall and a potential or actual lover. 'Lyndall' is with Waldo, 'Lyndall's Stranger' is obviously the actual lover, and 'Gregory's Womanhood' involves Gregory and Lyndall.

Part of the nineteenth-century code of womanhood was that women should be seen to be without appetite and insubstantial. Dorothy Jones has suggested that 'since overt hunger for any kind of food figured forth unmentionable desires for sexuality and power, delicate appetites became a mark of femininity' (25). This meant in material terms that 'the ideal of female fragility diminished women' as they needed to be thin to illustrate their lack of appetite (Jones 26). To be small in stature greatly enhanced this impression. In order to conform to the nineteenth-century ideal of feminine beauty, Lyndall must be small, and so that we are really convinced, her size is emphasised constantly. This emphasis, in each of the scenes mentioned above, serves to remind the reader that the male who is with her is experiencing her as a beautiful and attractive woman. It explains her appeal. However, it also has the effect of objectifying her for the reader, so that Lyndall becomes for us someone to gaze upon and perhaps desire. This can be seen as a function of the gendering of the narrator: Ralph Iron is, after all, a male name. Ralph Iron can be seen as just another male who gazes on Lyndall as an object of desire, thus heightening the appeal and tragedy of the story. Somehow, though, the female author, Olive Schreiner, becomes implicated in all this, especially when the second edition of *African Farm* (1891) was published under the authorship of 'Ralph Iron (Olive Schreiner)' and the third edition (1910) was just under her own name, without the male pseudonym (First and Scott 371). Schreiner's implication means that she once again illustrates 'the contradiction which ... is the condition of feminism' (De Lauretis 26). She is both compliant with, and resistant to, patriarchy. In *African Farm* 'Schreiner stylistically exacts the price that her sex must pay to be loved at the same time that she thematically protests against it' (Blake, 'Olive Schreiner' 85). To her ambivalence about Christianity and romance is added her ambiguity about the construction of femininity. Lyndall herself illustrates this well, if with irony. Having critiqued the construction of women as those who are to '*Seem!*' and appear pleasing to men, she then complies with this in her own life: 'of course, being a woman, I have not often time for such amusements. Profession duties first, you know. It takes a great deal of time and thought always to look perfectly exquisite, even for pretty woman' (*AF* 199).

Lyndall's description of the construction of gender in the growing female is in marked contrast to the way gender is constructed in the other females the reader is exposed to in the text. It is clearly not a description of the upbringing of Tant' Sannie, or even of Em, but rather of the middle- or upper-class girl of English South African background. Though Em has an English lineage, she follows most of the expectations and lifestyle laid out by Tant' Sannie. Despite the presence of Tant' Sannie as the only available mother figure, Lyndall never accepts her as such. Lyndall's culture of femininity is clearly that of the English finishing school, and is quite at odds with the Boer model as presented by Tant' Sannie. Gordon suggests that Tant' Sannie 'offers a parody, an absurd exaggeration, of "matronly" qualities', and Monsman concurs, stating that 'Tant' Sannie parodies matriarchal power, including aspects of fertility' (Gordon 161, Monsman, 'Olive Schreiner' 592). Although both Monsman and Gordon see her as a figure of parody, it is possible to see her presenting an alternative to the model of femininity which so constrains Lyndall. Judith Raiskin proposes that Tant' Sannie should be seen as 'a gleeful Wife of Bath whose choice of her third husband is boisterous yet shrewd' (102). Certainly Schreiner was sharply aware that Boer women had a different status in their society from English women. She wrote later in *Thoughts on South Africa* that

> the Boer's system of relations in matters of sex is just.
> We know of few social conditions in which the duties and enjoyments of life are so equally divided between the sexes, none in which they are more so. (Schreiner, *Thoughts on South Africa* 200)

To prove the point, Schreiner outlines the more equitable laws of inheritance which were quite different from British laws at the time. She also shows that though their areas of work were different, women and men contributed equally to the labour of farm life. This reverses what Schreiner saw as the main evil of English middle-class life: the lack of meaningful labour for women.

There are two factors which prevent the reader from taking Tant' Sannie seriously as an alternative model of femininity, however. The first is that though we have seen Schreiner's acknowledgement of the relative equality of the sexes in Boer society, she still sees their society as primitive and inferior to British society of the time. The edifice of social Darwinism is the structure within which her discussion of Boer women occurs, and in spite of their particular gender relations, she sees them as being out of time, in contrast to 'our nineteenth-century societies' (Schreiner, *Thoughts on South Africa* 197). This is a society in the 'second stage of complexity', not completely primitive but not equal with the highest aspects of European culture (Schreiner, *Thoughts on South Africa* 196). As such, it cannot provide role models. The second more obvious factor which discounts Tant' Sannie as an alternative model of femininity is her role as persecuting adult to the young orphans. In this she is to be equated, as previously mentioned, with Mrs Joe, the abusive sister of Pip, and with Mrs Reed, the unjust guardian of *Jane Eyre*. She is just as cruel and unfair as them, as she encourages and is amused by the whipping and general oppression of Waldo. She is thus a textual obstacle to the development of the young protagonists, and as such is viewed by narrator and reader alike in the most unfavourable way. Because Schreiner has treated her adult persecutors in a comic fashion, they are also figures of exaggeration. Tant' Sannie's 'success', and that of Blenkins, are the final proof that nothing is just in the world of the Karroo, and that even if some women find equality, it will be predicated on the overall injustice of their racist society.

The other commentary the text provides on the construction of gender is through the presence of Gregory Rose. If Lyndall is the mouthpiece for feminist rhetoric, he, at least at first, verbally reinforces traditional nineteenth-century views of gender, often in direct reaction to her. His name is a curious one. Gregory Nazianzen Rose not only includes a woman's name but also the name of a fourth-century saint, Gregory Nazianzen or Nazianzus. The original Gregory Nazianzen grew up in Cappodocia and later studied with Basil and the Emperor-to-be Julian, in Athens. It is somewhat curious that Schreiner has connected this historical personage with the character of Gregory. However, the connection does provide some, if idiosyncratic, illumination. It is similar to the naming of Bonaparte Blenkins. The 'Bonaparte' signifier only seems of relevance when read in relation to Emerson's essay on Napoleon Bonaparte, in which Napoleon is described as representative of the aspirations of the middle-classes:

> He had their virtues and their vices; above all, he had their spirit or aim. Their tendency is material, pointing at a sensual success,

> and employing the richest and most various means to that end ... subordinating all intellectual and spiritual forces into means to a material success. To be the rich man, is the end. (Emerson, *Representative Men* 220)

Emerson was able to reassure himself that such an aim would not ultimately succeed. In light of Napoleon's end, he could write, 'Every experiment ... that has a sensual and selfish aim, will fail' (Emerson, *Representative Men* 252). In keeping with her practice of overturning the master narratives, though, in Schreiner's *African Farm* the two sensualists, Blenkins and Tant' Sannie, succeed while those occupied with the intellectual and spiritual die.

Gregory is connected with his namesake in several ways. He is introduced to us as a man who has been forced by his father into an occupation he does not want to pursue: 'You know he has made a farmer of me instead of a minister, as I ought to have been' (*AF* 176). Gregory Nazianzen suffered a similar fate, but his father 'ordained him priest by force and when he least expected it', according to Butler's *The Lives of The Fathers, Martyrs and Other Principal Saints*, which was presumably Schreiner's source (Butler 486). Not that Gregory Nazianzen disliked the spiritual life: he liked it so well that he did not want to be burdened with the duties of a pastorate. He, like Gregory, wrote many letters, and like Gregory's many of them were self-pitying and self-justifying. It is in the letters of Gregory to his sister that we first begin to hear his views on gender boundaries and his concern with maintaining them. When complaining of his forced occupation, Gregory writes, amply illustrating the opposite, that he has 'borne it all, not as a woman, who whines for every touch, but as a man should — in silence' (*AF* 176). He later goes on to tell Em that 'no woman *can* love as a man can', and 'I will love you as long as I live' (*AF* 178, 179, emphasis in original). Though he insisted that Em would see that he is 'a man, one who keeps his word' (*AF* 179), what she actually discovers is that in relation to her, at least, he is weak, shallow and vacillating. Irony is the dominant tone which accompanies any description of his words and actions, at least while he is at the farm, so that he is not taken seriously by Lyndall or the narrator. When he makes generalisations about women, they tend to be more applicable to himself, such as when he tells Em, 'You women never *do* know your own minds for two days together' (*AF* 223, emphasis in original). Em has just broken off the engagement because she can see that Gregory has become obsessed with Lyndall, yet his inconstancy is projected onto her. His concern with gender boundaries is further reflected in comments about the impropriety of Lyndall's behaviour. The fact that she spends time with Waldo when they are not engaged, that she drives alone, and that she drives the horses in a masterful way — 'It's so unwomanly' (*AF* 206) — are all offensive to Gregory. In his comments about marriage, he closely reflects Gregory Nazianzen: 'If I had a wife with pride I'd make her give it up, *sharp*. I don't believe in a man who can't make a woman obey him' (*AF* 206-207, emphasis in original). Nazianzen, after Saint Paul, told wives, 'In the first place, honour God; then respect your husband as the eye of your life, for he is to direct your conduct and actions' (Butler 494). Marriage, not unusually, is seen by both as a relationship of dominance and submission. However, in all his comments about gender and roles, Gregory somewhat overstates the case, reflecting an anxiety about gender which is expressed ultimately in his cross-dressing.

Gregory's character is one in transition, and so it is contradictory in many respects. In this he closely resembles the character summary given Nazianzen by the late nineteenth-century *Chambers's Encyclopaedia*:

> His character and temper, ardent and enthusiastic, but at the same time dreamy and melancholy, hard, but also tender, ambitious and yet humble, and all his instability and vacillation between a life of contemplation and of action, are vividly depicted in his writings. (*Chambers* V, 414)

Gregory's chief vacillation is between gender roles, and it is notable that even his character seems transformed when he is wearing women's clothes. He is not the only one affected: the narrator immediately shifts from the ironic tone and presents us with a Gregory who is to be taken seriously, even admired. Monsman suggests that 'Gregory's clothes-as-symbol are paradoxically an unveiling of the inner self' (Monsman, 'The Idea of "Story"' 263). Lyndall also claims a conventionally feminine nature for Gregory, though the reader at this stage is not presented with any evidence to support the view, other than his preoccupation with gender boundaries:

> 'There,' said Lyndall, 'goes a true woman — one born for the sphere that some women have to fill without being born for it. How happy he would be sewing frills into his little girls' frocks, and how pretty he would look sitting in a parlour, with a rough man making love to him! ... '(*AF* 197)

Lyndall is careful to point out that though some women have to fulfil this role, they are not 'born for it'. She maintains her stance that gender roles are not intrinsic but rather learned and enforced. Gregory thus becomes a symbol of the restriction these roles place upon males, just as Lyndall demonstrates the restrictions on females. Du Plessis sees the whole scenario created by Gregory nursing Lyndall as one which speaks against these restrictive gender roles:

> The transvestite — trapped between male and female — nurses a dying feminist — trapped in a crossfire of thralldom and quest: a strong tableau of sexual and social marginality. The whole 'story of' the '*African farm*' concerns aborted change, dying ideologies, inchoate resistance. This combination of material shows the author's conviction that conventional gender roles repress human growth and social progress. (28)

That gender is a vital aspect of personal identity is shown when Gregory addresses the sky, saying, 'Am I, am I Gregory Nazianzen Rose?' (*AF* 270). When roles are so limited that there is only one way of being male, and one way of being female, Gregory actually has to assume another gender in order to act out a different role. In doing this, he puts his very identity into doubt. The character transformation could not be more complete. From being an immature, self-absorbed and arrogant young man, Gregory becomes a mature, sensible, caring and serving 'woman'. He becomes a living demonstration of the kind of love Lyndall aspires to, when she says 'One day I will love something utterly, and then I will be better' and 'happiness is a great love and much serving' (*AF* 242, 280). His love for her transforms him to the point that he is now able to serve, an ability we have seen no evidence of till then. It also causes him to abandon his insistence on male domination: 'He had forgotten that it is man's right to rule' (*AF* 245). This is another reason for his being named after a saint, and perhaps the most relevant one. *Any* saint would have done, the point being that the life of service is considered a saintly one. He becomes, to Lyndall at least, Saint Gregory. He also shows the positive aspects of the woman's traditional role of service, in that it fills society's needs for care and tenderness. His maleness shows that these roles need not be confined to women. Though this is not a lasting transformation in Gregory, it does hint at how gender relations might form other configurations in the future, a point reiterated in Schreiner's later works. His performance of gender has a certain unfortunate economy though, as his 'bodily and spiritual transformation, while facilitating the birth of the New Man ... remains firmly predicated on female self-immolation in the form of the death of the New Woman Lyndall' (Heilmann 126). There will be no 'New Man' and 'New Woman' living in equality in the life of this text.

However, the limitations of Gregory's service, which is a form of worship, are also demonstrated, as the human idol is always mortal.

The transforming power of his love for Lyndall is only able to sustain him when she is alive. After her death, he returns to the farm and to the male role, though apparently without his earlier arrogance. There is also something inherently unbalanced about his relationship with Lyndall. Once again, the domination/submission model is apparent, though this time the woman is dominant. The ultimate demonstration of this is in Lyndall's dying command that Gregory marry Em. The reader wonders what right Lyndall has to order the affairs of others, especially when she has played a role in destroying Em's aspirations. In this text women never find solidarity in each other. They seem rather to restrict each other, as Tant' Sannie constrains Em and Lyndall, and the finishing school teachers limit Lyndall. Lyndall, if inadvertently, restricts Em by attracting Gregory, and caps it by assuming she knows best with regard to Em's future. One might prefer that Em refuse Gregory and show some sign of self-assertion, but like Emerson's lesser spirits she is resigned though profoundly disappointed. Perhaps this aspect of the narrative is the final demonstration of the emptiness of the romance plot, as we *are* left with a couple at the end of this text. They are young, and are about to marry, but both are deeply disappointed with the whole idea of romantic fulfilment. Em has to marry one who no longer loves her, and Gregory comes back to a life in which Lyndall is absent, and his caring 'woman's' role is no longer possible. The romance plot, robbed of its content, is more of a burden to them than a fulfilment. As the consummation of the narrative, it is empty, and is evidence of Schreiner's final rejection of romance conventions.

2.4 Gendered ends: death and the collapse of meaning in the colonial world

Does Schreiner leave anything intact at the end of her bleak examination of European narratives in the context of colonial society? I believe she does, but defeat would seem to be the overriding reality of *The Story of an*

African Farm. Two areas which still hold some, if limited credibility, are those of art and the unity of the universe, and in the world of this text they are closely related. Jane Wilkinson has said that 'Art and nature, two of the novel's major themes, are in fact inseparably linked in a dynamic and complex relationship that runs through the entire work, knitting together its different characters, symbols, moments and motifs' (107). Though this is true, there is a differentiation in the way 'art' and 'nature' interact with Waldo and Lyndall, and this is a further comment on issues of gender. None of Lyndall's stated artistic inspirations comes to fruition, though she is presented as a developing artist. Perhaps 'her ultimate work of art, the only complete creation that is allowed her, is her long and lingering death' (Wilkinson 111). She is not even allowed the usual form of female productivity, children. Wilkinson suggests that 'the death of the child ... symbolizes all the thwarted energies the woman artist bears within her' (111).

In contrast with this, Waldo has some creative success. His two early creations, the shearing machine and the carving interpreted by his Stranger, are pointedly said to have taken nine months to produce. Waldo even calls the machine 'his child — his first-born' (*AF* 106). Though Waldo has his machine sadistically destroyed by Blenkins, he is allowed at least the fruition of artistic creation. Lyndall on the other hand is completely sabotaged by the romance plot and the fact that the possibility of functioning as a woman artist seems so utterly remote. If Duncan's Elfrida battles to find place and recognition in the metropolitan centres, in Schreiner's Karroo the woman artist appears to be little more than a fantasy. Waldo's second creation, the carved post, allows him to connect metaphysically with another human being, who can express verbally the thoughts he could only carve. His work improves with the production of a small carved box, which he makes for Lyndall. She predicts that he 'will invent wings, or carve a statue that one might look at for half an hour without wanting to look at something else', so we see Waldo not so much as a thwarted artist but as a developing one (*AF* 230). Whereas she never really begins, he is on the way. This gives him affinity with other artists such as the San painter, and makes him responsive to the music he hears in the Botanic Gardens. In fact, he is so responsive that it takes away his sense of difference: 'When I was listening to the music I did not know I was badly dressed' (*AF* 260). When vocation, quest and romance are emptied of meaning in the text, art remains as a balm, and as a reflection of the beauty of nature.

Art is also one of the few active things pursued by Waldo. It seems that for him, passivity is a pre-condition which makes him receptive to seeing beauty and harmony in the natural world. However, this passivity stops him from pursuing learning and justice. His first move towards his final state of apparent harmony with the rest of the natural world occurs when he seeks to get at the box of books which has been left in the loft. They are a legacy of Em's father, and have until now been a symbol of all the growth and learning Waldo yearned for. They become a kind of grail in Waldo's *Bildung*, the key to his transformation from ignorant farm boy to sophisticated artist and thinker. However, just as he is about to get access to them through the loft window, he is caught by the sight of the night sky filled with stars. He has been driven by a sense of injustice, and by his need for meaning and a replacement for his lost God. It is this drive which seems to be mocked by the stars and the size of the universe:

> A thousand eyes were looking down at him, bright, and so cold.
> There was a laughing irony in them.
>> 'So hot, so bitter, so angry? Poor little mortal!'
> He was ashamed. (*AF* 119)

In light of the knowledge that the stars have been shining since the beginning of the earth, Waldo not only puts his suffering and desires into perspective, he abandons them:

> What did it matter about the books? The lust and the desire for them had died out. If they pleased to keep them from him they might. What matter? It was a very little thing. Why hate, and struggle and fight? Let it be as it would. (*AF* 120)

While this brings him a sense of peace, it holds no promise of social change. From this point on, in the face of suffering, disappointment and loss, passive acceptance will be the only method of response which is successful for Waldo. This means, ultimately, the abandonment of serious self-education, and resignation to the failures of vocation and romance.

Waldo then has moments which bear home to him the apparent unity of the created world, moments which are epiphanic, providing a counter to the sordid reality of human life around him. One of these occurs when he gazes at the pigs after feeding them: 'Taken singly they were not beautiful; taken together they were. Was it not because there was a certain harmony about them?' (*AF* 111). He goes on to consider that this harmony might be 'the secret of all beauty' (*AF* 111). While Waldo has these thoughts, they are undercut by the intervention of human malice in the person of Blenkins, who trips Waldo into the sty. The disunity of human society is all too apparent in this world, making a vision of the harmony of the universe just that: a vision rather than a reality. However, it is this vision which sustains Waldo. Later, in 'Times and Seasons', the narrator/Waldo sees the pattern of a tree trunk repeated in the blood-vessels of a gander, in a thorn-tree 'against the sky in mid-winter', in the flow of water from a dam, and in the antlers of the horned beetle, asking 'are they not all the fine branches of one trunk, whose sap flows through us all?' (*AF* 153). Wilkinson has pointed out that this passage, with its 'unifying metaphor of a tree', draws heavily on Darwin, seeing all existence together as 'a living thing, a *One*' (Wilkinson 112, *AF* 153, emphasis in original). While this is so, especially with regard to the tree metaphor, this particular vision of unity is also a central concept of Emerson's *Nature*, in which he writes:

> Every particular in nature, a leaf, a drop, a crystal, a moment of time is related to the whole, and partakes of the perfection of the whole. Each particle is a microcosm, and faithfully renders the likeness of the world. (Emerson, *Nature* 22)

Being written before Darwin, this is less a logical description of interdependency than a belief in metaphysical unity, and as such its origins are more spiritual than scientific. Thus to Waldo, the fact that Blenkins tips him into the pig-sty is unimportant compared with the moment of epiphany, because 'matter is a phenomenon, not a substance' (Emerson, *Nature* 30). The pig-sty illustrates Emerson's assertion that 'where the particular objects are mean and unaffecting, the landscape which they compose, is round and symmetrical' (Emerson, *Nature* 14).

Through a series of such moments, Waldo is established as a truly Emersonian hero. Even his inability to articulate much of what he experiences is reflective of Emerson, who wrote, 'Of that ineffable essence which we call spirit, he that thinks most, will say least' (Emerson, *Nature* 30). Waldo is thus the spiritual opposite of Blenkins, who, like Bonaparte after whom he is named, seeks only 'sensual and selfish' objects in a non-spiritual world (Emerson, *Representative Men* 252). Waldo's receptivity to nature is also an expression of the Emersonian hero. When he returns to the Karroo after his journey, Waldo writes to Lyndall, 'I was drunk; I laughed; my heart was beating till it hurt me', at the sight of 'the hills with the blue coming down to them, and the karroo-bushes' (*AF* 255). He makes explicit the connection between natural beauty and art, when he asks Lyndall 'What is it? The sky, and your face, and this box — the same thing is in them all, only more in the sky and in your face' (*AF* 197). Though he has made the box himself, he sees the beauty of nature in it, illustrating Emerson's statement that 'in art, does nature work through the will of a man filled with the beauty of her first works' (Emerson,

Nature 15). Art is thus part of the unity of the universe, and the artist a servant of nature.

Lyndall's death presents the most serious challenge to Waldo's understanding of the unity of all life, for in the experience of grief he feels most strongly the need for a belief system which provides him with a conscious hereafter. After going through the extremes of protest and anger, Waldo cannot find a belief which really satisfies the depth of his loss. This is another occasion for Schreiner to go through the range of views current on the afterlife and to reject them, especially those associated with Christianity. The only thing that brings peace to Waldo is his old method of utter passivity and resignation, with its accompanying loss of a sense of self to the unity of all things:

> [H]is soul passed down the steps of contemplation into that vast land where there is always peace; that land where the soul, gazing long, loses all consciousness of its little self, and almost feels its hand on the old mystery of Universal Unity that surrounds it. (*AF* 290)

The necessity for Waldo to abandon all desires seems finally to disqualify him as a *Bildungsroman* hero. There would appear to be little chance of growth and development in one who is utterly passive, yet this is the quality which is endorsed by the narrator: 'In that deep world of contemplation all fierce desires die out, and peace comes down' (*AF* 290). In fact, the abandonment of development and even of human connection is required to experience this somewhat Gnostic salvation through 'Nature'. The narrator informs us that

> [w]hen that day comes, that you sit down broken, without one human creature to whom you cling, with your loves the dead and the living-dead; when the very thirst for knowledge through long-continued thwarting has grown dull; when in the present there is

> no craving and in the future no hope, then, oh, with a beneficent tenderness, Nature enfolds you. (*AF* 298)

If there is no desire, there will be no disappointment. While this may bring Waldo to a brief state of peace, it is peace at the cost of all development.

Schreiner's interpretation of Emerson's *Nature* is an individual one in that it chooses to emphasise passivity as a path to peace. As is indicated by the references made to 'Self-Reliance', Emerson was not advocating the passive in all things. Her choice of Emerson as a guide is nevertheless a revealing one. Having thoroughly critiqued the master narratives of Europe by overturning them, she turns for meaning to Emerson, an American. Though even Emerson's ideas are undercut to some extent, the sense of 'nature', along with 'art' does retain some value in the text. The United States at the time was one of the few examples of a 'postcolonial' society, for though Native Americans were clearly still being colonised and dispossessed of their land, and there was no equality for African Americans, it *had* broken ties with Britain, the colonial power. As a writer in a colony, Schreiner found a fresh and meaningful element in Emerson's writing which she could not find in her European heritage. The strong engagement with Emerson can be seen as a further rejection of Europe as the centre, and an acknowledgement that models for emerging nations must come from elsewhere.

Waldo and Lyndall both die young and largely unfulfilled, yet even in their deaths gender creates difference. Lyndall dies utterly alone, reliant only on herself and her own principles. In this she fulfils Jean Marquard's understanding of Schreiner's writing, in which 'her single great theme … is the solitude of the human spirit' (38). There is no sense of external comfort for Lyndall, for though she is loved, she draws little comfort from the love of others. She rather seeks her own vocation and love-object, and fails to reach either. She dies in the grey dawn she fears, in cold and bleakness, after much physical and emotional suffering. Waldo, on the other hand, has given up all desire. Though he has been as disappointed as Lyndall, he has not had to contend with the strictures of gender. He has resigned himself to his disappointments, profound though they are, and abdicated the role of developing hero, a surrender never made by Lyndall. It is in this state of passivity and acceptance that Waldo dies, happy and at peace. He dies in the sun, in a state of unity with the natural world around him, with the chickens as representatives of his fellow creatures. He also dies with a feeling of nurture that is denied Lyndall, as he knows the 'beneficent tenderness' of Nature (*AF* 298). As Gordon has stated, 'The narrative cannot sustain the illusion that a man's and a woman's souls follow the same paths. They cannot be "essentially" alike' (199). He dies feeling at home in the universe, she dies looking inward, with her only comfort coming from her self-love. However, even the peace Waldo feels is undercut in the narrative. While it affirms his passivity as a path to peace, the fact that this state cannot be maintained is acknowledged by the narrator: 'Desire, ambition, and the fierce agonizing flood of love for the living — they will spring again' (*AF* 299). All the elements which create the *Bildungsroman* hero are still there; they are just dormant. Waldo's death comes at a temporary lull, so the appearance of difference in death between Lyndall and Waldo is perhaps not as clear as it seems. Had he lived, the narrator seems to be assuring us, he would have known further pain and disappointment.

While outlining the violence and constriction of South African society, Schreiner gives no reassurances about the possibility of transformation. Waldo's 'salvation', as he experiences it, is not one which has a social implication. He may come to personal peace, and a sense of the unity of the universe, but somehow society is the only group of creatures outside of his vision. Likewise Lyndall disqualifies herself from bringing change to her society, though she is able to analyse it. In the end, Schreiner's *African Farm* is very much a world without a meaningful future. Those things which signified meaning in Europe — quest, vocation, romance — have been shown to be empty in the world of the Karroo, even irrelevant. Rather, the colonial society has been shown to be violent, unjust and utterly restrictive, especially toward its artists and its women. Robyn Visel has said that the text does not deal with the 'white invader's violence against the African people' but rather 'focuses on the settler culture's violence against its own children, in particular its female children' ('We Bear the World and We Make It' 115). This is true, but enough is said to make it clear that the whole society is built on continuing acts of violent racism. In such a society, the illusion of a just world, which underpinned the English *Bildungsroman* in particular, cannot be sustained. The form, in a colonial setting, and with a female protagonist, is forced to collapse, and *The Story of an African Farm* stands most clearly as an anti-*Bildungsroman*.

3

Sara Jeannette Duncan

A Daughter of Today

3.1 Introduction

When Sara Jeannette Duncan set out in *A Daughter of Today* to write a study of a female egoist, she had no real models in the heroines of Victorian fiction. While Jane Eyre and Dorothea Brooke may have longed for personal and romantic fulfilment, neither was sullied with the sin of complete self-absorption. Though the New Woman[18] in 1890s fiction may have expressed discontent with the institution of marriage and with sexual double standards (shocking enough attitudes in themselves to many contemporary readers), few things transgressed the Victorian cult

---

18   While the term 'New Woman' appears to have been first used by the writer Ouida in 1894, and then pejoratively, she was herself quoting Sarah Grand's essay 'The New Aspect of the Woman Question' (610), both of which appeared in the *North American Review*. Grand does not capitalise 'new woman', as later writers would, but uses it only once in passing (271). It is Ouida who makes it the focus of her article, and features it in the title. Despite the novelty of the term, most of Ouida's audience could recognise in the term a useful summary of a range of ideas that had circulated in the previous decade, whichever side of the debates they were on. The implications of various uses of the term, and the ways in which it consolidated, are traced in Anne Ardis, *New Women, New Novels* (12), Sally Ledger's *The New Woman* (9-34), and Talia Schaffer's 'Nothing But Foolscap and Ink' (39-52).

of femininity as surely as the depiction of a female egoist. Even feminists of the day justified their emancipation and education in terms of service and self-sacrifice, as they envisaged a healthier and more informed group of child bearers, taking the race to new heights. For example, Elizabeth Wolstenholme Elmy wrote in 1894:

> The woman risks her life for the perpetuation and progress of the race. It is because women are resolved to be mothers in the highest, and no longer in the ignoblest sense of that term, that they now demand for themselves and for each other the fullest opportunity of self-development. (Wolstenholme Elmy qtd in Bland 157)

Becoming better mothers was also one of Mona Caird's arguments for the education of women, in her 1892 article, 'A Defence of the So-Called "Wild Women"'. The suggestion that a woman could want something for herself, with no element of service to others to justify her desire, was not given currency in arguments for female emancipation, and would not have been considered a reason for granting it. Self-sacrifice was integral to an understanding of the feminine, and its accompanying suffering considered almost sanctified, by feminists as well as others.[19]

In spite of this, Elfrida Bell is not completely without literary antecedents. The American heroines of Henry James provide the ground on which the character of Elfrida is built, and Elfrida's independence of mind and mistaken understanding of herself link her in particular with Isabel Archer in *The Portrait of a Lady*. What sets *A Daughter of Today* apart is that it is an attempt to depict such a heroine developing as an artist. In fact, all three main characters are artists, two of them being women. As

---

19 For example, there is a constant valorisation of suffering in the fiction of Olive Schreiner, not only in *The Story of an African Farm*, but also in much of the short fiction. The pursuit of self-sacrifice as a source of pleasure is expressed clearly by the feminist character in 'The Buddhist Priest's Wife' (1892), when she says 'the most absolutely delicious thing in life is to feel a thing needs you, and to give at the moment it needs' (Schreiner 114).

part of the explosion of New Woman fiction, many alternative roles and outcomes for heroines were being explored in the fiction of the nineties, as has been widely observed.[20] Many of these turned on questions of the morality of marriage. The issue of women's work was raised but almost always subsumed by the romance or marriage plot, or seen as secondary to it. As a female *Künstlerroman* this novel had few literary precedents, and this was in several ways a groundbreaking book.[21] It does not chart the artist's accommodation to society, but rather ends with the artist's death. However, suicide does not preclude artistic success, and the narrator informs us that Elfrida's posthumously published *An Adventure in Stageland* was a success. In its focus on London's literary scene, *A Daughter of Today* recalls Gissing's *New Grub Street* (1891), in which many of the characters are writers. The degree of success experienced by these writers seems to be in inverse proportion to their genius and integrity, an understanding of artistic life shared by the more Bohemian characters in *A Daughter of Today*. Duncan is in marked contrast to Gissing, however, in her portrayal of the female writer. Rather than presenting her literary women as pale and tired hacks who lead unnatural lives and harbour no strong professional ambitions, Duncan depicts two healthy, opinionated and well-informed women who take their work seriously and have it seriously received. Even Ella Hepworth Dixon's *The Story of a Modern Woman*, so similar in many ways to *A Daughter of Today*, and published in the same year, depicts its heroine as not quite suited to artistic life. Mary Erle, after abandoning her

---

20 See, for example, Sally Ledger's *The New Woman: Fiction and Feminism at the* fin de siècle, and *The New Woman in Fiction and in Fact*, edited by Angelique Richardson and Chris Willis.

21 Certainly this was true of fiction, though women's poetry had explored for the previous century the role of the poetess. This was a major preoccupation of Felicia Hemans, who, as Angela Leighton has noted, was 'The first woman poet to embrace, so wholeheartedly, the woman artist as a subject for poetry' (Leighton 33). However, Hemans' female poets pay the price for their art through romantic disappointment, and are usually portrayed as longing to trade their fame for domestic bliss.

artistic studies, falls in to writing, but her publishers insist that she write for the popular market rather than writing the realist novel she would prefer to produce. Her doctor diagnoses her with a nervous illness, the implication being that supporting herself by writing is 'unnatural' and 'not fit for girls' (Dixon 176). Not so Janet and Elfrida, who thrive until Elfrida experiences failure.

Elfrida is more than a depiction of a female writer, however. She is presented as something of a phenomenon. That she is intended to be considered a particular product of the times, is indicated by both the title of the novel itself and the characteristic attributed to her by both her potential suitors: *'fin-de-siècle'* (*DT* 118, 151). If Elfrida is a product of her times, the artistic persona she cultivates is also, and is inextricably linked to her egoism, which takes on the character of a moral imperative. Such a view of art and morality is presented with some irony by Duncan, but also with understanding. The narrator shows that each character's morality and art is lacking in some way. Contemporary reviewers found Elfrida's individualised morality either fascinating or repulsive. While the reviewer from *The Nation* saw her as 'fresh, original and really delightful' and a 'fascinating personality' ('More Fiction' 473), *The Athenaeum* was repelled by 'the ill-breeding of her gospel of art and life', thus repeating the class judgements of Janet and Kendal in the novel itself ('New Novels' 705). Elfrida's view that the London literary scene was 'bourgeois' seems to be borne out by the reviewer from the *Saturday Review*, who wrote:

> We are not much impressed when the heroine lives in familiar intercourse with improper persons, appears in tights on the stage for 'copy' ... or talks disagreeably about the effects on her of the propinquity of 'a human being who would give all he possesses just to touch your hand.' We do not think we should be peculiarly anxious to touch Miss Elfrida Bell's hand. (Qtd in Tausky, *Sara Jeannette Duncan* 110)

In creating an unconventional and, to some, offensive heroine, Duncan drew on a range of sources. While I disagree with much of Janice Fiamengo's reading of this text, in which she seems most concerned to draw out its presumed moral lessons, her chief point — that Duncan can be seen to have written 'a fiction of self' (13) in which she was 'killing off an earlier version of herself whose views and behaviour she had since renounced' (19) — still holds. Elfrida's chief flaws appear to be the result of extreme youth as much as any other single factor. Duncan, in her early thirties, married and living in Calcutta, was in a position to look back on her earlier ambitious self and to reassess her own choices as well (Fowler 211). In giving her heroine her mother's maiden name, she makes this identification explicit, and rather poignant (Fowler 217). There are other sources for elements of Elfrida's character, though. In her biography of Lily Lewis, journalist and Duncan's travelling companion on her round-the-world travels, Peggy Martin argues that Lewis is the model for Elfrida. Lewis had lived in Paris and returned there after their trip, and she held similar views on art and life to Elfrida's (Fiamengo 13-14).

Despite the likelihood that both Duncan's younger self, and Lewis, the travelling companion of her youth, provide aspects of Elfrida's character and opinions, the most influential model for the heroine, and the one likely to be known to Duncan's readers, is the text which 'caused a sensation in Europe and even more so in America' (Parker and Pollock vii): *The Journal of Marie Bashkirtseff* (*The Journal*). With no model for the complete female egoist in fiction, Duncan turned to autobiography. *The Journal* had been published in France in 1887, and in England in translation in 1890, and had elicited some shocked responses. What shocked was not the expression of feminist sentiment or sexual desire, which had been expurgated largely from the text by Marie's family, but the statement of female ambition, exemplified by such statements as: 'I am my own heroine' (Bashkirtseff 31). Such statements also make explicit her awareness that in the act of writing her journal she was constructing herself as a character just as one might if writing fiction. When the moral crusader, reviewer and editor W.T. Stead, reviewed the journal, his conclusion was that 'She was very clever, no doubt, very fascinating, but woman she was not' (546). Many reviewers considered Bashkirtseff so transgressed the bounds of femininity that she could not be considered 'woman'. In his review of the journal in *The Nineteenth Century*, W.E. Gladstone is willing to attribute only negative female characteristics to Bashkirtseff: 'Womanish she was in many of woman's weaknesses; and she did not possess the finer graces which we signify by the epithet feminine' (605). This prompted Marion Hepworth Dixon's response in the *Fortnightly Review*, in which she is almost exclusively concerned to prove Bashkirtseff's femininity, using the term 'womanish' to excess. She claims that for once, in Bashkirtseff, we are presented with 'a real woman, as distinguished from the sham women in books' (276). Dixon rejects the construction of femininity as it has occurred in nineteenth-century fiction in favour of someone less ideal and more real. Her experience was based on her and her sister Ella's shared studies with Bashkirtseff in the Académie Julian in Paris (Fehlbaum 1). I agree with Michelle Gadpaille, who, in revising what she describes as 'the consensus about Duncan's model for Elfrida', asserts that 'Bashkirtseff furnished Duncan with a model for representing interiority for a woman artist' ('Aesthetic Debate' 3).

In drawing upon Bashkirtseff as the inspiration for her heroine, Duncan has not made Elfrida Bell as extreme as many other New Woman heroines of the 1890s, especially in terms of her sexual experience. In spite of this, Elfrida is deeply transgressive of feminine codes in the same way that Marie Bashkirtseff was: she is an ambitious egoist. Where egoists have existed in English fiction, their plots have reflected 'that pattern of egoism, despair, and self-knowledge — the ordeal of moral education — which is at the heart of so much of nineteenth-century fiction' (Halperin

247). Their egoism has existed for reform, whereas Elfrida's is a fact of her personality. In a knowingly ironic comment on her departure from other nineteenth-century novels, Duncan has Elfrida comment after she has seen the portrait that reveals her egoism, 'Don't think I shall reform after this moral shock, as people in books do' (*DT* 250). Bashkirtseff's *The Journal* and Duncan's *A Daughter of Today* are usefully read in tandem and I will be using *The Journal* as a contemporary source on a number of the issues raised by Duncan, as I suggest Duncan herself did. Both deeply reflect their generation's various obsessions with art, genius, women and death.

Duncan was in a somewhat unique position from which to enter the New Woman debates which were taking place in the fiction and journals of the 1890s. As a Canadian married to an Englishman and living in Calcutta, she was doubly removed from the intellectual furore which was occurring in London. As a Canadian, she had the dubious status of being colonial, and having married into Anglo-Indian society, shared the sense many Anglo-Indians had of being misunderstood at 'Home'. This has particular implications for the narrative voice of *A Daughter of Today*, as I shall discuss. Being an outsider to London literary life did not prevent Duncan from confidently presenting an impression of it, just as she had done many times in various settings in her journalism and travel writing. Her impression is based on three visits covering some months, and the experience of considerable literary success.[22] Duncan had created an American heroine before, but she is very different to Elfrida Bell. Mamie Wick, in *An American Girl in London*, is bright, genuinely cheerful, direct and largely without guile. None of Elfrida's affectation or outlandishness

---

22 Her first book, *A Social Departure*, had come out to very positive reviews and went into many editions. It is an account of a journey around the world, undertaken by Duncan and the previously mentioned Lily Lewis, without the aid of protector or chaperone. Several of the early novels are similar to her initial non-fiction work in that they are fictionalised forms of travel writing.

attends her: she is much more a representative American of the type which was so popular in English society in the late nineteenth century, especially when accompanied by a disposable income. What Mamie has in common with Elfrida is her love of independence, seen to be part of her birthright, and a different understanding of social customs. In examining ideas of individual freedom, Duncan shows her debt to Henry James, which is also obvious in a plot structure revolving around the courtship of the American Mamie by an Englishman. Many of Duncan's novels are light comedies of manners, though they almost always come with a satirical bite and invariably with a cool ironic detachment. *A Daughter of Today* still demonstrates the irony, but it is toned down, and directed towards the heroine as much as to any other character. The reviewer from *The Athenaeum* notes the change of style: 'The bright and sparkling books by which Miss Duncan made her reputation may quite possibly prejudice some of her admirers when they find Mrs. Cotes offering them a serious piece of work in a serious mood and demanding their best attention' ('New Novels' 705).

Duncan had worked as a journalist for several North American newspapers and magazines, including *The Globe* (Toronto), *The Montreal Star*, and *The Washington Post*.[23] Her ability to create a quick impression of a milieu had been a feature of her journalism and travel writing. She used this ability in the Paris section of *A Daughter of Today,* for although she had visited Paris briefly with her husband Everard Cotes in 1891,

---

23   Marian Fowler's *Redney: A Life of Sara Jeannette Duncan* is an excellent source of biographical information. As a biography, however, it is marred by an obstinate determination to read Duncan's fiction as an expression of various supposed personal neuroses, for which Fowler provides little or no evidence. Some of this biographical information, and certainly a different approach, is found in Thomas Tausky's *Sara Jeannette Duncan: Novelist of Empire*. A small example of Duncan's journalism has been republished as *Sara Jeannette Duncan: Selected Journalism* and edited by T.E. Tausky. Janice Fiamengo examines Duncan's journalism in the context of contemporary Canadian women's journalism in *The Woman's Page*.

her main source, especially for details of the painting school, appears to be Bashkirtseff's *The Journal*. My evidence for this assumption is purely textual, and is based on the way Duncan is so faithful to the descriptions in Bashkirtseff.

In embarking on this novel Duncan was consciously writing 'nineties' fiction. In dealing with aesthetes, Bohemia, decadence, suicide and the New Woman, she was confronting, deliberately, the issues which made this period so distinctive and self-conscious. However, her treatment of them is ironic and distanced, and in dealing with New Woman questions she avoids allowing the plot to turn on issues regarding the sexuality of the heroine. By taking this approach, Duncan is able to examine other questions relating to nation, art, and women's choices. Such a focus resists the direct equation of women with sexuality which is so prevalent in other fiction from the period, and calls for a greater degree of subtlety to be introduced into feminist debates.

3.2 The heroine as artist: *Künstlerroman* and the New Woman

Sarah Jeannette Duncan's *A Daughter of Today* does not contain a veiled *Künstlerroman*, such as may be found in Olive Schreiner's *The Story of an African Farm* or Henry Handel Richardson's *The Getting of Wisdom*, but purports from the start to be an account of a young woman's artistic development. Elfrida Bell has grown up in the small town of Sparta, Illinois, one of five small towns in the US to have inherited the name. Duncan's choice of the name does not appear to be arbitrary: Sparta comes to represent for Elfrida the all too pragmatic culturally bereft Other. For Elfrida is the child of the cultural centre 'Athens', which for her is located in Europe: in Paris, or at the very least London. Sparta has only her, and its difference from her, to offer: 'Elfrida allowed one extenuating point in her indictment of Sparta. The place had produced her, as she was at eighteen, when they sent her to Philadelphia' (*DT* 13). She initially attends the local High School, and one of the first things the reader learns about Elfrida is that she has been quoting Rousseau's *Confessions* in her school English assignments. This prompts her shocked teacher Miss Kimpsey to inform Elfrida's mother, who thinks 'her mind ought to develop along the lines that nature intended' and will not restrict her (*DT* 7). As Gail Cunningham points out in her overview of New Woman fiction, 'more important than formal education ... are the heroines' reading habits' (47). Elfrida is typical of New Woman heroines; during the course of the novel she covers a good deal of what was considered the 'new realism': Zola, Tolstoy and its milder representatives such as Meredith and William Dean Howells. Significantly, as noted earlier, Duncan herself is writing Elfrida's tale in a newer, more realist mode. In this interview with her teacher, Elfrida's mother demonstrates a strong investment in a view of Elfrida as exceptional, possibly even a genius. Having said 'I shouldn't be surprised if Elfrida did anything', she goes on to say, 'it *must* be art' (*DT* 8, emphasis in original). The rather nervous Miss Kimpsey does not appear to have contributed to Elfrida's increasingly avant-garde view of life and art, but she has provided the example of a self-supporting working woman. The next view the reader has of Elfrida's education is when she returns from a year at art school in Philadelphia, with good reports and a personal 'style of her own' (*DT* 11). Her ambitions have been fuelled, probably falsely, by the fact that she has won a medal for a charcoal of Psyche, and the narrator comments, in very journalistic style: 'In view of its inaccuracy the committee had been guilty of a most irregular proceeding in recognizing it with a medal, but in a very young art school this might be condoned' (*DT* 18). It is during this period away from Sparta, which the reader does not see, that Elfrida's understanding of herself crystallises, and she draws 'a vague and many-shaped idea of artistic living' (*DT* 15).

She is not alone, as the protagonist of a *Künstlerroman*, in finding her original town and environment unsympathetic to her artistic aims and indifferently unhelpful in assisting her to realise them. A move from a provincial environment to the metropolis is found often to be part of the educational requirements of the hero of a novel of development. In Elfrida's case her situation is slightly complicated by the fact that she is a woman and not from Europe. The reader is not privy to the domestic discussions which result in Elfrida's move to Paris to study art, but we do know that her father wants her to 'settle down here in Sparta', which for him means marriage, with painting as 'an interest' and possibly even a source of income, through teaching if necessary (*DT* 11). Her mother aims higher than Sparta for Elfrida, in both marriage and art, and so it is undoubtedly because of her influence that Elfrida is able to go. The irony of Elfrida's rejection of Sparta is that it is the pragmatic small town pursuit of security and business which enables her to leave by providing her with both an education and an income.

Being a woman does not appear to be an enormous hindrance to Elfrida's initial pursuit of her art, though it becomes more of an issue once she arrives in Paris. What is likely to hinder her more is the limitation in plots available to female protagonists. Admittedly, nineties' heroines are beginning to stretch the marriage or death outcomes which have been theirs throughout the Victorian period. The reviewer of the 'New Novels' section of *The Athenaeum* notes with regret that the contemporary heroine is a 'self-assertive, heartless, sexless thing whom various writers have recently brought into fashion and almost tempted the public to regard, as the typical modern woman' ('New Novels' 770). However, heroines whose choices in some way challenge nineteenth-century constructions of femininity still can be portrayed in the end as neurotic, sick or suicidal:

> While the very name of the New Woman naturally associated her with the dynamic radicalism of the nineties, the novels in which she appeared seem to go beyond the demands of realism in their emphasis on failure, despair and death. To be driven to suicidal

> depression or madness is almost an essential part of the experience; though ostensibly used to show how genuinely difficult it is to escape the established order, it is also, as in the poetry of the nineties, savoured for its own sake. (Cunningham 77)

With such overtly Decadent outcomes, much of the New Woman fiction seems to suggest that to break out of the bounds of conventional femininity is to invite retribution. Some of it is actively seeking to say this, but even those authors who were in favour of wider opportunities for women create the opposite impression with their emphasis on unfavourable ends. Elfrida's suicide, rather than resulting from any 'unnatural' behaviour on her part, would seem to have resulted from a lack of available plots, once she had worn out the two she was involved in: her *Bildung*, and the romance plot. She both fails to get the man and to find a place for herself as a great artist, and this leaves her with nowhere to go in terms of the narrative. A life of ordinary mediocrity not being her style, a slightly romantic suicide, the final Bohemian act, is the preferred option.

Though initially her escape from the Philistia of Sparta is a broadening experience, the limitations of Elfrida's options gradually are brought to bear upon her. However, the limitations of the metropolis never lead her to reconsider the low regard in which she holds Sparta. The reader returns to Elfrida's education after she has spent a year in Paris at a mixed art school. Not only is the milieu adopted by Duncan, but more significantly, Elfrida's character and the nature of her ambition are taken from Bashkirtseff. Upon her entry to Paris, her feelings about the world she has left harden to the point that 'she found it unnecessary to tell herself that she would never go back there' (*DT* 24). For Elfrida, as for Marie Bashkirtseff, former life is seen as a waste of precious time: 'when she thought of it, it was to groan that so many of her young impressionable years had been wasted' (*DT* 25). Taking on 'art' as a religion is the most significant aspect of Elfrida's Paris experience, causing her to judge others and herself by the standards of Bohemia:

> She entered her new world with proud recognition of its unwritten laws, its unsanctified morale, its riotous ideals; and she was instant in gathering that to see, to comprehend these was to be thrice blessed, as not to see, not to comprehend them was to dwell in outer darkness with the bourgeois, and the 'sand-paper' artists, and others who are without hope. (*DT* 24-25)

Paris, however, is also where she begins to experience the limitations of the woman artist, as Bashkirtseff had done. Following the description of Julian's studio in Bashkirtseff's *The Journal*, the fictional Lucien's studio, which Elfrida attends, is divided, with male students downstairs and females upstairs. Bashkirtseff's Julian tells her that 'sometimes his female students are as clever as the young men' which establishes downstairs as the superior school (275). A result of this is that if any of the women are judged to have done excellent work, it is taken downstairs for the opinion of the young men. The response to an early sketch of Bashkirtseff's is 'that the others said at the men's studio that I had neither the touch, nor the manner, nor the capabilities of a woman' (292). Bashkirtseff is always finding her femaleness separated from her ability, as if the two are mutually exclusive. The response 'that it looks like a man's work' becomes standard when men consider her work to be good (464). She is aware also that if she looks too feminine, it will detract from her being taken seriously and even suggest fraudulence on her part: 'I was so pretty and so well dressed that they will be convinced that I don't paint my pictures alone' (674). Duncan reflects this situation in her portrayal of the studio, when Lucien tells Nádie, the Russian girl, 'In you, mademoiselle ... I find the woman and the artist divorced' and takes her painting downstairs for the approval of the men (*DT* 21). When it comes to Elfrida, it is her lack of 'male' qualities which signals her lack of success: 'Your drawing is still lady-like, your colour is still pretty, and *sapristi!* you have worked with me a year!' (*DT* 23).

Such practice contributes to an understanding of 'art' and 'woman' as mutually exclusive categories, an understanding that was still widespread in the late nineteenth century. Considering the Larousse definition of '*artiste*', Louly Peacock Konz, writing about Bashkirtseff, suggests that 'Larousse's definition of "artist" implies that women might have been thought of as literary artists or even as artistic persons but that they were unlikely to be considered great visual artists' (95). To become a female artist involves the stress of moulding two supposedly incompatible categories, two subjectivities which by their current definitions could not coexist. It is not surprising that the 1890s, with its preoccupation with women, art, and morbidity, should produce a female *Künstlerroman* ending in suicide. The attempt to blend the categories of 'art' and 'woman' could be seen to be a process in constant risk of imploding. This risk is compounded by the connection between egoism and the artist. In her personal account of Bashkirtseff, Marion Hepworth Dixon notes in passing that 'the egotism of the artist is a bye-word' (277), and certainly in the late nineteenth century the two are combined in the category of the 'genius', whose difference allows for otherwise transgressive behaviour. The problem for the female artist is that the qualities of the egoist, while they might be found to be acceptable in a 'genius', so contravene the discourse of femininity as to make the category of 'female genius' a contradiction in terms. Such values were not confined to the visual arts. While the male students praise Bashkirtseff for 'talent and vigour, nay even brutality in drawing, and so much perseverance', these qualities are seen by these men to be male characteristics (292). Whatever they like in art is by definition male. Inferior work is female. Just such a view is expressed in Henry James's well-known review of Zola's *Nana*, where he states:

> A novelist with a system, a passionate conviction, a great plan — incontestable attributes of M. Zola — is not now to be easily found in England or the United States, where the storyteller's art is almost exclusively feminine, is mainly in the hands of timid (even

> when very accomplished) women, whose acquaintance with life is severely restricted, and who are not conspicuous for general views. (James, 'Nana' 241)

James maintained these views twenty years later, when he wrote in a similar vein to Duncan in response to receiving a copy of her 1896 novel, *His Honour and a Lady*:

> I think your drama lacks a little *line* — bony structure and palpable, as it were, tense cord — on which to string the pearls of detail. It's the frequent fault of women's work — and I like the rope (the rope of *the direction and march of the subject*, the action) pulled, like a taut cable between a steamer and a tug, from beginning to end. (James, 'To Mrs. Everard Cotes' 131, emphases in original)

James does not consider the notion that what a female writer values and wants to achieve in her work might vary from what a male writer aims for. He values action and 'a great plan' (though one might argue that there is sometimes little of both in his own work). Therefore, female writers who lack these attributes are inferior, and inferior *as a group*, James suggests.[24] The self-assured arrogance of these statements with their images 'bony structure', 'tense cord' and 'taut cable', suggest an aesthetics built on male sexuality, from which the female artist is by definition excluded, unless by chance she should demonstrate freak male characteristics. Should she do this, she would then be invalidated as 'woman', as Marie Bashkirtseff was in Stead's eyes.

Elfrida is not defeated initially by the conflict between the discourses of femininity and art or by the male artist as arbiter of both, though these forces contribute to her ultimate downfall. The initial setback in her

---

24 To be fair to James, the rest of his letter oozes charm, and he calls *His Honour and a Lady* 'your consummately clever book' (James, 'To Mrs. Everard Cotes' 131). Interestingly, he also ponders whether the Boer War signals the end of the British Empire and assumes that Duncan's India is a sign of its life.

Künstlerroman is her slow realisation that she has little talent for painting. Like Bashkirtseff, she had chosen painting from several possibilities, deciding that 'She would not write novels, or compose operas: she would paint', thereby expressing a bland assurance that she is capable of any of these (*DT* 17). When she gives up painting, the decision is precipitated for her by her parents' change in financial circumstances. The need for income makes writing the only practical choice other than returning home, which for Elfrida is out of the question. With writing novels being a longer-term proposition in terms of income, she must make the short-term choice to begin with journalism. This involves some complex negotiations in terms of her ideals. Initially, as it is not her chosen 'art', journalism is 'a cynical compromise with her artistic conscience, of which she nevertheless regretted the necessity' (*DT* 35). 'Art' must be the chief motivation for all her actions. Soon, though, she is able to decide that 'her solemn choice of an art had been immature and to some extent groundless and unwarrantable', and her pursuit of writing can become for her the pursuit of 'art', as painting had been (*DT* 54). Her *Künstlerroman*, after a brief setback, is once more on course.

Elfrida seeks advice from men at various crucial points in the narrative. Frank Parke is the first of these, and he advises her to go to London to pursue journalism, rather than attempting it in Paris. She takes this advice, abruptly, without letting anyone she knows into the secret. Later it is a man with the unlikely name of Golightly Ticke and the sub-editor Rattray who devise the plan which sees her joining a chorus line to gather novelistic material, thereby scandalising her potential romantic object Kendal, her literary friend Janet and Janet's father. In the matter of realising her lack of painting talent, it had been her Paris painting companion John Kendal who was blunt enough to confirm her suspicion. For Elfrida there are no female mentors in this book, and Janet, who ideally could have provided her with support, is instead regarded as a competitor.

This attitude extends to other women who write. When Elfrida attends a gathering which includes female journalists, her chief thought is that 'she would win, if it were only a matter of a race with *them*' (*DT* 108, emphasis in original). Duncan gently satirises these women, noting how important supper is to the evening, and commenting on 'the varying numbers of buttons off their gloves' and their 'indefinite and primitive ideas of doing their hair' (*DT* 108, 107). However, in pointing out the poverty of these female journalists, Duncan demonstrates the real difficulties of actual working women's lives and the pay inequities they experienced. Despite friendliness from these women, Elfrida does not take up the opportunity to receive advice, support or help from any of them. A lack of female solidarity is shown to be a contributing factor in Elfrida's demise, and confirms, rather than resists, the heterosexual paradigm in which women are pitted against each other as rivals.

This paradigm is confirmed, when, after many rejections, Elfrida finds an opening when she quite deliberately delivers an article in person, with the intention of using her sexuality to influence its reception. She is honest and straightforward with herself about her intentions, and justifies them with the thought that her former friend Nádie in Paris 'had no scruples' except about her art (*DT* 69). This choice clarifies further Elfrida's growing belief that art takes precedence over life: 'it was a much finer thing to be scrupulous about one's work — that was the real morality, the real life' (*DT* 69). Her move results in a regular column in *The Illustrated Age*, which may not be as highbrow as Elfrida would like, but is a start. Before this, however, she has had her pocket picked of her last eight gold sovereigns, an experience which throws her into the full realisation of her position as an independent woman who must provide for herself. Coming from a relatively secure financial background in which she has known no real poverty, Elfrida is able to drink in the sensation of being penniless as an experience of authentic artistic life: 'She saw herself in the part — it was an artistic pleasure — alone in a city of melodrama, without a penny, only her brains' (*DT* 75). This experience is short-lived, though, as she soon charms Rattray from *The Illustrated Age* and receives her opening in journalism.

Throughout the text, the narration raises the question of Elfrida's talent. Does she have what it takes to be an artist and is there anything of the genius about her? The narrator, and various characters, discuss her work in detail with these questions in mind. She herself acknowledges her lack of painting talent, but the narrator allows readers to consider the standard of her journalism as well. The first piece to catch Kendal's eye, however, is an art review Elfrida does for *The Decade*. The narrator acknowledges, as Kendal does not, that 'it dismissed with contempt where it should have considered with respect, how it was sometimes inconsistent, sometimes exaggerated and obscure' (*DT* 88). What excites Kendal is 'the delicacy and truth with which the critic translated into words the recognizable souls of a certain few pictures', and 'the young mocking brilliant voice' of Elfrida's writing (*DT* 88-89, 88). The narrator gives us a picture of an emerging talent which has considerable limitations, but also has a special spark. The limitations emerge when Lawrence Cardiff assists her in revisions of an article on 'The Nemesis of Romanticism', which on first assessment he finds 'hopeless — hopeless' (*DT* 178). The only way it can be redeemed, in his eyes, is to rewrite it completely, which Elfrida tearfully refuses. This leads her to a longer-term plan for her apprenticeship in writing: 'I mean to have a success — one day. But not yet — oh no! First I must learn to write a line decently, then a paragraph, then a page. I must wait, oh, a very long time — ten years, perhaps; five, anyway' (*DT* 184). This plan is short-circuited because Rattray and Ticke are determined to speed up the process with a scheme of their own. Elfrida is honest about the fact that she has no 'leading idea' and has 'had hardly any experience', but the temptation to impress Janet and Kendal is too much for her, and she agrees to the scheme (*DT* 185). Her skill is in the quick impression, in capturing a fleeting feeling, and the decision to dip into another lifestyle, the chorus line, and record her impressions of it, actually uses her talents well. It is a form of travel writing, involving not a change of country but of class and lifestyle, 'slumming' in a very particular setting. The reactions of the Cardiffs and Kendal are based on these class and lifestyle factors, and on national mores, and reveal them to be, at heart, British snobs. In an assessment of Elfrida's talent, the generally unfavourable reactions of Kendal and the Cardiffs are balanced by the reception Elfrida's posthumous work receives. Published six months after her death, *An Adventure in Stageland* 'met with a very considerable success' (*DT* 280).

Throughout Elfrida's artistic development, the reader has the opportunity to observe the development of another female artist, Janet Cardiff. Not only are they both involved in journalism, but both have a book published during the course of the novel, and much of their time together is spent in debating the virtues of different literary styles and figures. The narrator, who occasionally appears as 'I', but who does not otherwise figure as a character in the text, does not obviously endorse one method or woman over the other. *A Daughter of Today* stands out in that so much attention is given to the relationship between the two women, at the expense of the romance plot. Rarely are the nuances of women's friendships given as much importance in the literature of the period. Within the world of the romance plot, female friendship is often pushed into the area of competition as female characters vie for the attentions of the hero. This demonstrates the patriarchal assumptions inherent in the romance plot, as the heterosexual bond is seen as the primary aim of women, of much more value than friendships between women. It is partially the case in this text when John Kendal becomes the romantic focus for both women. However, their artistic rivalry is their first source of conflict. Janet Cardiff and Elfrida Bell are very different women, who are drawn together by their admiration for each other's writing and their friendship with John Kendal. From the start, there is an inequality in their relative status in Janet's favour, caused by her greater experience in her field, her age (she is twenty-four, while Elfrida is only twenty), and by the fact that she is functioning within her own group in terms of nationality, class and culture. Their friendship blossoms, largely because of their shared intellectual interests — their 'disinclination to postpone what they had to say to each other' — but both also maintain a distance caused by self-consciousness and sensitivity (*DT* 129). Though they discuss ideas about art, they do not discuss the creative process, which is different for both. The reader has no real insight into this process in Janet, reflecting her own closeness about it. She does not share her feelings about art either, other than in an abstract way: 'As for Janet's own artistic susceptibility, it was a very private atmosphere of her soul. She breathed it, one might say, only occasionally, and with a kind of delicious shame. She was incapable of sharing her caught-up felicity there with anyone' (*DT* 130). The writing of her novel, kept secret from all but her father and publisher, is not revealed to the reader either until it is almost finished. In contrast, Elfrida's artistic responses dominate her life, and when she writes her novel the reader is privy to both the process and its motivations, as she thinks of

> the long midnight hours alone with Buddha, in which she should give herself up to the enthralment of speaking with that voice which she could summon, that elusive voice which she lived only, only, to be the medium for; that precious voice which would be heard one day — yes, and listened to. (*DT* 210)

Strangely for an era of growing female solidarity, there is none to be had in this story. Elfrida's sense that Janet is ahead of her fuels a competitiveness which ultimately cripples their relationship. Initially Elfrida offers homage, but it is taken over by jealousy. This homage appeals to Janet's more restrained ego at first — 'she had found Elfrida's passionate admiration so novel and so sweet that her heart was half won before they came together in completer intimacy' — but palls when it does not seem to develop into affection: 'she was sick of Elfrida's admiration, it was not the stuff friendships were made of' (*DT* 189, 190). Janet does not feel the same sense of competition as Elfrida but she is protected from it by her position of superiority. She is ahead of Elfrida in so many ways. She has an established reputation in the better magazines and journals of her day. She is able to write analytically while Elfrida is not. She has been surrounded by a literary culture all her life, and is comfortable with its values and mores, while Elfrida struggles with and questions them. When her novel is published before Elfrida has even had a chance to begin hers, it is the final straw in Elfrida's frustrations with her friend. Competitiveness is one of the strongest signs of egoism in both Elfrida and Bashkirtseff. Artistic rivalry is a large element in Bashkirtseff's *The Journal*; it drives Marie's ambitions and motivates her in her work, but it also paralyses her by causing her to think she will never catch up. When Bashkirtseff observes her rival Breslau's work, she writes, 'I am discontented at not being the best at the end of one month' (291). Elfrida is similarly frustrated and finally explodes at Janet, 'You have everything! You succeed in *all* the things you do — you suffocate me, do you understand?' (*DT* 224). Elfrida has some cause to feel that Janet sustains her advantage over her by withholding important information about herself, such as the fact that she is having a novel published, and that she has fallen in love with Kendal. In the end, it is these two facts, together with the scathing review of her manuscript, which drive Elfrida to choose suicide. If the narrator finds Elfrida lacking because of her self-absorption, she also finds Janet lacking in her reserve and her ultimate snobbery.

In many ways these two women are made to represent two sides of a literary debate which was taking place in the late nineteenth century, the type of debate which they have on first meeting. In it they discuss the merits of the new realism and, in a particularly North American slant, the place of W.D. Howells in relation to it. Zola functions as the unstated benchmark for this realism, when Elfrida says of Howells's characters, 'his *bêtes humaines* are always conventionalized, and generally come out wearing the halo of the redeemed' (*DT* 114). This evokes, as the backdrop to their discussion, Zola's novel of 1890, *La Bête Humaine,* a reference point which is picked up by Janet when she suggests that only the Latin temperament can provide such studies. While Elfrida pleads for 'some real *romans psychologiques*' from Howells, Janet suggests that

> I don't think the English and American people are exactly calculated to offer the sort of material you mean ... pure unrelieved filth can't be transmuted into literature, and as a people we're perfectly devoid of that extraordinary artistic nature that it makes such a foil for in the Latins. (*DT* 114)

In a direct challenge to Zola's commitment to the 'rigor of scientific truth' in fiction (Zola 162), Janet asserts that as far as psychological oddities go, 'Phenomena are for the scientists. You don't mean to tell me that any fiction that pretends to call itself artistic has a right to touch them?' (*DT* 115). Elfrida's response is to claim the realist method as art itself: 'Art has no ideal but truth, and to conventionalize truth is to damn it!' (*DT* 115). This comment reveals the greatest limitation in Elfrida's approach to life and art: she sees no truth in the conventional. Janet, on the other hand, finds Howells's representations of the conventional to have 'a tremendous appearance of sincerity, psychological and other' (*DT* 114). In accordance with these views, Janet goes on to write a novel with, in her own words, 'an effective leading idea' (*DT* 175). If, as she suggests, the author it most evokes is Hardy, then she is not as conservative as she or Elfrida make her out to be. At the time *A Daughter of Today* was written, Hardy's most recent publication had been *Tess of the d'Urbervilles* (1891), which while not obviously a work of the new realism nonetheless challenged the morality and gender stereotypes of the day. Yet because Janet does not espouse the values of European realism, Elfrida considers her to be conventional. If Elfrida is on the cutting edge of art, as she seems to see herself, then Janet is on the side of the literary status quo, with her reputation in the better journals and her family's social position in literary London. By creating two divergent portraits of the woman artist, Duncan rejects the New Woman stereotypes current in the fiction of the nineties. She refuses to depict the female artist as a type. Instead, she creates individual women who make different choices in their art as well as in their lives, and who both gain artistic success in their own ways.

The only art the reader really 'views' in the text is that of the visual artist, John Kendal, via Duncan's use of ekphrasis. His style is presented as impressionist, yet in his best work, the portrait of Elfrida, he seems to fulfil Duncan's own ideas of what is best in art. Though she tended to defend the realism of Howells and James in her journalism,[25] Duncan saw through Zola's commitment to scientifically presenting nature in fiction. Realising the impossibility of this, she 'rejects the view that realism simply copies life and says instead that realism is a selective art' (Dean, *A Different Point of View* 48). Misao Dean demonstrates how nineteenth-century Canadian idealism also tempered Duncan's own approach to realism:

> She salvaged the romantic 'idealities' that Canadians derived from their literary dialogue with Victorian poetry even while she wrote

---

25 However conventional Howells may have appeared to Elfrida, he was a radical enough exponent of realism to require defence in the Canadian press during the eighties. T.D. MacLulich notes Duncan's approach in her journalism: 'Duncan appointed herself as the chief Canadian champion of the fiction of Howells and James, whom she often defended against the attacks of those she viewed as censorious Philistines' (MacLulich 73). However, while she praised the style, Duncan was not such a devotee as to remain completely uncritical, as her review of James's *The Bostonians* shows. Duncan emphasises the exquisite refinement of his expression 'but condemns his ridicule' of the suffragists and comments on his paucity of ideas (Duncan, 'Grandmotherly Repose' 105, 104).

within the growing dominance of materialist realism, writing against the assumption that only those things that can be explained by physical cause and effect are real. (*A Different Point of View* 43)

Thomas Tausky suggests that 'elements of realism and romance co-exist, sometimes happily, sometimes uneasily, in her novels' (Tausky, *Sara Jeannette Duncan* 41). Duncan is interested in the underlying ideas rather than the mere recording of detail, which she sees as the weakness of naturalism — so her style, in this novel at least, sits between the two. In light of this, Kendal achieves his highest when he gets beyond his technique and expresses an idea through it:

> He had submitted it to his idea, which had grown upon the canvas obscure to him under his own brush until that final moment; and he recognized with astonishment how relative and incidental the truth of the treatment seemed in comparison with the truth of the idea. (*DT* 260)

In Kendal's best work then, he would seem to be similar in approach to Janet (and to Duncan herself), further separating Elfrida from both her friends.

The role of the male artist as arbiter of women's art, exemplified by the previously quoted comments of Henry James, is pursued in *A Daughter of Today* by several male characters. Elfrida's first experience of this is in the atelier, where not only male taste but male style is the benchmark in the valuation of the woman students' work. As a male artist, John Kendal feels he is in a position to inform Elfrida of her lack of talent for painting. Later his chief interest in her is as an object of study. Demonstrating a stereotypically traditional male European approach, Kendal wants to make an evaluation of her, as he tends to do with most people: 'What he liked best to achieve was an intimate knowledge of his fellow-beings, from an outside point of view. Where intimate knowledge came of intimate association, he found that it usually compromised his independence of criticism' (*DT* 43). In his initial relations with Elfrida, Kendal 'was willing enough to meet her on the special plane she constituted for herself — not as a woman, but as an artist and a Bohemian' (*DT* 46). But this is in Paris, where Kendal seems able to put aside his respectable English background. When he returns to England, his views are more conservative. She shows her insight into his art when she reviews it in *The Decade*, prompting them to have a more serious and equal conversation than they have ever had. Kendal, though, is not sure about the change: 'Already she had grown less amusing, and the real *camaraderie* which she constantly suggested her desire for, he could not, at the bottom of his heart, truly tolerate with a woman' (*DT* 97). The equality of an artist-to-artist relationship is beyond him, and he prefers to use her in the much more traditional role of muse, to produce his best work. While earnestly insisting to himself that he is not sexually attracted to her, he nevertheless feels 'the pleasure of coming upon her suddenly' and 'a desire to talk with her about all sorts of things, to feel the exhilaration of her single-mindedness, to find out more about her, to guess at the meanings behind her eyes' (*DT* 121, 122). However, it is his desire to analyse, to pin down and control, which is his strongest impulse towards Elfrida, and he thinks 'eagerly of the pleasure of proving, with his own eyes, another step in the working out of the problem which he believed he had solved in Elfrida' (*DT* 204). Kendal is limited in his response to Elfrida as a person, because to him she is always a woman, and as a male artist he always sees himself as her judge. That she is a 'problem' is typical of the way debates about issues of gender were cast in the late nineteenth century. It was the 'Woman Question' rather than a discussion of gender, even though much of it was taken up with addressing issues of masculine practice and morality. The way Kendal positions himself in relation to Elfrida is also reminiscent of the approaches of many colonial male travel writers to peoples or environments which the writers saw as embodying the Other. Various narrative strategies were used to induce 'the fantasy of dominance', as Mary Louise Pratt describes it (*DT* 124).

Chief among these was maintaining the illusion of the impersonal as a means of increasing the authority of the narrative voice. Kendal does this mentally, and it is his favoured strategy for constructing Elfrida as Other.

While the reader does not have the opportunity to peruse either Janet's or Elfrida's work, we do in a sense have the chance to 'view' Kendal's, and it is his two portraits of Elfrida which the narrator describes most closely. In the first, he deals with his embarrassment at her public adulation of the novelist, George Jasper (presumably intended to be a figure based on George Meredith). Kendal's classification of her is apparent in the title of this work: '*A Fin de Siècle Tribute*' (*DT* 151). While this sketch helps him to forget the incident, he is still troubled by the need to understand Elfrida fully. It is in his posed portrait of her that he believes he achieves this. It is also in this work that he feels 'an exulting mastery' and 'a silent, brooding triumph in his manipulation, in his control' (*DT* 246, 247). The whole scene, in which Elfrida's last sitting for Kendal is described, is imbued with an erotic power which derives from her objectification and his sense of control. The realisation they both have when viewing the portrait, that Kendal has caught Elfrida's essence, her egoism, marks a different climax for each of them. Once Kendal is sure that he has mastered her in his art, his fascination with her disappears. He has had her, so to speak. However, her response to the recognition of his mastery is sexual submission: 'Her self-surrender was so perfect' (*DT* 252). Afterwards, she admits to herself, 'I would have let him take me in his arms and hold me close, close to him. And I wish he had — I should have had it to remember' (*DT* 254). When the memory of her desire causes her to blush, she dismisses the embarrassment by reaffirming her creed that sexual desire is just another appetite, as valid as hunger. In a very similar fashion to Schreiner's chapter 'Lyndall's Stranger', this scene captures in miniature the dynamics of the romance plot, which eroticises the imbalance of power between men and women, and Elfrida shows herself to be willing, if temporarily, to submit to it. Kendal's presence throughout most of the book makes the romance plot a possibility, if not a main focus. Elfrida's offer to give up her book, at the moment of her sexual submission, is a classic statement of the either/or choices of heroines in the fiction of this time. If the *Bildung* plot were allowed to reach fulfilment, it would be at the expense of the romance plot, and vice versa. All too often, the heroine in search of artistic pursuits would realise the unnatural course she was taking, and give up her career/art/education and devote herself to a man who was pursuing his career/art/education.[26] In this she would find fulfilment. Duncan's ironic comment on her gesture to this type of romance plot, in which *Bildung* is truncated, is to have Elfrida reflect to her confessor, the statue of Buddha, 'It was a lie, a pose to tempt him on. I would never have given it up — never!' (*DT* 254). However, Elfrida is swayed enough by the pull of the romance plot to have doubts: 'It is part of my soul, Buddha, and my love for him — oh, I cannot tell!' (*DT* 254). When Kendal rejects her, the romance plot collapses, without Elfrida having to make the either/or choice.

Kendal has used her as his inspiration for his best painting — 'It had already carried him further in power, this portrait, it would carry him further in place, than anything he had yet done, and the thought gave a sparkle to the delicious ineffable content that bathed his soul' — and has now had enough of her (*DT* 260). His best has been achieved through penetrating her being and revealing what he has found, and to complete the impression that some sort of ravishment has occurred, he admits to Elfrida, 'I've taken something you didn't intend me to have' (*DT* 251). In

---

26 A Canadian example of this classic 1890s plot is Joanna Wood's *Judith Moore; or Fashioning a Pipe* (1898), in which Judith, under the weight of her unnatural life as a famous singer, collapses physically and is only restored by retirement under the care of a simple farming man whom she marries. The implication throughout is that although she has an astounding voice, the pursuit of a career actually makes a woman sick, because it is not her purpose in life. As a reminder of past mistakes, Judith is unable to have children, but is more than content with her husband.

classic romance style, where rape or the threat of it is often eroticised, Elfrida's response is sexual submission, as we have seen: 'Well, I give it to you — it is yours quite freely and ungrudgingly ... You have a right to your divination' (*DT* 251). His moment of achievement has occurred in the act of defining her, and suggests that to some extent, Duncan is creating a scenario in which the success of the male artist is dependent on his containment of the female artist. The space in which he operates is space which has been taken from her.

The other male artist who operates in this way is George Jasper. He is the famous author whom Elfrida embarrasses at a public function by bowing to him and kissing his hand. He appears once more, briefly yet significantly. As an adviser to a publishing company, he is called upon to review Elfrida's manuscript. Supposing that the author will not be reading his opinion, and having had an 'extremely indigestible' dinner in uninteresting company, he vents his spleen on the manuscript: 'in writing his opinion of it to Mr. Pitt, which he did with some elaboration a couple of hours later, he had all the relief of a revenge upon a well-meaning hostess without the reproach of having done her the slightest harm' (*DT* 278). It is Elfrida's receipt of this opinion which precipitates her suicide. With the failure of the romance plot, she still has her art, but the apparent failure of her *Bildung* plot means that there is nowhere for her to go. Her suicide is the only way out for her after the failure of both plots: she dies choosing her own path, as she has done throughout the text. Male artists have had a huge impact on her choices, however, and while they have realised their brutality, they appear to feel no regret.

Everything which happens to Elfrida, as a female artist, is of course tempered by Janet's experience, which is not nearly so extreme. She is still well under male control, however, which increases markedly when she and Kendal become engaged. To be fair to Kendal as male artist, part of his blithe assumption regarding his right to control comes from his shallow experience of life and his position of privilege. When Janet considers him, she asks herself rhetorically, 'who had ever refused him anything yet?' (*DT* 177). When he has devastated Elfrida with not only sexual rejection, but also the definitive portrait, he feels 'the keenest pang his pleasant life had ever brought him' (*DT* 253). During the course of the novel, his status changes from student artist in the Quartier Latin, who 'made his studies for his own pleasure', to landowner with an estate in Devonshire (*DT* 43). He begins as 'the flower of Lucien's'; he ends as a member of the landed gentry (*DT* 44). Success is a sure assumption for him. However, given Janet's independence of mind, which she has demonstrated very adequately in her dealings with Elfrida, and her 'innate dominance', it is strange that as soon as Kendal proposes to her, he assumes that he has a right to direct her thinking and her actions (*DT* 220).

This is most clearly demonstrated when Elfrida, having heard of Janet and Kendal's engagement, responds with a bitter letter to Janet complaining of her duplicity. Kendal's response to the letter is to laugh out loud, being concerned neither with Elfrida's aggrieved feelings, nor Janet's, but only with the more absurd aspects of Elfrida's self-conception. He is preoccupied primarily with his role as judge and critic. The relationship between Janet and Elfrida is certainly not a factor in his thinking. While Janet is concerned that she has not been entirely straightforward in her dealings with Elfrida, Kendal is not prepared to admit to either his fascination, or his knowledge that he has hurt her. In response to Janet's comment that she thought he was attracted to Elfrida, he says 'It's a man's privilege to fall in love with a woman, darling, not with an incarnate idea' (*DT* 271). Yet the reader knows that he has been tempted by Elfrida's readiness to submit to him sexually, surely making her much more than an idea. He has not been honest with himself or Janet, and the response this provokes in him is to force Janet to express his anger to Elfrida. The letter he dictates is a measure of his rejection and dismissal of Elfrida. In it he diminishes the importance of the relationship between the women in a way neither of them feel, and destroys any possibility of its restoration. He does not leave Elfrida even the chance of looking back on her friendship with Janet with any sense of its value. His letter is designed to destroy what has been, as well as what could be. Kendal acts to reassert the primacy of the heterosexual bond, in the face of the importance of bonds between women, in particular those between women artists. This is underscored in the account of Kendal's dictation by the fact that it is interspersed with descriptions of the couple's lovemaking, causing the relationship between the two women to be further displaced, at least in the mind of Kendal. He concludes this scene with the question, 'now don't you think we have had enough of Miss Elfrida Bell for the present?' (*DT* 274).

However, Janet's concern about Elfrida reasserts itself to the extent that she sends Kendal away when he comes to her seeking sympathy about the portrait Elfrida has destroyed, in order that she might go to Elfrida herself with a true account of her feelings: 'she thought of the most explicit terms in which to inform Elfrida that her letter had been the product of hardness of heart, that she really felt quite different, and had come to tell her, purely for honesty's sake, how she did feel' (*DT* 279). It is then that she finds Elfrida's body. Female friendship having been displaced, the heterosexual bond is reinforced in the marriage of Janet and Kendal. However, the narrator mentions two factors which partially destabilise it. The first is that Elfrida is significant enough in Janet's life to cause her to make the journey to Sparta, Illinois, to pay some kind of homage, reparation, or both at the graveside. The second is a silence which intrudes into the Kendals' 'idyllic life in Devonshire', which serves to destabilise the apparent completeness of their life as a couple: 'But even in the height of some domestic joy a silence sometimes falls between them still. Then, I fancy, he is thinking of an art that has slipped away from him, and she of a loyalty she could not hold' (*DT* 281). Elfrida, the rebellious female artist, who has served as inspiration for him, and stimulation and comrade for her, has been reduced to silence. This novel has *not* been silent about relationships between women, which, as noted, are generally represented as adjuncts to male/female courtships. In *A Daughter of Today*, the story of Janet and Elfrida is primary, and though it is silenced finally, it still serves to unsettle the complacencies of both the male artist and the heterosexual bond as focus of the romance plot.

If part of Kendal's artistic inspiration has come from Elfrida, then it is not surprising that after her death his art should be in decline. His use of a beautiful woman as muse is a conventional ploy for artists over the centuries. Her death does not completely explain his decline, however. There is a sense in which his nationalism is in conflict with his art, and I shall discuss this more later. The narrator seems to suggest that the life of a landed gentleman is incompatible with the production of serious art works. Kendal's artistic capacity is likely also to be seriously diminished by his lack of emotional depth. He rejects the Bohemian approach to art, which, though it might at times be pretentious (and it certainly is represented as that), does provide stimulus and the rawness of experience, which he apparently needs in Devonshire. Can a wealthy, happily married and contented man paint well? In terms of nineties' conceptions of the artist, the answer is probably 'no'. His unwillingness to let go of his respectable scruples is another factor in his capacity, or lack of it. While he finds Elfrida to be perfectly acceptable in Paris, London 'made her extreme in every way' (*DT* 119). He is shocked to his core when Elfrida joins the chorus line, and can find no justification, artistic or otherwise, for her actions. Yet in her function as muse, she brings out the best in him, in all her extremity and difference. Paris, also extreme and different for Kendal, has the same effect: 'Paris and the Quartier stood out against [London] in his mind like something full of light and colour and transient passion on the stage' (*DT* 119). He recognises that he has needed its stimulus: 'he had brought out of it an element that lightened his life and vitalized his work, and gave an element of joyousness to his imagination' (*DT* 119). In opting for a life of convention, thereby abandoning the likelihood of encountering strong stimulus, whether through lifestyle, travel or friendship, Kendal loses the capacity to produce work which, it seems, cannot come from within.

Kendal's need to control and fix the two women is mildly reflected by Lawrence Cardiff, though Cardiff's desire to control Elfrida is a much more besotted one than Kendal's, and he finds himself completely out of his depth with this 'New Woman'. His attitude that romantic involvement gives him the right of control is similar to Kendal's, the difference being that he fails to gain romantic commitment from Elfrida. In his proposal, control is his foremost thought: 'I have no right to intrude my opinions — if you like, my prejudice — between you and what you are doing. But I have come to beg you to give me the right' (*DT* 199). He goes on with assurance that his position will carry the day. He is charming, intellectually more experienced, and successful, and sees himself in the role of mentor: 'we will write a book — some other book — together' (*DT* 200). His concept of marriage is clear in his statement 'I want to possess you altogether', and early in the interview he 'smiled masterfully', and addressed her with the diminutive 'little one' (*DT* 200). But his illusions about her and his ability to prevail are modified when she rejects him: 'at the end of that time Lawrence Cardiff found himself very far from the altar and more enlightened than he had ever been before about the radicalism of certain modern sentiments concerning it' (*DT* 200). He continues to pursue her, however, with the assumption that after marriage she would learn to love him. His misreading of the situation — of the plot — is made explicit when she responds with horror, 'I should feel as if I were acting out an old-fashioned novel — an old-fashioned, *second-rate* novel!' (*DT*

228, emphasis in original). Though Cardiff initially assumes that he has control of Elfrida, he does not achieve it. He comes into conflict with a nineties plot, which leaves him, a bastion of the older Victorian literary establishment, floundering.

The attitude to marriage which Elfrida expresses throughout is one that was not uncommon in the fiction and essays of the period. Schreiner's *The Story of an African Farm*, appearing as it did in the year following *The Married Woman's Property Act* of 1882, helped to bring the marriage debate into the literary arena, where it stayed for some time. Thomas Hardy and George Meredith both continued to address this question, as did most of the writers of the so-called New Woman fiction. Elfrida's views are not unique, but they are at the more extreme end of the spectrum. She draws on the analysis voiced by Lyndall in *African Farm* which critiques marriage as a degrading exchange in which sexual favours are traded for economic support, a 'legal prostitution' (Egerton 155).[27] A less extreme statement of the case is made by Mona Caird, who wrote that 'Friendship between husband and wife on the old terms was almost impossible. Where there is power on the one hand and subordination on the other, whatever the relationship that may arise, it is not likely to be that of friendship' (827). She does go so far as to refer to marriage as 'common bondage' (827), words echoed by Elfrida when she responds to Cardiff's proposal: 'there is not for me the common temptation to enter into a form of bondage which as I see it is hateful' (*DT* 229). In her short story 'Virgin Soil', which was published in the same year as *A Daughter of Today*, George Egerton's character Florence, a young wife, states the anti-marriage case strongly:

> [I]t must be so, as long as marriage is based on such unequal terms, as long as man demands from a wife as a right, what he must sue from a mistress as a favour; until marriage becomes for many women a legal prostitution, a nightly degradation, a hateful yoke

---

27 See footnote 12 on page 35 for the genealogy of this concept.

under which they age, mere bearers of children conceived in a sense of duty, not love. (155)

Debate about the 'morality of marriage', to borrow Caird's title, continued in the journals and fiction of the 1880s and 1890s, with the opponents of feminism, such as Mrs Lynn Linton, bolstering their arguments with appeals to 'nature', and supporters such as Caird arguing from the perspective of liberalism. Elfrida's analysis seems in part to draw on materialism, in her suggestions that 'The spirituality of love might be a Western product', and that romantic love is but a passion humanity 'shares with — with the mollusks' (*DT* 154, 158). She also sees marriage as a hindrance to her art, and wonders that Janet should not feel the same: 'of course, the men are not affected by it. But for women it is degrading — horrible! especially for women like you and me, to whom life may mean something else. Fancy being the author of babies, when one could be the author of books! *Don't* tell me you'd rather!' (*DT* 157, emphasis in original). Once again for women, there are only either/or choices. Where men can pursue love, marriage, parenthood *and* career, women are reduced to choosing between these options, rather than combining them. Very few authors, if any, from the period, seem able to conceive of a heroine combining roles in a way which is entirely commonplace for heroes. For heroines, the element of sacrifice is still found to be an integral part of their constitution, even for an egoist like Elfrida.

If there were no contraception available, that would make more sense of the need to choose between marriage and art. However, although it is not discussed in the text, the references to 'free unions' suggest the increasing information about, and use of, contraception that were occurring at this time. The 'free union' is a growing part of Elfrida's philosophy of sexuality, though it is obviously difficult for her to completely break out of the traditions in which she has been raised. However, her commitment to a Bohemian lifestyle, and her analysis of conventional morality, demand it of her. When Nádie tells her she has a lover, and that 'We have decided about marriage that it is ridiculous', Elfrida 'had not even changed colour, though she had found the communication electric' (*DT* 28). Later when she admits to herself her sexual desire for Kendal, she blushes, even though according to her new creed, sexual desire is entirely ordinary: 'I might as well be ashamed of wanting my dinner!' (*DT* 254). The British public is not so ready to part with its morality, however. When Elfrida writes 'the graphic, naked truth about the Latin Quarter', Rattray the sub-editor feels compelled to reflect 'that their public wouldn't stand *unions libres* when not served up with a moral purpose — that no artistic apology for them would do' (*DT* 100). Like Lyndall before her, a 'free union' is ultimately what Elfrida comes to desire in her relationship with Kendal. Even after he has rejected her, she thinks this the most likely outcome:

> He will marry some red-and-white cow of an Englishwoman who will accept herself in the light of a reproductive agent and do her duty by him accordingly. As I would not — no! Good heavens, no! So perhaps it is as well, for I will go on loving him of course, and some day he will come back to me, in his shackles, and together, whatever we do, we will make no vulgar mess of it. (*DT* 254)

This sounds like the plot of a different New Woman novel, but Elfrida has misread the situation, and does not realise that this 'cow' will be her friend Janet.

In contrast to Elfrida's commitment to a new morality is her obliviousness to the damage she may cause others by encouraging their sexual interest and affections, when she has no intention of returning them. This is evident even while she is still in Sparta, when she is involved in 'one or two incipient love affairs, watched with anxious interest by her father, and with harrowed conscience by her mother, who knew Elfrida's capacity for amusing herself' (*DT* 25-26). In this aspect of her character, she is once again reflective of Bashkirtseff, who wrote: 'it is amusing when you feel that you are making some one love you ... *The love one inspires is a sensation unlike anything else*' (308, emphasis in original). Elfrida's chief response to such a situation is the same: amusement. When Rattray's attraction becomes obvious, 'Elfrida laughed a little', and when Cardiff comes to declare his love and beg her to leave the chorus line, she sees him as an interesting plot development in her book: 'She hid her face in the pillow to laugh at the thought of how deliciously the interference of an elderly lover would lend itself to the piece of work which she saw in fascinating development under her hand' (*DT* 101, 195-196). Elfrida is certainly not the only heroine of her time to be guilty of such attitudes. Henry James's Isabel Archer had 'yielded to the satisfaction of having refused two ardent suitors in a fortnight', and 'had tasted of the delight, if not of battle, at least of victory' (James *Portrait of a Lady* 145). Elfrida follows her in this, but is even more flippant, as befits her greater egoism. Likewise Elfrida's competitive drive and need to succeed make 'what ... the poets are pleased to call love' a 'game' (*DT* 159). Like Bashkirtseff and Isabel, Elfrida finds the exercise of power to be the thrilling aspect of this game: 'It is worth doing — to sit within three feet of a human being who would give all he possesses just to touch your hand — and to tacitly dare him to do it' (*DT* 159). For, as she thinks, 'it's splendid to win — anything. It's a kind of success' (*DT* 159). For Elfrida, and for Bashkirtseff, part of growth and education is to 'look considerations of sentiment very full in the face', and to realise the constructed and artificial nature of the romantic discourse of the day and to exploit it for pleasure and sensation (*DT* 153). The fact that this allows both heroines to manipulate certain men is part of its charm. While wanting the independence of the modern heroine, neither is prepared to abandon the age-old means by which some women have always gained a power that would otherwise have been denied them.

In her role as daughter, Elfrida is in marked contrast to Janet. When the reader first encounters her, it is through the eyes of both her teacher and her mother, and in the first two chapters we have the chance to see how much Mrs Bell is constructing Elfrida in the role of artist or genius. The same self-conscious affectation that we later encounter in Elfrida is evident in her manner, when she says 'I often wonder what her career will be, and sometimes it comes home to me that it *must* be art. The child can't help it — she gets it straight from me' (*DT* 8). In suggesting that Elfrida's talent has come from herself, Mrs Bell gives us the only real clue as to why she has such an investment in Elfrida's career. She has been unable to pursue her own talent, as she states: 'there were no art classes in my day' (*DT* 8). Duncan is ironic at her expense, the narrator commenting that 'Mrs. Bell's tone implied a large measure of what the world had lost in consequence' (*DT* 8). Her own lack of choices could be seen to motivate her belief in Elfrida's destiny: 'I wish *I* had her opportunities' (*DT* 8, emphasis in original).

Mrs Bell views Elfrida's young life as a potential biography, another *The Journal of Marie Bashkirtseff* perhaps, as she tells Miss Kimpsey, 'She has often reminded me of what you see in the biographies of distinguished people about their youth — there are really a great many points of similarity' (*DT* 8). Once again, the resemblances to the Bashkirtseff account are apparent. Throughout Marie's life, she was made to feel different because of her various talents, a difference she both enjoyed and resented. Her difference was reinforced by the words of fortune-tellers and cultivated by the household, which was largely made up of members of her mother's extended family. After Marie's death her mother was so concerned to construct a picture of young genius blighted that she changed her age throughout the manuscript to make her appear younger, and removed passages which detracted from the legend, particularly those which suggested any discord between Marie and herself. While Mrs Bell does not have a journal to publish, she does have a memory to cultivate, and she employs judicious editing techniques similar to those used by Madame Bashkirtseff.

When Elfrida leaves Paris, she refuses to tell her parents where she has gone, ostensibly in order to prevent them from sending money they cannot afford to spare. Her letter provokes 'the suspicion that its closing paragraph was doubtfully daughterly', but their view of their relation to Elfrida keeps her parents from admitting this. In reality, now that they are no longer supporting her financially, she has claimed her independence and rendered them redundant (*DT* 55). The act of casting off her parents, though done in the politest of terms, allows her to participate fully in 'the picturesqueness of the situation in which she saw herself, alone in London, making her fight for life as she found it worth living, by herself, for herself, in herself' (*DT* 60). When she hears that her parents are considering moving to England, and hope to have her living with them again, it is the loss of self-determination that she fears: 'She saw the ruin of her independence, of her delicious solitariness' (*DT* 146). In a rejection of what literally happened to Bashkirtseff, she refuses 'the *role* of family idol', envisaging that it would entail, as it did for Marie, 'the household happiness hinging on her moods, the question of her health, her work, her pleasure, being the eternally chief one' (*DT* 146, emphasis in original). She wants adulation, but only from the right people, and her parents do not know enough about her values to qualify. Uninformed adulation is merely an inconvenience.

The role of Elfrida's former teacher, Miss Kimpsey, is that of go-between and then of substitute daughter, as she visits Elfrida in England. Miss Kimpsey returns with the opinion strongly expressed by Elfrida, that England would be bad for Mrs Bell's health, and more expensive than Sparta. Elfrida is going about the business of destroying 'the prospective shrine' (*DT* 146). For her, family have no tie to compare with that enjoyed between true Bohemians: 'They had no such claim upon her, no such closeness to her as Nádie Palicsky, for instance, had' (*DT* 148). This is why she cannot understand Janet's concern about the emotional strain her father is going through because of his attachment to her. Janet begs her to make an end of the affair, but to Elfrida nothing should bother Janet while she is experiencing artistic success, particularly her father's emotions: 'You have your success; does it really matter — so very much!' (*DT* 246). To her parents, Elfrida is perfectly charming and perfectly distant, and should she be anything else, they have such an interest in maintaining a particular view of her that they will not let the facts interfere with their interpretation of things. In a sense, her suicide allows them to go on deceiving themselves in an uninterrupted way. There is nothing to contradict a construction of Elfrida as a tragic young genius: instead of destroying the shrine, Elfrida has fixed it. The ironies of the final pages could not be more complete. Elfrida's body is returned to the Sparta she abhors; a red granite monument is constructed in her memory; in a show of family solidarity her parents plan to be buried with her; and Buddha — the same one who has been chief confessor and who has been told that he would '*loathe* Sparta' — is finally placed in Mrs Bell's drawing room amongst the 'mournful Magdalens' (*DT* 102, 281, emphasis in original). To complete this, her parents have obediently placed the text she 'commanded to be put' on her grave, which reads '*Pas femme-artiste*' (*DT* 280-281, 281). They seem to have no idea of what this might imply, though, and it sums up the gulf separating Elfrida from them: they have no comprehension of what she is about, and she has not tried to enlighten them. Even her suicide note is an exercise in politeness, being 'charmingly apologetic', and her suicide itself, rather than challenging the understanding they have had of Elfrida, is explained away using the family tree (*DT* 280). By this time Miss Kimpsey has moved in with them, and to complete their lives, 'her relation to them has become almost daughterly' (*DT* 281). The final irony for Elfrida is that the enshrinement she tried to avoid can now run its course unchecked by reality: 'The three are swayed to the extent of their capacities by what one might call a cult of Elfrida' (*DT* 281).

The concept of the impossibility of the woman artist, which fills not only *A Daughter of Today* but the text on which it draws so heavily, *The Journal of Marie Bashkirtseff*, is brought to the fore in the epitaph which is inscribed on her monument. 'Impossibility' results from the clash between the discourses of femininity and the artist. The inscription, '*Pas femme-artiste*', remains somewhat ambiguous (*DT* 281). Janet reads this as a mistaken comment on Elfrida's lack of real womanhood, and when she visits the grave, 'hopes in all seriousness that the sleeper underneath is not aware of the combination' (*DT* 281). However, the novelist allows it to stand, an oblique commentary on the fact that to become an artist was, in terms of the late nineteenth century, to contravene the codes of femininity, and to cease to be a real woman. The impossibility of the woman artist is confirmed by the narrative, as although the reader has seen two woman artists functioning throughout the text, in its denouement they both seem to have been swallowed up by nineteenth-century women's plots. Elfrida is dead and Janet is married, with no mention of her work. Nádie Palicsky has disappeared from the story and the *Künstlerroman* plots of both heroines appear to have come unstuck under the influence of their romance plots. The discursive clash between the categories of 'woman' and 'artist' is worked out at the level of plot, with the result that 'artist' disappears under 'woman', the ultimately defining factor for a female character. But the inscription can also be read as a defiant assertion against this. Elfrida seems to be asking from the grave not to be considered first as a woman but as an artist, just as a male artist would be. To claim for her the status of artist — rather than woman — on the last page of a novel whose plot forecloses opportunities for women artists, is to protest not only at the circumstances that led to Elfrida's death but also against the plots available to women in the *Bildungsroman* form.

Just as Duncan represents both female characters as having different approaches to their art, so they are shown to be very different in their approach to romance. These differences define them as heroines. I have discussed in particular Elfrida's stated philosophies about marriage and sexual relationships. She expresses these in her attitude to her growing attraction to John Kendal, an attraction she shares with Janet. Although she could not be described as aggressive in her pursuit of Kendal, she certainly does not sit back and hide her attraction, as Janet does. When the opportunity arises, after her portrait is finished, Elfrida makes her feelings quite clear to Kendal, as she does her willingness to submit to him, at least sexually. She has resisted soundly any romantic plots until this point, preserving herself against them in order to maintain the freedom to pursue her art. Janet, on the other hand, is completely passive in relation to letting anyone know her feelings, especially Kendal. She waits for his declaration, fearing that it will be regarding Elfrida rather than herself. She is self-sacrificial in her attempts to maintain the relationship with Elfrida, as well as in waiting for Kendal. In light of the fact that Kendal is a traditional Englishman, and the romantic hero, a passive romantic partner is what he is looking for, and what he gets. While Janet is scarcely traditional in terms of her career, she is in terms of romance, and in this romance plot, as in most others, the traditional heroine succeeds. In the marital plot, it is the heroine's passivity which is rewarded. The artistic career of the romantically successful heroine is an area of silence in this text, as romance and art continue to be incompatible for women. However, while the narration does not mention Janet's work after her marriage, the silence about it *could* be read as a silence of possibility.

In her representation of Elfrida's artistic growth and persona, Duncan is concerned to show the influence of nineties trends 'while simultaneously exposing the limitations of Aestheticism and Decadence for women artists at the *fin de siècle*' (Ready 95). Elfrida's tragic end fits in well with the cultivated understanding of her as genius that is shared by her mother and Miss Kimpsey, and partly by herself. Her father, early in her life, is still hoping for 'normality' for Elfrida, but her mother interprets all her actions through the lens of her supposed genius: '[Art] led her into strange absent silences and ways of liking to be alone, which gratified her mother and worried her father' (*DT* 15). As Elfrida's idea of artistic living solidifies, she develops a self-consciousness which dominates her approach to everything she does. Her manner becomes a creation in itself: 'She stood and sat and spoke, and even thought, at times, with a subtle approval and enjoyment of her manner of doing it' (*DT* 15). She becomes absorbed in her own beauty, and like Bashkirtseff, sees her image as something almost separate from herself. Marie records her self-admiration on many occasions, in terms such as, 'I am charmed with myself. My white arms beneath the white wool, oh, so white! I am pretty; I am animated' (37). Likewise, Elfrida 'took a keen enjoying pleasure in the flush upon her own cheek and the light in her own eyes', and 'she paused before the looking glass, and wafted a kiss, as she blew the candle out, to the face she saw there' (*DT* 16). This self-consciousness means that both Bashkirtseff and Elfrida strive to project a certain image of themselves onto others. While Bashkirtseff records, 'I spend my life in saying wild things, which please me and astonish others' (317), the reader has the opportunity to observe Elfrida at this pastime almost continually. Some of this preoccupation with self could be seen to be a function of age: no one is so self-absorbed as a teenager, and Elfrida is only twenty-one when she dies. Bashkirtseff's maturation brings a change in her journal also. However, in both these character portraits, self-consciousness is presented as an element of ego which feeds the artistic impulse and gives drive to its possessor. It may be repulsive to others, but it is productive. Ego also flows into the competitive spirit, which is seen particularly between Marie and Breslau, and between Elfrida and Janet. The positive aspect of this is its motivating power, and the sense it provides of being in an artistic community, which is not created fully by the proximity of male artists.

In forming herself as an artistic creation in her own right, Elfrida is guided by the late-nineteenth-century Aesthetic movement, in particular by its more morbid nineties version, whose particular reading of Pater led them to value the appreciation of beauty and the development of their own aesthetic sense above all else. Though Lawrence Cardiff recognises, when he lends her *Marius the Epicurean*, that this is the source of her ideas, such concepts have become so much a part of the currency of the Decadence that their origin does not have a great impact on Elfrida. The narrator, stepping back for a moment, comments, 'I cannot say that this Oxonian's tender classical recreation had any critical effect upon her; she probably found it much too limpid and untroubled to move her in the least' (*DT* 128). Certain of Pater's somewhat modified ideas had been taken up by the Aesthetes of the nineties, in ways which are well demonstrated in Oscar Wilde's *The Picture of Dorian Gray* (1891) by the philosophies of Dorian himself. In a minor way, Elfrida's 'little eastern-smelling box, which seemed to her to represent the core of her existence', reflects Dorian's collections of aesthetic materials (*DT* 163-164). Elfrida approached this box with religious fervour, gathered her best pieces of writing, 'and put them sacredly away with Nádie's letters and a manuscript poem of a certain Bruynotin's, and a scrawl from one Hakkoff with a vigorous sketch of herself from memory, in pen and ink, in the corner of the page' (*DT* 163).

Her best works are all impressions, as would be expected. Just as Kendal's paintings would be more appreciated by the British public 'if they were a little more finished', and by a patron of the arts if 'the foreground weren't so blurred', so Elfrida's best work is represented by what is regarded as 'an odd, unconventional bit of writing' (*DT* 86, 87, 163). The pieces of her writing that reach the prerequisite standard of the treasure box are 'an interview with some eccentric notability which read like a page from Gyp, a bit of pathos picked out of the common streets, a fragment of character-drawing which smiled visibly and talked audibly' (*DT* 163). Dean notes that 'Artistic "impressions" are the object of *A Social Departure*, Duncan's first book which 'was published in 1890, at the beginning of the decade in which the role of "impressions" in the ideology of cultural decadence would be elaborated' (Dean, 'The Paintbrush and the Scalpel' 83). Elfrida is thus using a method and style which had been Duncan's own. While the narrator observes Elfrida's collection of impressions with some amusement, it is also with acknowledgment of their merit, as the above description of the character study shows. In the piece, Elfrida is able to bring the person to life, suggesting that her talent is real despite her pretentiousness. Pretentiousness does not make her any less a part of nineties artistic life; in fact, it probably qualifies her more than any other single characteristic as a child of Decadence. Another expression of the Decadent creed is the seeking out of sensations. Bashkirtseff captures this idea, when she writes:

> I return at half-past six, so tired and completely worn out that it is quite a luxury … You don't believe it can be? Well, to my taste, every complete sensation, pushed to its utmost limit, even if painful, is an enjoyment.
>
> I remember when I hurt my finger once, the pain was so violent during half an hour that I enjoyed it. (652)

Though she does not specifically relish the experience of physical pain, Elfrida has come to experience sensation as pleasure. When Cardiff arrives to put his proposal she feels the rush of adrenalin which comes from apprehension, but she has learned to take enjoyment from it: she 'took the card with that quickening of her pulse, that sudden commotion, which had come to represent to her, in connection with any critical personal situation, one of the keenest possible sensations of pleasure' (*DT* 95). Her immersion in the Decadence can be seen to contribute to her end, as it invites extremity of feeling and behaviour.

In Marie Bashkirtseff's *The Journal*, the actual writing process becomes a means of creating a space in which to experience the self. Though Elfrida does not keep a journal, her conversations with her bronze statuette of Buddha perform a similar function. Just as in writing the journal Bashkirtseff experiences a subjectivity which is different from that she knows in her family, so Buddha comes to represent a space that is Elfrida's own, and in which she can explore herself and her art. Elfrida imbues the statue with the characteristics of an all-knowing impartial judge, with whom she can discuss her work, and who will see through her disguises. 'You are always honest, aren't you?' she tells it (*DT* 59). With Buddha in this guise, she has to justify her actions in taking the job at *The Age* by explaining to it that it is not for the money, but so that they can stay in London, that 'we are going to despise ourselves for a while' (*DT* 102). The persona she creates for Buddha becomes implicated in this way in her decisions. Janet, not knowing its role in Elfrida's life, appeals to it when she is attempting to win back Elfrida for the sake of her father. It looks on critically while Elfrida reads Janet's book, taking Elfrida's part in every instance. The fact that our final view of it is in Sparta amongst Mrs Bell's other calculated ornaments and pictures underlines the irony that though Elfrida has sought to create an enduring space for herself, it has at best been temporary and is soon submerged into family ideology.

As well as being the result of the collapse of both romance and *Bildung* plots, Elfrida's suicide is also the logical outcome of her creation of herself as a nineties artist. As Kathryn Ready notes, 'Her suicide marks the fullest expression of her Decadence' (100). Prior to this, she participates in behaviours which would make a heroine such as Bashkirtseff ill, but in her own new world fashion, they add to her health: 'she could slip out into the wet streets on a gusty October evening, and walk miles exulting in [art], and in the light on the puddles and in the rain on her face, coming back, it must be admitted, with red cheeks and an excellent appetite' (*DT* 14-15). Such a jaunt would have brought on a consumptive attack in Bashkirtseff. Likewise, the late nights which adversely affected Marie's condition have no obvious effect on Elfrida. She stays up late employed in activities such as kneeling before an open window in the moonlight reciting Rossetti for the sheer romance of it, and 'in the morning she had never taken cold' (*DT* 16). Consumption, that favourite condition of nineteenth-century heroines, is not to be hers, but she can create her own tragedy. Throughout the story she has toyed with suicide, as a way out of situations. The question is, what does her actual suicide signify? Is it the martyrdom of true genius or the impossibility of the woman artist? Or does Elfrida's suicide merely demonstrate the excesses of Bohemian values, and the thwarted will of a spoilt young woman?

Intimations of Elfrida's end come early in the text. Even before the poison ring is introduced, the connections between suicide and the female artist are drawn by the landlady: 'I only 'ope I won't find 'er suicided on charcoal some mornin', like that pore young poetiss in yesterday's paper' (*DT* 64). Behind this comment lies almost a century of preoccupation with connecting the female artist and death, a connection inscribed and reinscribed in many works. Madame de Staël's *Corinne: or Italy* (1807) began the trend with its portrait of the famous poetic improviser, who dies of grief when her lover chooses a more conventional woman. The poetry of Felicia Hemans celebrates many scenes from *Corinne*, again tempering the artistic success of the heroine with her romantic loss and consequent death. Angela Leighton suggests that behind this plot is the nineteenth-century version of the Sappho myth. This was, of course, a Sappho myth free from the suggestion of lesbian lovers. Rather, she is the archetypal figure of the woman poet who, on being rejected by her male lover Phaon, throws herself to her death from the Leucadian cliff. Such a figure came to dominate nineteenth-century depictions of the female artist. As Leighton notes, 'Sappho's leap connects female creativity with death, in a pact which the Victorian imagination finds endlessly seductively appealing' (35). Death then can be seen as almost a compulsion for Elfrida, a proof of artistic sensibility.

The poison ring is described by Elfrida as 'a dear little alternative' — she does not say to what — and a way of preventing her becoming 'less attractive than [she] is now' (*DT* 66). Though Golightly Ticke is 'involuntarily horrified' when she shows it to him, his Bohemian opinion, when he has recovered, is that it is 'awfully chic' (*DT* 66, 67). Considering suicide is shown to be a fashionable game in the Bohemian world, and one which Elfrida increasingly plays as she considers it a feasible response to disappointing situations. Kendal's revelations, both of his perception of her egoism in his painting, and his lack of response to her attraction to him, provoke a consideration of suicide. For her, it is 'the strong, the artistic, the effective thing to do', but initially a lack of courage keeps her from it (*DT* 253). Later, when the thought of the portrait becomes unbearable, she decides one of them must go. As she records in the note she leaves for Kendal, 'I have come here this morning … determined either to kill myself or IT' (*DT* 276). In the end, it is the portrait which she destroys, as 'death is too ghastly' (*DT* 276). Neither the loss of Kendal nor the revelation of her egoism is enough to overcome Elfrida's natural repulsion at the thought of death. The importance of the romance plot is thus diminished as it does not force the denouement of the novel. The matters which do bring it to its climax are those which have occupied the body of the text: Elfrida's relationship with her fellow artist, Janet, and her own artistic development. When both of these seem cut off, Elfrida has nothing else to do but to take the step which Bohemia has decreed to be a noble one. This narrative direction demonstrates that the *Bildung* plot is more significant in this novel than the romance plot, and the relationship between the two women artists supersedes the romantic relationship.

The irony of Elfrida's end is that it was prompted by two written responses, both of which misrepresent the true opinions of their authors. Janet's letter was dictated by Kendal, and did not reflect her feelings at all, and Jasper's 'reader's opinion' had more to do with 'two or three extremely indigestible dishes' he had eaten for dinner than the merit of Elfrida's manuscript (*DT* 278). In light of her apparent artistic failure, and the rejection and denial of their relationship by Janet, Elfrida finally swallows the poison. Dean claims that Elfrida 'destroys herself rather than face the discipline she would have to learn in order to be whole', and it is certainly true that Elfrida has found failure, or at least lack of instant success, difficult to cope with throughout the text ('The Process of Definition' 143). However, her suicide could be seen as just another extravagant artistic gesture of the sort that Elfrida has spent her life performing, or indeed, in terms of her aesthetic code, the noble thing to do. Pierre Cloutier raises the question as to 'whether Elfrida crosses or does not cross the paper-thin boundary line separating tragedy from gratuitous extravagance' (35),[28] and certainly the seriousness with which she regards herself might tend to suggest the latter. Elfrida's suicide is in character: it is extreme, and just when Kendal feels he has her defined and placed, she escapes his definitions once again, going on even after her death to disrupt not only his domestic harmony but also his artistic inspiration. In terms of it being the end of the woman artist, it is significant that the event is precipitated by the words of two male artists. Elfrida's suicide, beyond being the melodramatic gesture of an egocentric young woman that it

---

28 Although Cloutier's essay has been roundly criticised by Thomas Tausky for its misreading of *A Daughter of Today*, and given that Cloutier's mistake in attributing Canadian rather than US origins to Elfrida Bell is inexcusable, it is nevertheless an interesting study (Tausky 'The Citizenship'). Not only is it the first modern essay published on this text (to the best of my knowledge), but it also places the novel within the context of late nineteenth-century Decadence, an important one given scant attention by either Tausky or Dean, the most prolific Duncan scholars. More recently, Ready and Gadpaille have returned to questions of Decadence in Duncan.

undoubtedly is, is also a refusal of the space allotted to her by male artists: a refusal to be defined, and limited, as a woman artist.

While *A Daughter of Today* raises questions about the compatibility of the concepts of 'woman' and 'artist', it also confirms a dichotomy between *Bildung* and romance for the heroine. Elfrida is not allowed in her lifetime to succeed at either, though she has some artistic success posthumously. This dichotomy is not as strongly drawn in this novel as it is in some others from the period, although at the point of surrendering to Kendal, Elfrida's first thought is to offer him the sacrifice of her work. The fact that Janet is able to succeed in love while functioning as an artist is a sign of hope for future heroines, though the text is silent about any subsequent work Janet might produce. Whether the ending is punitive is questionable. Certainly the reviewer from *The Nation* felt that Elfrida's end could have been avoided, and was merely a concession to those offended by Elfrida's behaviour and views:

> To leave a final impression that her fresh, original, and really delightful heroine has been after all merely a lay figure, from whom the trappings are stripped with almost vindictive exposure, is a wasteful and ridiculous excess of consideration for the requirements of a novel as understood by literary Philistia. ('More Fiction' 473)

However, if the end is not a punitive gesture, and I feel it is not, then it is a serious comment on the difficulties of the female artist, and the role of the male artist in circumscribing her. Perhaps Duncan is illustrating the story she records in an article written while she was still a journalist, and had not yet begun writing fiction:

> I remember once entertaining, and unguardedly expressing, at the age of nine, a wild desire to write a novel.
> 'Put it out of your mind, my dear,' nodded a placid old lady of the last century over her knitting. 'Novel-making women always come to some bad end.' ('Review of *The Bostonians*' 33)

3.3 Death as Denouement: discursive conflict and narrative resolution

'Exactly on March 15th, the punkah wallah arrived with the hot weather, to pull the rope on the punkah, the large fan kept going day and night', Marian Fowler tells us (208). Duncan 'spent the whole year in Calcutta in 1893, suffering through the hot weather in August before the temperature became bearable again in November' (Fowler 215). It was a productive year. Not only did she correct the proofs of *The Simple Adventures of a Memsahib* but she wrote *Vernon's Aunt*, swiftly followed by *A Daughter of Today*. Fowler presents us with an image of Duncan sweltering in Calcutta in pursuit of her art, the other memsahibs having fled to the comparative comfort of the hills. She does so without irony, though it is an image which captures many of the ambivalences inherent in the position of the white woman writer in the colonial situation. While benefiting from the labour of the colonised, Duncan writes a narrative of feminine self-determination in the face of patriarchal restriction, a narrative which seems blind to its own colonising impulses. This has been a major criticism of First World feminism over almost five decades. A range of scholars have criticised its agenda as being primarily concerned with individualised self-fulfilment, which rises on the back of the Third World. Such a view of First World feminism is exemplified by Gayatri Spivak's classic reading of *Jane Eyre*, in which the possibility of Jane's personal and romantic fulfilment is predicated on the exploitation of slave labour in the West Indies. This exploitation provides the economic means which allows Jane her independence, and Rochester his wealth. Spivak's concern is to 'situate feminist individualism in its historical determination', and though she does not actually attribute the rise of First World feminism to the growth of imperialism, the two are imbricated in a text such as *Jane Eyre* (Spivak 244).

While *A Daughter of Today* continues the tradition of *Jane Eyre* in its representation of female *Bildung*, its participation in, and its response to, the discourse of colonialism is much more ambivalent. Given that there exists 'profound imbrication within the human subject of multiple, and often contesting, discourses' (Donaldson 6), *A Daughter of Today* both advances and resists the discourses of colonialism. In Duncan's text, the process by which alterity is used to maintain power relations is observed closely, but it is not treated as a given: it is often resisted, especially in the areas of gender and nation. However, characteristically of a postcolonial text from the Second World, the narrative position is often ambivalent and the resistance offered partial.

Duncan's anti-imperial strategies are mostly narratorial and nationalist in character, the most obvious narratorial strategy being the use of irony. Irony creates distance between the narrator and the perspective of the characters. Irony always has a victim, and as Dean points out, it 'conventionally excludes its victim' (*A Different Point of View* 19). It is not just Duncan's characters who become the victims of her irony; it is also those who are unable to participate in the narratorial point of view. They are necessarily disempowered by this process. At the same time the value systems shared by the narrator and those who share in the ironic view are confirmed: 'irony has the effect of consolidating a sense of community among those readers with the inside knowledge necessary to decipher it' (*A Different Point of View* 21). This can be a political strategy when the irony is directed at 'the representatives of imperial power' and the community being consolidated is the community of those on the fringes of the Empire (*A Different Point of View* 21). In *A Daughter of Today*, every character is the victim of some level of irony, particularly the main characters. This is significant in terms of their nationalities, and continues the practice evident in Duncan's other international fiction. The main characters in this text are either English or American. There is no Canadian character but the critique of the characters of the other two nations can be read as implying a Canadian narratorial position. Dean suggests that 'Duncan's initial project in her fiction ... [was] the definition and criticism of Britain and the United States' through portraying the limitations of representative characters ('The Process of Definition' 148). England and the US certainly needed to be assessed by Canadians, as they dominated the economy and culture of Canada. This preoccupation, initially evident in *An American Girl in London* and continued to a lesser degree in *A Daughter of Today*, reaches its peak in *Cousin Cinderella*, the only one of these international novels to have a Canadian as a main character. It is perhaps curious that there are so few Canadians featured in Duncan's work, and only one text actually set in Canada. Though regretted by many Canadian scholars, this lack is explained by a former colleague of Duncan as 'but another evidence, however, of the disabilities common to the status of a dependency and of the national effacement that is forced upon a clever and aspiring writer, who is only a Colonist' (Adam 473). However, the process of critiquing the character of the English and Americans is a subtle means of asserting a Canadian perspective. Both are viewed intimately, yet from outside. Only Canada has such a view of both nations. The perspective on Britain forms a link with other British colonies, such as Australia, as the commonality of the invader/settler colony's experience of Britain is shared. Irony also creates a double text because of the possibility of both a literal and an ironic reading, which enables a text to undermine subtly the values it might otherwise appear to espouse. This makes it useful not only to a colonial who is trying to gain literary acceptance in the cultural 'centre' but also to a woman who is trying to succeed in a male-dominated literary establishment while still questioning such hegemony.

Duncan was a strong believer in the influence of nation upon character, so she appears to have been comfortable in using individuals as representative types, as Henry James often did. This enabled her to examine aspects of a national culture through the medium of these representative characters, although she also allows characters themselves to give their own national summaries. Some such statements made by characters act as hypotheses, which the text goes on either to confirm or deny. One of these hypotheses is that held by the French art students regarding the English understanding of art and society, and the effect this understanding will have on Kendal's art. Nádie and her lover forecast that the conventional and feudal nature of English society will quench Kendal's inspiration and prevent his further artistic development. While in France, Kendal enjoys great recognition and success at the Salon, but outrages his fellow students with 'his preposterous notion that an Englishman should go home and paint England and hang his work in the Academy' (*DT* 41). Nádie's lover puts the supposed narrowness of English taste and artistic understanding down to the class system: 'It is *trop arrangé*, that country, all laid out in a pattern of hedges and clumps, for the pleasure of the milords. And every milord has the taste of every other milord! He will go home to perpetuate that!' (*DT* 41-42). Though 'Kendal was more occupied with impressions of all sorts than is the habit of his fellow-countrymen', he is nevertheless more comfortable with British manners, and rejects 'French' displays of emotion (*DT* 45). After Lucien, the art master, has literally shed tears on Kendal's coat in an effort to dissuade him from returning to Britain, Kendal is sure that 'He could not take life seriously where the emotions lent themselves so easily' (*DT* 42). And in confirmation of his decision to return, his consummate piece of work is done in England, and it is a portrait. However, Kendal's art *does* recede; the reader is left to decide whether it is English society, his rejection of Elfrida or other factors which are to blame for this. His choices about Elfrida are based on his rejection of her 'difference', and his growing preoccupation with land ownership. In terms of Nádie and her lover, these are seen to be 'English' characteristics, and tend to confirm their perspective. It does not happen exactly as they have foreseen, with Kendal controlled by those who commission him to paint portraits, but instead he becomes one of the respectable controllers himself. The inability of the English characters to be open to those with different values comes in for serious scrutiny, and is a big contributor to the breakdown of the relationships between Elfrida and both Janet and Kendal.

In this way, English national characteristics are critiqued by a Canadian narratorial position. This continues in the representation of the arrogance of Kendal, Janet and Cardiff. Kendal is observed objecting to Elfrida's behaviour because she has let Golightly Ticke come to her room and smoke, a pastime he himself has been quite happy to indulge in. He is somewhat consoled when he reflects 'that it was doubtless a question of time — she would take to the customs of civilization by degrees, and the sooner the better' (*DT* 128). He not only fails to see the distinction he draws between himself and Ticke, which is class based, but he also shows an unquestioning belief in the superiority of English upper middle-class customs as 'civilisation'. This assumption of superiority, a 'born to rule' attitude, is also a part of Janet's approach to Elfrida. In their contact after both have been less than candid with each other (Janet regarding the publication of her book and Elfrida about her jaunt with the chorus line), Janet's attitude is clear: 'Janet's innate dominance rose up, and asserted a superior right to make the terms between them', and when she spoke, there 'was a cool masterfulness in the tone' (*DT* 220, 221). This attitude is also seen in Cardiff's approach to Elfrida, until she rudely awakens him with her refusal of marriage. It is Elfrida's decision to work in the chorus line which really unites Kendal, Janet and Cardiff in stuffy disapproval. Though aware of their perspective, and embarrassed by her knowledge of the conventional view of her actions, Elfrida is able to bring a broader understanding to her experience. While Cardiff, Kendal and Janet merely look down on and disapprove of the Peach Blossom Company and her involvement with them on the basis of class and occupation, Elfrida is able to see them as a valid group with their own values and systems: 'If I didn't mean to write a word, I should be glad of it. A look into another world, with its own customs and language and ethics and pleasures and pains' (*DT* 198). The Cardiffs and Kendal prove themselves to be insular and petty, though they are represented as well-thought-of intellectuals in London. Elfrida alone has a perspective which is able to get beyond factors such as class, to see the people underneath, though she is limited in her ability to apply this perspective. As Gadpaille suggests, Duncan 'dares to have Elfrida erect her own rules, to put them before social rules and to refuse to compromise in the face of social pressure', while permitting 'her heroine to combine esthetic values with her morality in a way that reflects new fin-de-siècle mores' ('*As She Should Be*' 90).

Duncan is relentless in exposing the contradictions inherent in every character's position though. While Elfrida might show an enlightened view of the acting troupe, she has none when it comes to washerwomen. When Ticke complains that the washerwoman will not wash his clothes if he does not pay her, he comments, 'Washerwomen, as a class, are callous' (*DT* 103). The irony of Elfrida's reply — 'They live to be paid' — is that she has just taken a job she despises so that she will have enough money to survive in London (*DT* 104). She is not able to see that this may be the washerwoman's fate also. She is still functioning from the position of privilege. Her poverty is a self-imposed one, chosen that she might pursue her art and independence, and so that she might experience the unfamiliar thrills of deprivation. It is something she can withdraw from if she chooses: the washerwoman is unlikely to have this luxury. Elfrida's attitude to class varies depending on circumstance, while the attitude of the Cardiffs and Kendal is more fixed. The narrator portrays the Cardiffs and Kendal as representative of the English ruling classes in their attitude, and criticises their class as a whole when revealing the shortcomings of their individual values. Janet's stereotypically English reserve has a negative impact on Elfrida when she is surprised by the publication of Janet's novel, and then by Janet's engagement to Kendal. When Janet considers Elfrida's positive qualities, she thinks of 'her keen sense of justice' and 'her absolute sincerity toward herself and the world', whereas she is forced to acknowledge:

> It isn't that I didn't know all the time that I was disloyal to her, while she thought I was sincerely her friend. I did! And now she has found me out; and it serves me perfectly right — perfectly! (*DT* 239, 271)

Janet's reserve keeps others at a distance, and insulates her from the influence of others. Though 'she and her father declared that it was their great misfortune to be thoroughly respectable, it cut them off from so much', this is shown to be an empty complaint (*DT* 109). When someone lacking respectability or even conventionality appears, they both find it difficult to overcome the prejudices of their class, especially when such qualities are embodied in the person of Elfrida Bell. Of course, Elfrida is not given complete narratorial approval either. One of her besetting sins was seen by Duncan as characteristic of Americans. This was the sin of excess, which Tausky suggests can account for Elfrida's suicide:

> In one perspective, however, her suicide represents the tragic consequence of a peculiarly American sin — lack of restraint. When a parallel character in *Cousin Cinderella* is criticized for being 'very American', a genuine Canadian replies: 'Americans like being very. I don't believe they can help it'. (Tausky, 'The Citizenship' 128)

A Canadian narrative stance critiques Elfrida for being so extreme, as this is regarded as an American characteristic, which is self-destructive. However the irony evident in the narrative voice regarding Elfrida goes beyond her status as a character representative of the US and attaches itself more to her character, values and aspirations. I shall return to this.

While the English rather unconsciously Other Elfrida as an American, she is also implicated in the practice of Othering, and it is associated with her conceptions of art and the role of the artist. These conceptions are not peripheral to the outworking of the narrative: in a *Künstlerroman*, they are central. The way in which she Others is to dismiss all those with different conceptions of art to her own. Her form of Othering is a premeditated choice which in Elfrida's mind embodies artistic survival. It revolves around the binary opposition of Bohemian/respectable, which is closely linked to, but does not exactly correlate to, artist/bourgeois. Like many aspiring artists, Elfrida has found in Bohemia a code which buttresses her against the demands of respectable society, demands that detract from the pursuit of her art. Two of the major issues for artists in *A Daughter of Today* are how to gain inspiration and how to function in relation to prevailing public opinion. These are survival questions, linked to wider questions regarding the role of art and the artist in society as a whole. These issues were highlighted in the nineties because of societal restrictions on what writers could produce. This was apparent in specific instances, such as the obscenity trial of Henry Vizetelly in 1889 for publishing a translation of Zola, and in the power of the lending libraries to impose a virtual censorship by way of boycotting texts considered 'unsuitable' (Frierson 37). Negative reviews were a more subtle form of discouragement. As a young woman, Elfrida was just the sort of person who was to be 'protected' by these measures. If Elfrida herself was to be protected from *reading* certain fiction, how much more transgressive is her desire to *write* it. Writers increasingly felt that public opinion was a constraint detrimental to the pursuit of truth in art, and Elfrida's bitterness about the English public and its power must be read in this light.

The role of Bohemia in the formation of the nineteenth-century artist was often considerable, yet Joanna Richardson claims that in

England, 'There was no sense of a Bohemian movement; and there was no Bohemian colony', a circumstance she puts down to the class of English undergraduates — upper or middle — and English temperament, as opposed to French (460). Bohemia often functioned as a haven of creativity, transgression and excess, in which artistic inspiration could be found, community established, and compensations found for the poverty artistic life often entailed. The most obvious weaknesses were that while it contributed to success for some, 'it led all too often to the poorhouse, or to death' for others (Richardson 466). It also led to the pretentiousness demonstrated by both Elfrida and Ticke. While Ticke is more of an opportunist in his adoption of Bohemianism, Elfrida takes on the philosophy as a creed, reflecting the commitment described by Murger in *Scènes de la vie de Bohème*:

> They are the race of stubborn dreamers, for whom art remains a faith and not a trade ... If you point out to them, gently, that this is the nineteenth century, that a hundred-sou piece is Empress of humanity, and that boots don't fall ready polished from heaven, they turn their backs on you and call you bourgeois. (Qtd in Richardson 466)

The opposition of the artist and the bourgeois is reinforced in Bashkirtseff's journal, when the maid at the atelier states: 'I am no longer *bourgeois* — I am an artist' (275). Marie also shows the distrust of the artist for the public and its opinions, when she writes, 'The people in society, otherwise known as *bourgeois* will never understand me' (290). When Elfrida thinks that Janet's art 'belonged really to the British public' it is a serious criticism, because it means that it lacks the originality that the public would supposedly object to (*DT* 213). And when she goes on to decide that 'The book would be one to be recommended for *jeunes filles*', it is a damning description in terms of the Bohemian artist and most serious novelists of the nineties. Elfrida's understanding of art is a total philosophy, and she uses biblical language to describe it. Not to have this understanding would be to 'dwell in outer darkness with the bourgeois', while a 'fellow-being was not a Philistine' but rather 'of the elect' (*DT* 25, 58, 57). Because of this, the difference in their approaches to art make the relationship untenable for Elfrida, as she writes to Janet:

> [W]hat you said betrayed a totally different conception of art ... from the one I supposed you to hold, and if you will pardon me for saying so, a much lower one. It seems to me that we cannot hold together there, that our aims and creeds are different, and that we have been comrades under false pretences. (*DT* 242)

This form of Othering may be seen as a survival tactic by Elfrida, reflecting her need to bolster her choices against the many obstacles to her artistic achievement, but it nevertheless *is* Othering. Probably every form of Othering which occurs can be justified in certain terms; many have been, if one looks at the elaborate explanations which have been used to justify a range of oppressions such as institutionalised racism and sexism over the centuries. However, Elfrida never feels the need to justify her commitment to Bohemian values: to her they are self-evident.

While the narrator distances herself from Elfrida's wholehearted embrace of Bohemia, the text does hint that Kendal's abandonment of French Bohemia has been detrimental to his inspiration. Richardson's view that England lacked a real Bohemia is borne out to some extent by the fact that neither Kendal nor Elfrida seem to have access to the kind of artistic community they had known in Paris. There is artistic community, but it consists of people like Lawrence Cardiff, who is upper middle-class and establishment. Kendal's ultimate loss of inspiration would seem to suggest negatively that Bohemian values and community can be useful to the development of the artist, and that the extremes of its more financially insecure lifestyle are more conducive to the production of art than the securities, and responsible worries, of the upper-class landowner Kendal becomes.

In describing the Orientalism of the nineteenth century, Edward Said has stated that, 'Quite aside from the scientific discoveries of things Oriental made by learned professionals during this period in Europe, there was the virtual epidemic of Orientalia affecting every major poet, essayist, and philosopher of the period' (Said, *Orientalism* 51). In *A Daughter of Today*, Lawrence Cardiff and Elfrida Bell demonstrate these two different aspects of Orientalism. The reader is introduced to Lawrence Cardiff, 'a professor of Oriental languages at London University' (*DT* 111). Later his speciality is revealed to be Persian, which his daughter, unfamiliar with the specifics of his work, imagines is of 'a very decorative character' (*DT* 83). Janet's view is that of the public of her age; Oriental artefacts and light furnishings were decorative, fashionable and *en masse* Bohemian. Elfrida's room is a tribute to this trend, in which items of Eastern material cultures are taken from their cultural context, thrown together under the general description of 'Oriental' and used to bring 'chic' to the drawing rooms of the West. Her room contained an 'Indian zither', a 'Japanese screen', 'a little Afghan prayer carpet', Omar Khayyam on a Koran holder, the 'little bronze Buddha', and was filled with 'a mingled fragrance of joss sticks and cigarettes' (*DT* 58, 59). This is the fashion extremity of the populist version of nineteenth-century Orientalism, while Cardiff exemplifies its academic aspect, and both are ultimately unsettled in their complacent objectifications of 'the East'.

Cardiff is unsettled by the assertion of feminine self-determination when he encounters it in the form of Elfrida. Until this point, he is secure in his position as urbane gentleman academic, Orientalist and father. In terms of the Social Darwinism of his day, he is at the top of the evolutionary tree. The assurance this brings to him is demonstrated when he comes to save Elfrida from the supposedly youthful, feminine and misguided choices about life and art she makes in joining the Peach Blossom Company. His salvation is that she should marry him, and that they should write a book together, a book over which, judging by his earlier efforts at editing her work, he would maintain full editorial control. I have already discussed the mastery he assumes in his approach to Elfrida in relation to gender, but this mastery is a result of his whole social position: a combination of gender, race, nation and academic position. When Elfrida unsettles this, the structure which upholds him comes into question. The first hint of this is

> a sickening sense of impotency which assailed his very soul. All his life he had had tangibilities to deal with. This was something in the air, and already he felt the apprehension of being baffled here, where he wrought for his heart and his future. (*DT* 197)

Not only his sense of his own manhood, but also of his intellectual superiority are thrown into doubt by Elfrida's resistance. He is still sure that he will prevail, and assumes that he can persuade her. Even though her refusal is a severe shock, he is sure that 'She would change' (*DT* 200). However, after months of her dallying, with him unable to drag himself away, Cardiff is no longer in control, nor does he suppose himself to be. He takes what crumbs Elfrida offers him, is 'irritable or despondent', 'worn and thin' and in a state of 'habitual abstraction' (*DT* 235). His position at the top of the evolutionary tree has been shaken by Elfrida's refusal of her gender role, and he, having come from the position of intellectual superiority, has now 'lost all his reckonings' (*DT* 231). Her transgression of gender boundaries has unsettled him in all his dominant roles.

I referred earlier to the narrative stance of the text, in which Elfrida always seems to be kept at a distance from both narrator and reader. For readers, it is difficult to feel any sense of intimate connection with the heroine. Though we are sometimes privy to her thoughts, the process is rarely an engaging one. We observe Elfrida. She is an object of study, rather than a protagonist with whom one identifies, and this is directly the result of the narrative voice. Elfrida is presented to us as an example of *fin-de-siècle* life and culture, almost as an artefact or specimen; there is no passionate involvement with her aspirations on behalf of the narrator. There may be several reasons for this. I have mentioned the fact that Elfrida functions as a national representative for the US, and this in part separates her from the Canadian narratorial position. This certainly accounts for some of the narrator's distance but not for all of it. There is a level at which the writer is not prepared to endorse fully her heroine's feminist aspirations. Instead of entering into Elfrida's ambitions she has chosen rather to dissect them, even to portray them as occasionally ridiculous. Certainly Elfrida *is* at times melodramatic and almost always self-centred, and this is directly the result of Duncan's choice to portray a very young woman whose defining characteristic is her egoism. Of all of Duncan's oeuvre, this is the only female *Künstlerroman*. That she has chosen to portray the developing female artist as an immature egoist could be seen to reveal a very half-hearted support for the project of female emancipation, especially in the area of the arts. At the very least, it shows ambivalence about that project.

That she herself was functioning quite successfully as a female writer herself makes this more curious, but she is not alone in this. George Eliot provides a very strong precedent, in that she never allowed her heroines the romantic or vocational fulfilment she experienced in her own life. Her heroines are always contained by the narrative ends of her day, whatever their fictional aspirations may have been. In her everyday life as Mary Ann Evans, George Eliot was socially and professionally marginalised for her choices. Duncan, too, came to the literary centre of London as an outsider. Her status as a colonial, combined with the fact that she was a woman, made her incursions into London literary life doubly precarious. By not fully endorsing her heroine, she possibly sought to protect herself from some of the scathing reactions that literary women provoked. Her novel's potential for broad appeal was increased as well. Any glance at

Punch from the 1890s would demonstrate that the public ridicule of women, especially those seeking any form of emancipation or change, was thriving. By showing the more ridiculous aspects of Elfrida's code and behaviour, Duncan catered for those who were entertained by such ridicule. At the same time, her very subject matter, and the range of issues addressed, placed the novel directly in the area of New Woman fiction, thereby drawing on a quite different readership. In her desire to gain literary success in the Empire's metropolis, Duncan possibly distanced herself from her heroine in order to protect her own literary reputation. Her foray into the controversial area of New Woman fiction was marked by extreme caution. As with Henry Handel Richardson, irony became her chief subversive tool, and lest she be found out, she made sure that not even her heroine was spared its ravages.

I return to the image of Duncan writing her novel of female self-determination while the colonised *punkah wallah* works the fan that enables her to write in the heat. While in other works Duncan addresses issues of colonialism directly, with specific reference to the situation in India, in this novel she does not. The narrative is written from a Canadian perspective, as I have discussed, but Canada is not mentioned. Dominant discourses of the nineteenth century leave their mark on this text, and in the case of Orientalism and feminism, these discourses conflict with and undermine each other. Elfrida's *Bildung* is truncated. The irony of her suicide is that it comes about via one of her oriental artefacts, a piece of Persian culture taken quite out of context. The poison ring bears 'deep-cut Sanskrit letters' which are never translated by the 'professor of Oriental tongues', Lawrence Cardiff (*DT* 66, 83). Elfrida is killed by her 'chic' poison ring, and dies in 'the queer Orientalism of the little room' in London, the room of her own in which she has sought to realise her ambitions as a female artist (*DT* 67, 179). Even as Duncan's Orientalism is evident as she worked in Calcutta, the Orientalism in her text overtakes her narrative of feminist self-realisation, and contributes to the failed *Künstlerroman* of her heroine. The presence of many and conflicting discourses is reflected in the text, in which the discourses of Orientalism and late-nineteenth-century feminism serve to unsettle each other, and are implicated in the recourse taken by the narrative to deal with conflict: namely, the death of the heroine.

4

Henry Handel Richardson

The Getting of Wisdom

4.1 Introduction

By the time *The Getting of Wisdom* was published in 1910, the era of New Woman fiction had passed. The age of modernity had begun, and as Gail Cunningham notes, 'The word "Victorian" itself became, with remarkable rapidity, a synonym for stuffy puritanism, outmoded propriety' (154). However, while the impact of the New Woman heroines had some lasting effect on the fictional representation of women, it was limited. The sexuality of women continued to be explored in the new century, but any vocation other than romance seemed to be overlooked: 'The new type of heroine was, then, sexually aware but domestically inclined' (Cunningham 155). The debate about women occurred less in fiction and more in tracts and on political platforms, and became more concentrated on the question of women's suffrage than any other issue. When Henry Handel Richardson chose to write an account of one girl's schooling in the colonial city of Melbourne, she did so when such a topic was no longer in vogue. However, her relative distance from the height of the debates gave her an analytical clarity which most of the fiction of the 1890s lacked.

Richardson's apparently cool and ironic treatment of her subject does not make it any less political than the more emotional outpourings of earlier writers. If anything, its considered and subtle nature enhances its political impact. Poised between the heights of Victorian realism and modernism, Richardson is able to make use of new structural possibilities in the novel. Her engagement with the *Bildungsroman*, unlike that of Schreiner and Duncan, does not result in the complete curtailment of the heroine in death. Rather, as an early twentieth-century writer, she makes use of an open ending to create opportunities for her heroine, Laura, while outlining the many forces aligned against her.

Richardson's critical reception in Australia varied considerably during the twentieth century. Because of her expatriate status, some of her contemporary Australian writers and members of the literary scene regarded her with suspicion. Possibly inspired by jealousy, Miles Franklin suggested that the Mahony trilogy 'could have been written by someone who came out and studied the records', comparing it unfavourably with *Such as Life* which 'could only have been written by one with Australia in the bone' (qtd in Roe 283). Franklin also records that Firmin McKinnon, literary editor of the Brisbane *Courier Mail*, 'once gave a lecture decrying HHR as untrue to Australia' and that an editorial of *The Sydney Morning Herald* described Richardson as 'morbid and not representative of Australia' (Roe 297, 315). While suspicion of the expatriate writer continued through much of the twentieth century, in Richardson's case it served to place her outside the developing radical nationalist writing tradition which valorised certain modes of white masculinity to the detriment of women and those of different race. The exclusions of 'the *Bulletin* school', as this group has been dubbed, are well summarised by

The Bulletin magazine's subtitle: 'Australia for the white man'.[29] It was only when Richardson received international acclaim for the Mahony trilogy that she gained broad recognition in Australia, though as can be seen from Franklin's response, much of it was given begrudgingly.

In England, though she lived and was published there, other factors contributed to a view that Richardson was somehow outside the English literary tradition. When *Maurice Guest* was published in 1908, reviewers saw it most commonly as reflecting Continental rather than English preoccupations. Depending on the understanding of the reviewer, this could be portrayed as positive or negative. John Masefield described the novel as 'the best work of fiction published in this country during the present year', going on to place it squarely in the French tradition. He wrote:

> A book so strongly planned as this, so full of constructive energy, is unusual. It is not an English quality, this quality which plotted 'Maurice Guest': it is the great quality of the great French realists, of artists, that is, who are led away neither by sentiment nor by its negation, satire. (Masefield, *RP* n.p.)

This connection was made by reviewers of *The Getting of Wisdom* also, *The Athenaeum* suggesting that Richardson's 'method is microscopic, Zolaesque' (*The Athenaeum*, *RP* n.p.), while *The English Review* asserted that Richardson would 'probably admit that it is just to assign him a place in that school of fiction writers whose birthplace is in France and whose

---

29 Russel Ward's *The Australian Legend* (1958) perhaps best expresses the style of masculinity valorised by this group and their critical supporters throughout the century. Critiques of the radical nationalist tradition have become more widespread following Marilyn Lake's 'The politics of respectability: Identifying the masculinist context' and a collection of these are evident in *Debutante Nation: Feminism Contests the 1890s* (eds Susan Magarey, Sue Rowley, Susan Sheridan). What becomes clear from these critiques is that this version of national identity was always in dispute, especially in the women's fiction of the period.

leading exponent was Zola' (*The English Review*, *RP* n.p.). However, such an approach drew criticisms which are typical of those levelled at Zola in the late nineteenth century by some sections of the British literary establishment. One reviewer, obviously relieved not to be dealing with the subject matter of *Maurice Guest*, was soon disappointed in *The Getting of Wisdom*: 'Very soon, however, one discovers the fly in the ointment — the same devotion to a crude realism which, however true to life from one aspect, seems to dwarf and submerge all lovelier elements of our existence' (*Yorkshire Daily Observer*, *RP* n.p.). While such reviews recognise the influence of Richardson's literary education, steeped as it was in Scandinavian and German writing as well as French, they do serve the function of distancing Richardson from her English-speaking audience. Karen McLeod has complained of Masefield's review in particular, 'that it inevitably removes the author from any obvious place in an *English* literary map' (229, emphasis in original). Neither clearly within a range of literary traditions nor completely outside of them, Richardson's work straddles the discourses which have shaped her.

According to Delys Bird, the act of writing from outside hegemonic ideologies has an obvious distorting effect on narrative form. She suggests that *The Getting of Wisdom* is 'characterised by structural irresolution, thematic ambiguity and shifting modes of discourse: all qualities which can be seen to derive from women's experience in a culture in which they are dehumanised' (179). However, the 'weaknesses' Bird sees can be read differently. They can be seen as very individual assertions in the face of excluding traditions, as an attempt to find a voice despite a lack of hegemonic credentials. If, as a high cultural artefact, the novel can be seen to embody the interests of its culture's hegemonies, Richardson's literary practices also can be seen as a means of resisting at least some of those hegemonies, thereby serving as subversive strategies rather than weaknesses. Richardson's techniques and concerns identify her with other proto-modernist women writers: they are not peculiar to her alone. Gerd Bjørhovde describes some of the practices which were typical of those used by individual women writers from the late nineteenth century, who were stepping beyond the bounds of Victorian realism and experimenting with what were to become aspects of modernism. These strategies include an elusive narratorial stance, confusion of sex-roles, a move away from closure, and images of transition (171, 173, 176, 178). Though Bjørhovde makes no mention of Richardson, all of these concerns are present in Richardson's writing to some degree, linking her with proto-modernist women writers in Britain. Variance of point of view is another element that identified in the writing of this group of writers (Bjørhovde 184), and Richardson continually gives the reader multiple perspectives in her texts. Bjørhovde convincingly represents these elements and practices as resistive strategies, brought about by the collision between dominant nineteenth-century fictional forms and the fact of the woman writer who had somehow to negotiate them.

Two readings of Richardson with much to offer are those of Marian Arkin and Carol Franklin. Franklin has concerned herself with Richardson's intertextuality, and in so doing has emphasised the parodic nature of much of her work. Arkin asserts that 'All her works ... focus on enculturation as it intersects with gender and class' (121). In proposing a new reading strategy for Richardson's fiction, she also suggests that

> [a]n analysis of the gendering of certain attributes and values in these novels — and subsequent utilization of these gendered values and attributes by the Victorian hegemony within the novels — will reveal a much more subversive vision of gender and class than has been ascribed to Richardson previously. (121)

Three further readings have taken up these areas to some extent. Catherine Pratt's examination of gender and form has led her to the conclusion that because the protagonist 'is a woman the narrative cannot be a *Bildungsroman*' ('Fictions of Development' 8). While I read the novel differently, the collision of form and gender identified by Pratt is a major concern of *The Getting of Wisdom*. The fresh material Michael Ackland's biography brings to the study of Richardson is his closer examination of German thinking and culture on Richardson's work, and, like Franklin, he concerns himself with her contestatory strategies in relation to much of this (*Henry Handel Richardson: a life*). This is particularly so in his reading of *Maurice Guest*. Much of this material is also extremely relevant to Laura's progress, especially as so much of the philosophical and sexological writings referred to by Ackland are specifically misogynist in character. In many ways the most sympathetic reading is that by Axel Clark in his second literary biography of Richardson, as he traces the ways in which her writing 'was becoming more complex and sophisticated' in *The Getting of Wisdom* (*Finding Herself* 104). What is probably most surprising about Richardson as a major Australian writer is the lack of recent critical material addressing this novel, and indeed all of her work.

This analysis proposes to build on this earlier work, and to explore a reading which looks for 'the extraordinary challenge of her feminist and post-colonialist critique' in *The Getting of Wisdom* (Arkin 130). Richardson's critiques, like those of Schreiner and Duncan, are highly resistant yet at times highly ambivalent, reflecting the position of the white colonial woman writer as both within and outside of prevailing discourses.

The novel begins with a scene which encapsulates many of the issues discussed in the course of its unfolding narrative:

> The four children were lying on the grass.
> ' … and the Prince went further and further into the forest,' said the elder girl, till he came to a beautiful glade — a glade, you know, is a place in the forest that is open and green and lovely. And there he saw a lady, a beautiful lady, in a long white dress that hung

down to her ankles, with a golden belt and a golden crown. She was lying on the sward — a sward, you know, is grass as smooth as velvet, just like green velvet — and the Prince saw the marks of travel on her garments. The bottom of the lovely silk dress was all dirty —'

'Wondrous Fair, if you don't mind you'll make that sheet dirty, too,' said Pin.

'Shut up, will you!' answered her sister who, carried away by her narrative, had approached her boots to some linen that was bleaching.

'Yes, but you know Sarah'll be awfully cross if she has to wash it again,' said Pin, who was practical.

'You'll put me out altogether,' cried Laura angrily. — 'Well, as I said, the edge of her robe was all muddy — no, I don't think I will say that; it sounds prettier if it's clean. So it hung in long, straight beautiful folds to her ankles, and the Prince saw two little feet in golden sandals peeping out from under the hem of the silken gown, and —'

'But what about the marks of travel?' asked Leppie.

'Donkey! Haven't I said they weren't there? If I say they weren't, then they weren't. She hadn't travelled at all.'

'Oh parakeets!' cried little Frank.

Four pairs of eyes went up to the bright green flock that was passing over the garden.

'Now you've all interrupted, and I shan't tell any more,' said Laura in a proud voice.

'Oh, yes, please do, Wondrous Fair! Tell what happened next,' begged Pin and Leppie.

'No, not another word. You can only think of sheets and parakeets.' (*GW* 1-2)

Laura is the teller of the romantic tale, which not only harks back to the old world with its 'glade' and 'sward', but also to the old fairy tales of patriarchy where the 'lady' passively awaits her rescue/discovery by the 'Prince', whose value is taken as given because of his gender and his political position. Laura has cast herself as 'Wondrous Fair', a suitable name for the heroine of such a piece, whose main requirement is to be physically attractive according to dominant sexual ideals, and to be suitably inactive. Laura is in an awkward position, however, and she remains in it throughout the text, in varying degrees of discomfort. Her status as heroine links her to the dominant tradition which tied the role to conventionality in feminine behaviour. Even in the fairy tale, the active, initiating women tended to be evil: wicked witches, for example. In nineteenth-century fiction, passivity for heroines had taken more expansive forms. The ends tended to be the same, however: success for the heroine was always in terms of marriage. Activity, especially sexual, was, until late in the century, followed by death. Laura, as initiator and teller of the tale, will be at odds with this tradition, and hence her plot cannot go the way of nineteenth-century heroines. As a protagonist of the *Bildungsroman*, she must also take on the role of hero. While she is still in the grip of the old narratives, various forces impinge on her singular vision. Pin intrudes with everyday reality, the business of boots and linen, foreshadowing the later intrusion of Scandinavian realism into Laura's reading, which has consisted of the two dominant forms of romance, represented by Scott and *King Solomon's Mines* (*GW* 57, 140). Then the gaudy spectacle of the 'bright green' birds of the new world intrudes on swards and glades, breaking the spell of patterns of narrative which have come from the old world.

In her negotiation of gender enculturation, Laura also confronts the way in which the imperial project is imbricated into the gendering process. The narrator shows the boarding school to be a prime site for the production and maintenance of both the discourse of patriarchy and that of imperialism. Though there is ambivalence in Laura's response to these, to some extent she must resist both of them in order to create a space in which she can become the hero of her own story. This passage also raises the issue of the writer's relationship to his/her audience, as Laura's siblings add their interruptions to her tale. Laura finds at college that 'crass realists though these young colonials were, and bluntly as they faced facts, they were none the less just as hungry for romance as the most insatiable novel reader' (*GW* 148). When she concocts her story about her fictional romance with Mr Shepherd, she does so in response to the demand and taste of her listeners, as well as to secure their good opinion. The whole process by which she learns what is, and what is not, acceptable to the audience of fiction, reflects to some degree the kind of anxieties about authorship, readership and censorship which characterised the late nineteenth century and early twentieth century. The text's preoccupations are already apparent in these first paragraphs: the relationship of audience and artist; the choice of appropriate fictional genre; the contrast between the old world and its values and the new; and the politics of gender.

The Getting of Wisdom is prefixed by a quotation from the Book of Proverbs: 'Wisdom is the principal thing; therefore get wisdom: and with all thy getting get understanding'. On one level this is a straightforward indication of what is to follow: the story of Laura's acquisition of wisdom. On another level it is the signal of a more subversive narrative. Literary allusions are often used in Richardson's work as shorthand for fields of thought. They are a subtle yet clear signal for the aware reader, and this quotation from Proverbs can be seen as part of that practice.

The preface sets up a framework for what is a generally overlooked aspect of this work: its parody of other fictional forms. There are two levels at which parody functions in *The Getting of Wisdom*. The first is in the more usual sense of making a satirical point at the expense of another work. A biblical quotation could well indicate that what follows would be an instructional tale for young women in which moral lessons, of the sort to maintain the dominant gender and class status quo, would be learnt by a suitably compliant girl. Such reading was common in a Ladies' College in the 1880s, and considered particularly suitable reading for a Sunday. The lessons learnt by the heroine of such a text would prepare her ideologically and temperamentally for her role as wife and mother, though it would definitely not enlighten her with regard to matters of sexuality. Susan Warner's *The Wide, Wide World* (1850) is a good example of this genre.[30] One of the earliest bestselling US novels, it was widely read around the English-speaking world, its characters and scenes being reflected in much nineteenth- and early twentieth-century children's literature. Ellen, the heroine of *The Wide, Wide World*, embodies a self-regulating female subjectivity which is premised on an ethic of renunciation and submission. She often achieves her aims, but only through the path of tears, prayer, submission and self-control. Clearly, *The Getting of Wisdom* parodies such a work, as its moral lessons are more in the nature of surviving inequities of class, wealth and gender than about developing habitual submission, and part of Laura's achievement is to grow beyond the conformity expected of such a heroine.[31] However, these two heroines, Ellen and Laura, are not dissimilar, with their passion, pain and attempts at conformity close enough to ensure that the parody does not go unmarked.

Laura's resistive characteristics have not been universally noticed. Bruce Beresford, director of the film *The Getting of Wisdom* (1978), noted with surprise that "'Wisdom" was republished in a schools' edition

---

[30] *The Wide, Wide World* was first published under the pseudonym Elizabeth Wetherell in 1850 in the US and in the following year in Britain.

[31] In citing Warner's novel as an object of parody, I do not wish to deny that it contains some subversive potential in the portrayal of its passionate heroine. The very difficulties Ellen experiences in submitting to the role expected of her demonstrates the artificiality of the gender codes to which she is expected to conform. Her intense bonds with her mother and Alice, her mentor, celebrate aspects of women's culture, and suggest the primacy of female connections in a young woman's life, though significantly death curtails both of these relationships.

by Heinemann, who seemed unaware of the amorality of the central character or the sapphic overtones' (Beresford 26). Though the satirical style of parody in this novel is achieved with subtle irony, its denunciation of the forces which repress Laura is an angry one. While it mocks earlier moral tales of a girl's education and development, at the same time *The Getting of Wisdom* expresses strong outrage at the hypocrisy of moral standards at the school and in wider society, and the inequalities by which they function.

A second type of parody apparent in *The Getting of Wisdom* is that which acknowledges the value of an original yet reworks it to make a new point. Neil M. Flax describes this as 'romantic parody', which 'stands both inside and outside the original model, repeating it and criticising it, honoring and mocking it at the same time' (Flax 43). This practice of German romanticism has been defined by Friedrich Schlegel as 'a witty translation' (Flax 43). It is a device used in Goethe's *Faust*, one of the texts that Laura embarks on in her forays into the Stracheys' drawing room.

Carol Franklin has made a convincing case for Richardson's use of this manner of parody, mainly in relation to Richardson's short fiction.[32] Describing it as 'dialectical parody', Franklin outlines its effect:

> Structurally, by including the target text within itself the parody text draws attention to fictiveness. Meanwhile by its own literary colouration it refunctions the original to another purpose. The new piece will question the prior text. However, the very inclusion of a previous text within the parodic piece may also imply a certain amount of assent. ('The Resisting Writer' 233)

For Franklin, the obvious text to stand in such a relationship to *The Getting of Wisdom* is Norwegian Björnstjerne Björnson's *Fiskerjenten*, translated by Richardson as *The Fisher Lass* in 1896 (Roncoroni 137). Franklin reads

---

[32] For a clear exposition of Franklin's argument regarding Richardson's form of textual dialectic, see her 'The Resisting Writer: H.H. Richardson's Parody of Gogol'.

them both as *Künstlerromane*, a reading which, with regard to *The Getting of Wisdom*, does not have the combined weight of critical thinking behind it. However, most critics concede that there are elements of the artist in the making in *The Getting of Wisdom*, making this comparison more valid. I hope to demonstrate the usefulness of reading Richardson's work in this way.

Richardson's husband, J.G. Robertson, points to two literary models for *The Getting of Wisdom*. Björnson's novel is one of them; the other is *Jane Eyre* (Robertson 174, 75). What is significant in terms of Richardson's politics is the way in which she uses these sources, rewriting aspects of them to give a perspective which delineates the repressive forces aligned against female creativity in particular, and female self-determination in general. Part of this has to do with the dialectic between idealism and reality which runs through *The Getting of Wisdom* from beginning to end. In *The Fisher Lass*, the heroine Petra comes into her artistic vocation with the full support of her community, including 'mother, tutor, lovers' (Franklin, 'The Female *Künstlerroman*' 427). Richardson's work shows the utopianism inherent in such a closure, as Laura finds she has only herself to rely on. This is made more emphatic as *The Getting of Wisdom* echoes many scenes in *The Fisher Lass*, each time casting them in a new light which demonstrates the forces of repression working against Laura's desires. Richardson is concerned to portray accurately how persistent and systemic are the forces arrayed against the realisation of female vocation. Franklin claims that 'Björnson's stratagems and reconciliations are embarrassingly utopian. Richardson's analyses are painfully true. The differences are that Richardson sharpens and tightens the experiences, eliminating romanticism' (Franklin, 'The Female *Künstlerroman*' 427). What she delineates instead is the system of patriarchy at work in society, in particular in the society of the Ladies' College. *The Getting of Wisdom* is, at heart, a deeply feminist work, and these two types of parody, romantic and satiric, are two of the devices which demonstrate this.

In its relationship with *Jane Eyre*, as with Richardson's treatment of Björnson, it is the differences that are illuminating. The most obvious of these is the narrative stance toward the heroine. Readers of *Jane Eyre* are invited to identify directly with Jane in a way that *The Getting of Wisdom* never allows. This is because Brontë positions us to see reality almost exclusively through the consciousness of the heroine. McLeod notes that 'Charlotte Brontë's passionate identification with her heroine is tempered in Richardson's case by her ironic reappraisals of Laura's plight' (81). Though Laura would like to cast herself as a persecuted heroine — 'there was something rather pleasant in knowing that you were misunderstood' — the reader is never allowed to look at events purely from Laura's perspective (*GW* 8). In the episode in which Laura cuts off a clump of hair as a goodbye present, Richardson immediately shows us that Mother *had* understood and we are forced away from complete identification with Laura: 'Mother smiled a stern little smile of amusement to herself; and before locking up for the night put the dark curl safely away' (*GW* 8). In fact, in the first few chapters Laura demonstrates numerous wilful and obnoxious qualities, which serve to distance the reader. Such narratorial aloofness reflects Richardson's naturalist approach and the irony with which she wishes to present her subject. She repeatedly described *The Getting of Wisdom* to Nettie Palmer as 'a merry little book' (qtd in Palmer 29); the use of irony allowed the very painful episodes described in the text to be treated with something approaching humour. Many readers have failed to find it humorous at all, Germaine Greer complaining that 'the school is the instrument whereon the soul of Laura Rambotham is strung out for the torture' (11) and Brian McFarlane asserting that 'the comic episodes are only just amusing; and what really matters to [Richardson] is the pain associated with Laura's growth' (53). While Charlotte Brontë offers us Jane's pain, she does not portray it in such a way as to bring a smile to our lips. We are there with Jane in it. And while we feel that Jane is the victim of gross injustice while at school, in Laura's case it is not so clear. It is not extraordinary cruelty that she suffers; it is the ordinary processes of gendering against which she bucks. The reviewer from *Votes for Women* recognised this when she wrote, 'It shows the ambitious woman-mind hurling itself against obstacles set up by a world that is hardly ready for it' (*Votes for Women*, RP n.p.). She also has to confront her position as a white female in a small colonial city remote from the metropolis. As such, she is being educated for her position in the Empire, not as a full citizen and subject, but as one who has a clear and prescribed role. It is difficult to separate Laura's experience of gender enculturation from her inculcation as a member of the Empire, and the 'British' boarding school she attends exacts much of the individuality of its students to further the ends of Empire. Laura's painful development is the result of two things: she is being squeezed by expectations resulting from gender and Empire, and like *Jane Eyre* and every other *Bildungsroman* protagonist, her own artistic and highly individual personality brings her into conflict with the society around her.

4.2 Child to woman: gender enculturation in the Empire

Ambivalence about the role of mothers has long been an issue for women and for feminism. While mothers *are* generally the source of nurture for girls, this also means that they are the chief socialising agents. Because society is patriarchal, mothers become, at least in part, the enforcers of patriarchy as they socialise their children. Sara Mills suggests that 'within a Foucauldian framework, it is possible to see patriarchy as a system without intentions as a whole, which is supported by, resisted, given into or passively gone along with by both males and females' (18). Within such a framework, it is possible for an individual to support some aspects of patriarchy while rejecting others. This can be seen to be the case with Laura's mother. Of course, it is also a commonplace of feminist theory that 'the contradiction which … is the condition of feminism' is that it is impossible to function entirely outside of patriarchy, even for those committed to opposing it (De Lauretis 26). Hence Laura's mother is able to both comply with, and be resistant to, the patriarchal systems that surround her. Laura's relationship with her is, accordingly, highly ambivalent. When at the start of the story Laura runs from Mother's summons to hide in the garden, she is running from the news that 'she must now begin to give up childish habits and learn to behave in a modest and womanly way', things she does not want to hear (*GW* 10). Iris O'Loughlin points out that in the garden Laura 'has been unrestrained by gender, playing the roles of leader and creator and nurturer unselfconsciously' (69). Here she has tended her stray animals, organised her brothers and sister, and given free rein to her imagination. She has cast herself in the role of Romeo, to sister Pin's Juliet, and as Crusoe amongst the bamboo. Such active roles are, not surprisingly, male ones, and in the case of Crusoe, actively colonising as well. It is the place where Laura has explored and performed the subjectivity of the hero, and hence the safest place in which to resist Mother's threat of coming loss of autonomy and choice. However, Laura cannot stay in her Edenic garden; she may be able to put off some of Mother's admonitions, but going to school will bring the full weight of the institutions of Empire to the process of gendering that Mother attempts to facilitate.

Although some of the distance Laura displays toward her mother has to do with the conflict between their personalities, Laura's real point of resistance as far as her mother is concerned is when Mother seeks to prepare her for this growth from childhood into womanhood. She is drawn initially into a discussion about this by the promise of physical intimacy with her mother, which she does not experience in the same way as her sister does. Her sister Pin 'slept warm and cosy at Mother's side', while Laura slept alone in her own room (*GW* 9). In the manner of Jacobsen, the narrator here enters into Laura's consciousness to express Laura's longing and sense of loss when recording this fact. Having been attracted by this opportunity for physical closeness to her mother, Laura

> had gone into Pin's warm place, curious and unsuspecting, and thereupon Mother had begun to talk seriously to her, and not with her usual directness. She had reminded Laura that she was growing up apace and would soon be a woman; had told her that she must now begin to give up childish habits, and learn to behave in a modest, womanly way — all disagreeable, disturbing things, which Laura did not in the least want to hear. When it became clear to her what it was about, she had thrown back the bedclothes and escaped from the room. And ever since then she had been careful never to be long alone with Mother. (*GW* 10)

The price of physical intimacy with Mother is too great if it is to involve being pushed into the adult female role. When Laura is again offered the chance to join Mother in bed, prior to dressing, she reacts by dressing rapidly in order to avoid her. She runs to hide at the bottom of the garden, her eyes big, 'and as watchful as those of a scared animal' (*GW* 10). Realising that Sarah might come and force her to go, by dint of her superior strength, her one reassuring thought is that 'at least she was up and dressed' (*GW* 10). Clothes are a defence against Mother's power, which is seen by Laura to be stronger when there are no physical barriers between them. Laura is attempting to achieve her own subjectivity by striking out from her mother, and unclothed contact between them seems to risk a return to that pre-Oedipal state of union, in which ego boundaries are blurred, and identification strong. To assert herself against Mother (who appears to be forcing womanhood onto her and so reinforcing identification) Laura arms herself with clothing, thereby signalling her abandonment of the pre-Oedipal while actively resisting the imposition of the artificial constraints of gender.

Laura's avoidance of more words with Mother is preceded by an incident in which she imitates the actions of many nineteenth-century heroines before her: she cuts her own hair. Though hers is a far less dramatic gesture than those employed by heroines in, for example, *The Mill on the Floss*, *Little Women* or *The Woodlanders*, her act evokes a host of associations between hair and dominant modes of femininity. Admonitions to women not to cut their hair can be traced back at least to the New Testament, chiefly it seems because then, as in the nineteenth century, hair was read as a signifier of women's sexual status. Hair was to be covered, dressed and kept long as the sign of adherence to appropriate sexual codes. Hair can be seen, then, as a gender fetish, a sign of the sexualisation of women's bodies.

It would be simple to read Laura's act as one of defiance, in which she rejects the restraints her mother is trying to introduce into her life because of her sex. Certainly the act of cutting her hair can be read in this way. Because hair has had such a role in delineating female sexual status, the removal of that hair is a way of stepping outside such codes and refusing to bow to them. There is a level at which this would appear to be the appropriate reading of the incident. However, as hair is such a signifier of female identity, the act of removing it becomes one of extreme self-sacrifice. When Maggie Tulliver or Jo March perform the act of cutting their hair, it is temporarily shocking to those around them, but as a real rejection of gender stereotypes its potential is limited. This is because at the heart of all of these tearful haircuttings, the foremost motive is self-sacrifice, that most basic of all nineteenth-century feminine requirements. When nineteenth-century heroines cut their hair, they reinscribe their feminine role as one of giving up the self for others. Actually removing a part of one's person is a very strong acknowledgment of this, confirming the primacy of family interests over one's own. Laura acts to demonstrate her own capacity for such sacrifice, her own ability to conform to the self-sacrificial role: 'Mother should see that she did know how to give up something she cared for, and was not as selfish as she was usually supposed to be' (*GW* 6). Laura is both complying and defying. She infuriates her mother while making her peace-offering, proving her attempt to conform to her gender role while demonstrating that characteristic which is apparent throughout her school life: her inability to do so appropriately.

Ambivalence is also apparent in Mother's approach to the gender codes and practices of the day. This is seen in her reaction to the question of stays, which Laura raises in a letter home. It is clear that this element of the construction of the nineteenth-century woman has been missing from Mother's version of it. If Laura is correct, and 'all the girls wear stays', then Laura's mother, in rejecting this most restrictive aspect of feminine costume, has gone very much against the tide of popular practice (*GW* 48). In replying to Laura, she refutes one of the most widely held myths about the benefits of the corset: 'You dont [sic] need stays. I have never worn them myself and I dont [sic] intend you to either. Your own muscles are quite strong enough to bear the weight of your back' (*GW* 50). Though she sees her mother chiefly as one who is imposing restraint, Mother also provides Laura with a model of resistive femininity through her common sense rejection of the corset. The other way in which Mother facilitates Laura's divergence from the usual female codes is by her ambitions for her, ambitions which 'knew no bounds' (*GW* 74). Though Mother writes to Laura, stating 'I'd much rather have you good and useful than clever', Laura knows otherwise and takes

> the statement about the goodness and cleverness with a grain of salt ... Mother thought it the proper thing to say, and she would certainly have preferred the two qualities combined; but, had she been forced to choose between them, there was small doubt how her choice would have fallen out. (*GW* 73)

Tension in their relationship is accentuated by a strong will on both sides, and by the lack of understanding they show in their dealings with one another. They clash over Laura's clothes, for while they may indeed protect her from Mother, they are at the same time an expression of

Mother's imagination, which has 'wreaked itself' on her clothing (*GW* 85-86). Laura finally wins this contest, as 'she was stubborn: rather than wear the dress, she would not go back to the College at all' (*GW* 89). By this time she has found ways of avoiding 'Mother's searching eye' (*GW* 164). College obviously removes her physically, and the exchange of letters quickly establishes a new mode in their relationship. Her first two letters are honest accounts of her experience of school life, but Laura soon learns that this is not what Mother wants to hear. In order to maintain the relationship Laura adopts a policy of very selective reporting, which keeps Mother fairly well in the dark about what actually occurs at school. While Mother insists that the truth is what she wants to hear — 'Of course I don't mean that you are not to tell me everything that happens at school but I want you to only have nice thoughts and feelings and grow into a wise and sensible girl' — her reactions show that she actually does not want it (*GW* 52). Both of them are content to maintain the relationship on a functional level by means of Laura's practice of giving her mother the information she wants. This strategy illustrates Laura's point about truth: 'then truth wouldn't be any good any more at all, would it? If nobody used it?' (*GW* 183). Laura and her mother tacitly agree to do away with truth in the interests of peace. That this practice underlines much social intercourse is demonstrated when Mother accuses Laura of being impolite. Laura responds with 'You don't want me to tell stories, I suppose?' (*GW* 215). Mother's complaint — 'if a child of mine doesn't know the difference between being polite and telling stories' — implies that there is little difference in the two practices, only in their contexts (*GW* 215). As Laura finds is the case with written fiction, truth is a matter of social convention.

In her portrayal of the relationship between Laura and her mother, Richardson reflects an ambivalence common to many women writers of the modernist era. Susan Gubar, in an article on the female *Künstlerroman*, suggests:

> The generation gap between such childless women writers and their mothers resulted in a sometimes guilty, sometimes tender effort to reconcile radically disparate experiences. In their *Künstlerromane*, therefore, the relationship between the daughter-artist and her mother is far less easily resolved through rejection than it is in the famous *Künstlerromane* of their male counterparts. (49)

Such tenderness is apparent in Richardson's sympathetic portrayal of Laura's hardworking mother, but Laura's need to go beyond her mother's experiences and to create herself, necessitate the rejection of much that her mother embodies. And yet, complete rejection is impossible, and Laura maintains her uneasy relationship with her mother throughout the text. It is an intense relationship, which both empowers and restricts. Richardson in fact pre-empts writers such as Woolf and Mansfield who depicted the same type of ambivalence in the mother/daughter relationship of the artist daughter.

It is in Laura's attempts to conform to the very stringent requirements of the Ladies' College that we see most clearly the artificiality of the constructions of gender forced upon her by both staff and other students. She makes genuine attempts to submit to these constructions, but finds ultimately that she cannot ever quite succeed. Laura experiences the force of the school as an Ideological State Apparatus (Althusser), naturalising, as it does, the constructions of gender and colonialism in late Victorian Australia. McFarlane claims that '*The Getting of Wisdom* accepts as a fact that life is a stultifying process' (53). He also notes that '"the getting of wisdom", at least as it happens at the girls' boarding school, is not an expansive process but one of diminution' (52). The fact that the setting is a girls' school makes all the difference to what kind of wisdom can be gained, and what kind of narrative can be written about it. A boys' boarding school of the time was not, of course, a haven for free thought and self-discovery. According to John A. McClure, the virtually institutionalised tortures and humiliations of the boys' public school 'encouraged adjustment and conformity' and 'prepared the victim to assume an authoritarian stance: to obey orders, grapple himself to a powerful group, channel his aggression outwards against weaker parties' (15, 17). But to the Ladies' College is added the extra element of the process of feminisation, which is at heart a repressive one. In this way McFarlane's analysis fails to accentuate the most significant factor in Laura's environment: 'stultifying process' and 'diminution' are in evidence precisely because the book is set in a girls' school. Bird also ascribes to Richardson and *The Getting of Wisdom* an essential pessimism, claiming that 'One of its central tenets is that to be female is not to get wisdom, not to be free, not to achieve' (179). While I do not think this is true of *The Getting of Wisdom* as a whole, it certainly captures some of the effects of the process of gendering which it outlines. Gendering produces a world in which to be female is understood to have been passed over by wisdom and achievement.

Boarding schools for both genders were authoritarian and repressive, but different constructions of gender dovetailed. While young men were trained in a certain amount of physical aggression, young women in *The Getting of Wisdom* were trained in passivity and restraint. The 'diminution' McFarlane notes is principally the result of the process of feminisation. This reflects the process of colonisation, in which subject nations are feminised, becoming daughters. Feminisation necessarily means being placed in a position of inferiority and otherness, under control. However, the fact that Laura is who she is at the end of the book, that she is able to examine critically the forces that seek to shape her, show that she *has* gained a type of wisdom, and that she *has* begun to achieve. She is able to maintain some resistance to the forces of patriarchy in the school.

One of the main tactics of such forces is repression. Girls' schools of the Empire were especially concerned with disciplining the bodies of their pupils; there was little questioning of the widely accepted notion that young women were in need of external and internal restraint (Treagus, 'The Body' 138-150). O'Loughlin calls this 'the elusive code of restraint which underpins ladylike behaviour' (88). It is elusive in one way — Laura has difficulty working out what it is that is expected of her — yet plain at every turn, as it seems to involve the repression of all that comes naturally to Laura. This is demonstrated when after some time at school she has to eat with strangers, and is completely overawed because her 'natural, easy frankness had by this time all but been successfully educated out of her' (*GW* 119). The school has done its work: at this stage she will not knowingly contravene rules of class, gender and status by speaking frankly as she did in early school days with the Principal in his drawing room.

The atmosphere of the school is repressive, and its patriarchal agendas are closely aligned to maintaining class distinctions. Initially Laura is happy to be considered socially acceptable, and when she makes friends with Bertha and Inez is able to throw 'supercilious glances' at other girls because 'her new friends belonged socially to the best set in the school' (*GW* 75). However, she soon learns the injustice of such class values. The episode in which Annie Johns is expelled has been cited often as the situation in which Laura demonstrates her artistic development: she is able to analyse the situation from perspectives other than her own. However, it is also the situation in which Laura's social conscience appears to be awakened. When Annie Johns is called out the front to face what is a public humiliation, Laura becomes aware of Annie's possible motivations and the train of choices which led to her expulsion. She cannot feel the same self-righteous indignation as the other girls, 'particularly since the money had been taken, without exception, from pockets in which there was plenty' (*GW* 103). Laura can see that the other girls are blinded by their affluence into thinking themselves beyond such a crime. It is not an issue for them:

> How safe the other girls were! No wonder they could allow themselves to feel shocked and outraged; none of *them* knew what it was not to have threepence in your pocket. While she, Laura ... Yes, and it must be this same incriminating acquaintance with poverty that made her feel differently about Annie Johns and what she had done. For her feelings *had* been different — there was no denying that. (*GW* 107, emphases in original)

As Palmer notes, 'The apparently uniform security of the young ladies in the Melbourne boarding-school is riddled through and through by Laura's consciousness of poverty with its breath of social ostracism' (32). Such ostracism is taken to its logical conclusion in the expulsion, where the school's administrators ostracise far more effectively than the girls themselves could have done. Laura longs to fit in, to think in the same way as everyone else — in fact 'she genuinely despised herself' — but at the same time she cannot shut out her perceptions of injustice and of the moral complacency of the wealthy (*GW* 107). Critical perceptions clash with gender construction as Laura realises that there is something intrinsically unladylike about her insights. To perceive with thoughtful eyes is to break the gender code, and to refuse to be feminised. It is not as though Laura is choosing to be resistant. She is not a knowingly feminist heroine at this point, she just cannot manage the falseness required to be 'feminine'. Had her 'thoughts found words, they would have taken the form of an entreaty that she might be preserved from having thoughts that were different from other people's; that she might be made to feel as she ought to feel, in a proper, ladylike way' (*GW* 108).

Where this touches Laura even more closely is in relation to her own poverty, or lack of inherited wealth, with its consequence that her mother must work to support the family and to pay for Laura's education. This breaks two school taboos:

> Work in itself was bad enough — how greatly to be envied were those whose fathers did nothing more active than live on their money! But the additional circumstance of Mother being a woman made things ten times worse: ladies did not work; someone always left them enough to live on, and if he didn't, well, then he, too, shared the ignominy. (*GW* 96)

Mother's work must be kept a secret because it is so shocking in the eyes of the other girls, and becomes a weapon in the hands of Lilith. In this instance, breaking the gender rules is greater than the crime of a low birth: 'Laura knew very well that a good birth and an aristocratic appearance would not avail her, did the damaging fact leak out that Mother worked for her living' (*GW* 95-96). The governesses are in an awkward position, in authority over the girls yet clearly below them in class and position as they work for a living. The narrator certainly portrays this, following the mention of Mother's work with a conversation between three governesses about the drudgery of their work: '"Holy Moses, what a life!" ejaculated Miss Snodgrass, and yawned again, in a kind of furious desperation. "I swear I'll marry the first man that asks me, to get away from it. — As long as he has money enough to keep me decently"' (*GW* 97). Richardson is careful to show the contradictions and injustices inherent in this school setting, as well as to demonstrate the economic compulsions driving women to marriage.

Marriage as an escape from drudgery is a fraught practice, varying according to the class and wealth and of course person of the husband. However, whatever the reality of marriage, there is no doubt in the minds of most of the girls that marriage is the end at which they will arrive: 'For this *was* the goal; and the thoughts of all were fixed, with an intentness that varied only in degree, on the great consummation which, as planned in these young minds, should come to pass without fail directly the college-doors closed behind them' (*GW* 130, emphasis in original).

It is evident that the gendering process, preparing girls to choose to be submissive wives and mothers, has been effective. Sara Delamont points out that most girls' education in the nineteenth century did not even prepare girls for marriage, in the sense of giving them household skills. Rather 'It was a preparation for a flirtatous courtship, not for the marriage which it was hoped would follow' (Delamont 135). That marriage might actually work against their development is certainly realised by Laura: 'it was impossible to limit yourself to one single event, which, though it saved you from derision, would put an end, for ever, to all possible exciting contingencies' (*GW* 130). Yet this is what the girls aim for. The inculcation of patriarchal thought has been quite complete in most of these young women, and they have little chance of thinking otherwise, as this discourse saturates their world. This is the point at which Richardson is quite blunt about women's role in upholding patriarchy: in *The Getting of Wisdom* women are complicit, the enforcers of the day-to-day process of gendered enculturation. Women do not control the system they invest so heavily in, however: Arkin states that 'the getting of wisdom, the learning of the "facts" of life, is really the learning of the rules, rules which, Laura discovers, are *man*-made' (127, emphasis in original). For it is men who are in authority in the College, as elsewhere, but women in authority under them do the bulk of the day-to-day gender enforcement. The girls also, particularly through peer group pressure, are no less effective at spreading the hegemonic ideology than the female staff.

Because marriage is the goal of all, the girls have an 'intense interest in the opposite sex: a penned-up interest that clamoured for an outlet; an interest which, in the life of these prospective mothers, had already usurped the main place' (*GW* 113). Their interest also reflects a sexuality which is forced to develop largely in ignorance. These events occur in a college that appears to be modelled on Richardson's former school in Melbourne, the Ladies' College, which later became Presbyterian

Ladies' College. At the time it was regarded as one of the most advanced educational institutions for girls in Australia: it was not a finishing school. Like Richardson's school, Laura's college actually prepares young women for university entrance, yet a career other than marriage is not considered by many, and rarely comes to those who consider it, as the lives of Laura's school friends, Cupid and M.P., show. In spite of the fact that marriage and childbearing will be their major role in life, the girls have an appalling ignorance about sex, and what they do think can only be described as gothic:

> For out of it all rose the vague, crude picture of woman as the prey of man. Man was animal, a composite of lust and cruelty, with no aim but that of brutally taking his pleasure: something monstrous, yet to be adored; annihilating, yet to be sought after; something to flee and, at the same time, to entice, with every art at one's disposal. (*GW* 112)

Such a view is an extreme example of the sadomasochist element of heterosexual relationships of the time, brought about by lack of equality between the sexes.[33] The gap left by ignorance is filled with 'fancies', which are certainly not dispelled by actual social contact with males. Even those able to avail themselves of any of the sexological writings of the time (a virtually impossible task due to censorship and the fact that they tended to be accessible only to health professionals and scientists) would have had these ideas confirmed. Though he did not begin publishing in 1890, Britain's leading sexologist, Havelock Ellis, was forming his view of human sexuality in the period in which this novel is set, and his writings were becoming influential while Richardson was writing in the early 1900s (Clark, *Finding Herself* 105). Ellis's understanding of human sexuality, which filtered down through the medical professions, saw the male sex

---

33 I discuss this more fully in relation to *The Story of an African Farm* in Chapter 2, Section 2.3, especially as it applies to the romance plot.

drive as essentially sadistic and the female drive as correspondingly masochistic. He traced 'the zoological root of the connection between love and pain', finding in the animal world the justification for his gothic version of human sexual relationships, which asserted that 'men delight in inflicting' pain, while 'women pleasure in submitting to it' (Ellis, *Studies in the Psychology of Sex* 69, 104). There is very little in the milieu of the novel to counteract such views. Actual contact between schoolgirls and boys takes the form of highly stylised episodes in which honest and open communication is one of the *last* things to occur. Laura observes that there was 'a regular machinery of invitation and encouragement to be set in motion', yet she protests to Maria that in relating to a boy in this way, 'you never get to know him' (*GW* 128). Maria makes it clear that getting to know a boy is not the purpose of the exercise. However, both Maria and Evelyn, in advising Laura on the subject, admit that appealing to the male ego is an integral part of attracting a boy: 'Just you sit still, and listen, and pretend you like it — even though you're bored to extinction' (*GW* 199). Although some other girls remain aloof from these proceedings, most become adept at them, and Laura 'could not help admiring their proficiency in the art of pleasing, even though she felt a little abashed by the open pride they took in their growing charms' (*GW* 129). The summation of this is that attracting a boy involves pleasing him, listening to him (whether one is interested or not) and *not* getting to know him. This does not seem an appealing option to Laura, yet it fills the other girls' waking hours. Pleasing him means also that the perennial focus on women's bodies is replicated in the lives of these young women. For example, Tilly

> lived to reduce her waist-measure: she was always sucking at lemons, and she put up with the pains of indigestion as well as a red tip to her nose; for no success in school meant as much to Tilly as the fact that she managed to compress herself a further quarter of an inch,

no praise on the part of her teachers equalled the compliments this
earned her from dressmaker and tailor. (*GW* 129)

These activities concentrate on the body as the site at which the agendas of patriarchy are ultimately enacted, corresponding to the practices of imperialism, which uses the bodies of its subjects as labour and resource. Whether they are to produce, or reproduce, it is the body over which control is required in these imbricated systems. As Anne Summers observed in one of the early works of Australian feminism, the colonisation of women is not a metaphor, because 'women do possess a territory: their bodies' (Summers, *Damned Whores* 199).

As for the relationship to which these girls aspire — marriage — it is never portrayed in a positive light in *The Getting of Wisdom*. The pre-courtship procedures of the girls are satirised; so also are actual courtship rituals. Laura's ride with Godmother's daughter Georgina, her boyfriend Joey and Georgina's two young and mocking brothers shows how difficult it is for the couple to communicate when they are surrounded by the teasing atmosphere inherent in being chaperoned by two small boys. The fact that they are rarely alone means that they can rarely be honest with each other. Though Richardson points out the difficulties this creates, she does not waste sympathy on the lovers. The scene is charged with frustrated sexual tension, yet 'Joey and Georgy were silent, since, except to declare their feelings, they had nothing to say to each other' (*GW* 69). The paucity of the relationship is what she chooses to highlight, together with the problem that they must already be engaged before they can speak freely, on their own. The example of Laura's Godmother's marriage is even less inspiring: she and her husband only communicate through their children. It is significant that Laura's first shred of interest in the opposite sex occurs when she has a crush on the curate: 'Her feelings had, of late, got into such a rapt and pious muddle that it seemed a little like being out to meet God' (*GW* 136). This occurs when she is asked to stay for the weekend, as there is a family connection with the curate. Her interest is, however, quickly dampened when she observes his home life — including his abuse of his wife and sister, who are in fierce competition for his attention. Laura 'had seen an overworked, underfed man, who nagged like any woman, and made slaves of two weak, adoring ladies' (*GW* 145). None of these relationships is designed to provide Laura with a positive view of what almost all the girls see as *the* chief end of their lives: marriage.

Flirtation is a skill that escapes Laura, and while she finds this embarrassing, it ultimately helps to open up more possibilities for her fictional life. Her failure to play suitable flirtation games with the boy at the cricket, and with Tilly's cousin Bob, means that these boys despise her. Laura sees the unfairness of this, and rejects the female role assigned to her without her agreement. The fact that 'because he had singled her out approvingly, she was expected to worm herself into his favour, seemed to her a monstrous injustice' (*GW* 126). Bob's reaction — 'said she ought to have come in a perambulator, with a nurse' — shows that in these boys' eyes, a female who cannot please a man is an undeveloped female (*GW* 160). The process of female maturation is assumed to include centring on male wants and needs, but the inadequacy of this arrangement is brought home strongly to Laura.

One of the chief factors dominating the college is a culture of conformity which demands that the girls blend in, and not draw attention to themselves. This effectively enforces restraint in many ways. Certainly Mr Strachey's 'dignified air of detachment' and 'the very unseeingness of his gaze, inspired awe' (*GW* 78). By choosing not to see or acknowledge the girls, Mr Strachey makes them of no account, and reinforces his status. When Laura breaks this unwritten law and makes conversation with him, she is accused of 'gross impertinence' by Mrs Gurley, who of course is acting on the Principal's behalf (*GW* 82). Jan Morris describes 'aloofness' as an imperialist strategy, which precluded understanding of others, particularly subordinates, and was thereby a mechanism for maintaining power (143). The girls also enforce the belief that all should blend in, when they demonstrate their disapproval at Laura's readiness to display her sight-reading ability on the piano. This aspect of the public school ethos, that 'One did not, as a general rule, wish to appear too clever, or too enthusiastic' (McClure 226), comes as a surprise to Laura. Laura's first piece of wisdom is, in fact, that 'if you had abilities that others had not, you concealed them, instead of parading them under people's noses' (*GW* 83). This conformity serves to make the girls an homogeneous group, invisible as individuals, ready to fit in at all times. As a result, 'Laura began to model herself more and more on those around her; to grasp that the unpardonable sin is to vary from the common mould' (*GW* 84). The very unnaturalness of such a project is shown by Laura's reaction to her attempts to fit in. However much she may want to, she cannot do it:

> You might regulate your outward habit to the last button of what you were expected to wear; you might conceal the tiny flaws and shuffle over the big improprieties in your home life, which were likely to damage your value in the eyes of your companions; you might, in brief, march in the strictest order along the narrow road laid down for you by these young lawgivers, keeping perfect step and time with them: yet of what use were all your pains, if you could not marshal your thoughts and feelings — the very realest part of you — in rank and file as well? ... if these persisted in escaping control? — Such was the question which, about this time, began to present itself to Laura's mind. (*GW* 100)

Conformity is impossible for Laura, as it involves submitting to the artificiality of the female role. She is not at this point objecting from an articulated position: she simply cannot do it. Her companions, however, continue to judge one another by these narrow criteria. In this way the gendering process occurs, with the girls the unwitting accomplices in their own oppression.

The text also demonstrates the girls' partial responsibility for their own educational position and limited worldview and interests. Laura is deeply struck by the comments of Miss Hicks about the woman's brain, articulating as it does many nineteenth-century preconceptions about biological sex and mental capacity:

> 'I'll tell you what it is, Inez,' she said; 'you're blessed with a real woman's brain: vague, slippery, inexact, interested only in the personal aspect of a thing. You can't concentrate your thoughts, and worst of all, you've no curiosity — about anything that really matters. You take all the great facts of existence on trust — just as a hen does — and I've no doubt you'll go on contentedly till the end of your days, without ever knowing why the ocean has tides, and what causes the seasons. — It makes me ashamed to belong to the same sex'. (*GW* 75)

This passage highlights many of the issues women and girls confronted in the education system. Laura takes it to heart — 'She did not want a woman's brain, thank you; not one of that sort' (*GW* 76) — and she quickly concludes that the kind of brain she should develop is one which emphasises facts. Bird points out that this passage reflects 'the traditional, obfuscating male/female dichotomy which separates and categorises reason and intuition according to gender' (179). While it may express a view which embodies binary oppositions on which patriarchal ideology grounds itself, this comment from Miss Hicks also points out the way in which the girls are in some sense responsible for their inferior intellectual position. They lack the discipline of concerted thought and analysis, of asking why. While Laura may not be interested in 'why the earth went round the sun and not the sun round the earth', she does apply her mind to the conditions around her, and she sees the process of gendering at every turn (*GW* 76). However, Inez's reaction to these same comments shows her thorough grounding in class and gender. She considers the comment a compliment which proves 'she was incapable of vulgar inquisitiveness', her upper-class upbringing having taught her to value those things which will impede her intellectual development (*GW* 75).

However, there is a certain irony in Richardson's use of this example of the nineteenth-century 'science' of sexual characteristics, reflecting the narrator's sceptical attitude to these views. There is also a strong critique of the educational emphasis of the college. Miss Hicks's comment does not take into account the other aspect of the education the girls were offered: that it is basically a male-orientated curriculum based on a male-centred system of values. Why should it have intrinsic interest for girls? It is also part of an Empire-wide system of education which enforced very particular constructions of gender on males and females, constructions which ultimately served the maintenance of that empire.

4.3 Imperialism, the boarding school and the emerging nation

In *The Getting of Wisdom,* the Ladies' College is the site of the collusion of several discourses of power, most notably those of patriarchy and imperialism. Both of these employ fear and repression as tactics, as Laura discovers when she arrives at school. The person she first encounters is the head of the boarding house, Mrs Gurley. Richardson has her own private joke here in her use of autobiographical material. The boarding house headmistress from her school days was Mrs Boys: changing the name to Gurley could be seen as not merely a change of gender but a signal of the intent to reverse the gender hierarchies, or at any rate to show them for what they are. Mrs Gurley speaks 'with an air of ineffable condescension', while Laura's mother's friends are present (*GW* 31). When they have gone 'her pretence of affability faded clean away' (*GW* 33). She is shown to be a tyrant, whose look at the new girl Laura 'could not have been more annihilating' and who waits for a summoned girl 'like a beast waiting for its prey' (*GW* 36). In fact she is described as having a 'genius for ruling through fear' (*GW* 55).

The school's structure, its staff, and its attitude to education come in for severe scrutiny in *The Getting of Wisdom*, yet as far as educational institutions for girls went in the English-speaking world, this one would have been one of the more advanced. Represented as actively preparing girls for entry to university, the school seems to give them a similar academic opportunity to that available to boys. In spite of this, Richardson demonstrates how tied it is to imperialism and how narrow is its educational approach. Apart from the school's appearance — 'just like a prison' — it has hierarchies of information, with a clear favouring of facts over concepts and understanding (*GW* 30). One layer of the irony of her preface — 'with all thy getting get understanding' — is directed at this educational emphasis, showing that Laura will have to look beyond the school's curriculum to find this knowledge. When Laura realises that 'facts were wanted of her' she is able to oblige, but the narrator is disdainful about the value of such education, as exemplified by the two ways of knowing about Mt Kosciusko:

> Thus it was not the least use in the world to her to have seen the snowy top of Mount Kosciusko stand out against a dark blue evening sky, and to know its shape to a tittlekin. On the other hand, it mattered tremendously that this mountain was 7308 and not 7309 feet high: that piece of information was valuable, was of genuine use to you; for it was worth your place in the class. (*GW* 77)

It appears that Richardson did not have a high opinion her own schooling.[34]

One of the problems such a college would have had, and this is certainly true of the actual Ladies' College that Richardson attended,

---

[34] Richardson's sister Lilian, also a former Ladies' College student, appears to have shared this view, as together with her first husband, Otto Neustatter, and the man who was to become her second husband, A.S. Neill, she formed the alternative school Summerhill and devoted her life to it (Green 361). As is often the case, the male debt to such female participation is barely acknowledged by A.S. Neill in his account of the school. The name Summerhill appears to have come from the Richardson family tree (Green 361).

was that described by Delamont as 'double conformity' (140). Double conformity 'concerns strict adherence on the part of both educators and educated to two sets of rigid standards: those of ladylike behaviour at all times *and* those of the dominant male cultural and educational system' (140, emphasis in original). Nineteenth-century educational institutions for girls, even those created with some feminist objectives, were torn in trying to fulfil two often contradictory requirements. Many of those involved in girls' schools in Britain had no real feminist motivation. Marjorie Theobald notes that 'the promoters of schools on this model for their daughters wanted to redefine femininity, rather than challenge the patriarchal basis of Victorian society' (243). This is particularly true of the school that became PLC, as 'organised feminist agency in the establishment of the college was conspicuous by its absence' (Theobald 246). In its day-to-day operation, 'PLC adopted the model of the clergyman principal and the academic lay headmaster … with an all-male council dominated by the clergy' (Theobald 248). In addition to the 'male' curriculum, older and more traditional subjects for girls were offered at the actual Ladies' College. Subjects such as European languages, music, dancing and art had been termed 'accomplishments' in earlier schools for girls (Theobald 256). The fact that the Ladies' College offered them as 'extra' subjects, reinforces the notion that while girls might be encouraged to excel in traditionally male subjects, they were also expected to retain traditional signifiers of nineteenth-century femininity.

In order even to attempt to teach the male curriculum it was necessary to overcome some aspects of contemporary sexology, as exemplified by Miss Hicks' comment about a woman's brain. While Miss Hicks does not express a very extreme view on this, and her outburst would seem to be the expression of little more than exasperation, any comment about women's brains would have been made in the context of a succession of 'scientific' studies designed to demonstrate that there was something as particular as a woman's brain, and that it had serious shortcomings when compared with a man's brain. The chief English proponent and chronicler of secondary sexual characteristics was Havelock Ellis, but during her time in Germany Richardson was exposed to even more virulent attacks on the intellectual capacity of women. Michael Ackland notes the way in which the female characterisation employed in Richardson's *Maurice Guest* actively counters some of the ideas about women current in Germany at the time of its writing. He describes the ideas expressed by influential thinkers such as Schopenhauer, Strindberg and Nietzsche as 'generic, dismissive and often defamatory treatment of womankind' (*Henry Handel Richardson* 21). Though all of these writers express a misogynist perspective, the ideas of Otto Weininger are perhaps the most virulent, and had great currency in the years leading up to World War One, when *The Getting of Wisdom* was written and published. According to Weininger, 'woman, in short, has an unconscious life, man a conscious life and the genius the most conscious life' (Weininger 113). Women are therefore incapable of genius. In order to account for those women who have displayed intellectual or artistic capacity, Weininger asserts the presence of 'sexually intermediate forms' (70), women who are in fact more male than female: 'It is only the male element in emancipated women that craves for emancipation' (68). Overcoming the power of such views was absolutely vital for the success of female education, for the development of the heroine, Laura, and for Richardson herself in her career as a writer. In offering her contemporaries Miss Hicks's milder version of the inadequacies of the woman's brain, Richardson prods her audience toward considering the whole 'woman question'. Though one might see the 1890s as the time when these issues peaked, they were by no means irrelevant in 1910. There were still several years to go before women's suffrage was achieved in Britain, and many more on the Continent. Richardson herself was associated with this movement.[35] The narrator of *The Getting of Wisdom* suggests that Miss Hicks rejects these views about the woman's brain also, even though she voices them. Holding such views would damn both her and her hearers. Rather, she seems to be pointing out how easy it has been for the sexologists to categorise women in this way, when they so willingly fit the stereotype. However, the narrator goes further than Miss Hicks, for the reader is able to see that Inez's commitment to ignorance is socially constructed through class and gender, rather than intrinsic to her because of her sex.

Another line of attack against women in education, especially higher education, came from Edward Maudsley, who built much of his argument on the notion of 'energy conservation', a theory well-known in natural science and one which 'became firmly entrenched in popular science' (Atkinson 43). Herbert Spencer had expounded the idea in 1861 with his warning that 'Nature is a strict accountant and if you demand of her in one direction more than she is prepared to lay out, she balances the account by making a deduction elsewhere' (Spencer 217). Though by no means confined to ideas about the female constitution, Maudsley drew on this widespread understanding that 'the energy of a human body' had a 'definite and not inexhaustible quantity' and so was able to decry all kinds of female activities with the assertion that 'When Nature spends in one direction, she must economise in another direction' (Maudsley 467). For Maudsley it was clear that 'women are marked out by nature for very different offices in life from those of men', the chief of these being motherhood (468). Expending their energies on intellectual pursuits would

---

35 Richardson took part in one of the letter bombing raids in London. (They were filled with ink.) She had also been a member of the Dress Reform for Women group in Germany. A diary entry for the week of January 11-17 1903, records that Richardson joined *Karlsruher Verein für Reform der Frauenkleidung* in Karlsruhe (personal communication from Axel Clark). Her sister Lillian was jailed as a result of her suffragette activities (Ackland, *Henry Handel Richardson* 5).

tax those limited energy reserves, rendering them unfit for reproduction and inviting unspecified 'lifelong suffering' (473). Maudsley's notions were countered vigorously by the early proponents of women's entry into higher education, and one of their tactics was to argue that sport countered the drain of brain work.[36] The attitude of girls' educational founders is well-summarised by the opinion expressed by the feminist *Englishwoman's Review* in its overview of the debate:

> We may draw out less, as the medical alarmists counsel us to do, but we can only do so to the certain injury of women's future work; or we may put in more by giving our girls a greater physical vitality to start with ... girls, as well as boys, can work hard if they play hard too. ('Physical Training' 168)

Views about the inadequacy of a woman's brain must be rejected in the context of a female *Bildungsroman*, or the progress of the narrative will be curtailed utterly. In presenting us with an inquisitive, precocious and, above all, aspiring heroine, Richardson offers a model to counter the preconceptions of the earlier sexologists and their followers and those who opposed female education. In allowing her plot to progress in the way that it does, she refutes such thinking entirely. Richardson had some support in this project from other quarters. Even in the unlikely field of sexology, and while Weininger was highly influential (despite, or perhaps because of his early suicide), the case against him was being put by others. Jean Finot, in his *The Problem of the Sexes* (1912, English translation 1913), sought to destroy the arguments of Strindberg, Schopenhauer, Kant and especially those of Weininger. He particularly demonstrates how science had been used, falsely, to justify 'a comparative anatomy and physiology of the two sexes naturally unfavourable to woman' (Finot 98), and that such a misuse of method had been caused by the discourse he terms the

---

36 I deal with this debate more extensively elsewhere. See 'The Body of the Imperial Mother: Women, Exercise and the Future of "the Race" in Britain, 1870-1914'.

'superstition of man' (96). However, one of his most radical assertions is that 'Creative genius and intelligence have no sex' (99). It is only when such a view is held by a woman writer that she can, first, write, and second, write a female *Künstlerroman*. The scarcity of such fictions up until this time may be accounted for by the fact that the effort of counteracting such a weight of 'scientific' misogyny was very great. While the narrator does not dwell on Miss Hicks's statement, or even comment on it directly, its presence is overlaid with knowing irony as its sentiments are just another obstacle that Laura will have to overcome in the progress of her *Bildung*. Richardson did not reject Weininger's work in its entirety, though (Clark, *Finding Herself* 54-55). In *Maurice Guest* the character Schilsky writes a symphonic poem with his work *Über die Letzten Dinge* as its subject, and it might be argued that Weininger's view that bisexuality is universal could have had certain appeal for Richardson herself.

While Mrs Gurley is portrayed as dictatorial, she does not merely serve her own interests. She also stands for the male in authority over her, and for the hierarchies of which they are a part. Arkin suggests that the school is a 'world totally contingent on males, who "doggedly" guard the entrance to the free world outside' (126). All the positions of final authority are held by males, and all the 'serious' classes are taught by males. It goes without saying that all of these men are British. It is clear that the school's purpose is at least in part an imperialist one. The Principal, Mr Strachey, 'quelled the high spirits of these young colonials by his dignified air of detachment', while the efforts of the elocution teacher to instil a correct British accent in the 'emotionally shy young colonials' leaves the girls feeling 'half amused by, half superior to the histrionic display' (*GW* 78, 100). These colonising efforts are not completely successful. Just as the parakeets interrupt Laura's old world tale, so there is something irrepressible about the native-born Australians. For Kate Grenville, this school 'is a little bit of England desperately trying to keep Australia at bay. Laura represents that Australia: she's a bit rough, a bit uncouth, and her money comes from hard work, not inherited wealth' (62). The problem with Grenville's analysis is that Australia has never had one identity as a colonised nation, either in the time of *The Getting of Wisdom* or now. That it was a colony of Britain is undeniable, but the experience of that colonisation varied in ways dependent on class, gender and especially race. The white middle-class female protagonist of a colonial/postcolonial text will always be compromised in terms of her relationship with the indigenous peoples of the country, if only by her presence. In invader/settler colonies such as Australia, the roles of colonised and coloniser can, and do, intersect in one character. While Laura is not colonised to the degree that indigenous Australians have been/are being, she *is* assigned an object position which is designed to indicate her difference and consequent inferiority. I do not wish to participate in what Arun P. Mukherjee calls 'the post-colonialists' erasure' of '"race" as an analytic category', nor to imply that the experience of white women and indigenous peoples is the same (2). Rather I want to suggest that the strategies of sexism, racism and colonialism are similar, and often interconnected. Laura demonstrates the ambivalence of postcolonial resistance, especially that of a white female. She and her fellow students are not assigned the more objectifying 'native' or 'black', yet they are regarded as 'colonial'. They, in turn, apply this same colonising discourse of 'otherness' to those of lower class, or to the (briefly mentioned) Chinese and (still less mentioned) Aboriginal Australians. Laura is thus both colonised and colonising. She is also linked textually to colonisers through her identification with the role of Crusoe the subject, rather than Friday, the object, and by her later absorption in *King Solomon's Mines*, with its romantic portrayal of white imperialistic masculinity and the savagery and alterity of those of different race and sex.

Part of Laura's distaste for the educational emphasis of the school has to do with its unspoken but clearly demonstrated belief that English history is essential to the education of those living thousands of miles away from England. Morris describes the spread of English public schools across the Empire during the nineteenth century, claiming that they 'were assiduous and highly successful brainwashers' (141). Instilling the sense of Empire and loyalty to it was their object, and English history was the common thread which linked the diverse dominions in which they were placed. Laura's query — 'Why could it not have been a question about Bourke and Wills, or the Eureka Stockade, or the voyages of Captain Cook? ... something about one's own country, that one had heard hundreds of times and was really interested in' — demonstrates that she already has a sense of Australia's nationhood, and hence has an inbuilt resistance to being absorbed, even mentally, by Britain (*GW* 221).

Joseph Bristow describes the process by which geography and history were consciously introduced into the British public school system in the later part of the nineteenth century, in order to facilitate the absorption of 'tenets of imperialism' (20). Official advice to teachers in 1906 suggested that students would not know what 'distinguishes them from the people of other countries ... unless they are taught how the British nation grew up, and how the mother country in her turn has founded daughter countries beyond the seas' (Anon. qtd in Horn 42). Australian history does not serve the interests of Empire quite as well as British history, though even Laura's understanding of Australian history is largely about the 'discovery' of Australia and its interior. Such a view obviously ignores Aboriginal occupancy and intimate knowledge of the land. It is thus a history which perpetuates the notion that Australia was indeed *terra nullius*: legally unoccupied and hence open to settlement. In essence, the ideological function of Laura's ideal history curriculum and the one she was actually taught are the same: both provide a justification of invasion and colonisation by silencing the voices and stories of the colonised. While Laura resists the Empire on the one hand, she supports the ongoing imperialist activities of Australian settlers on the other.

Though when we first meet Laura she is telling a tale set in the old world, she does have a growing sense of the reality of the new nation, and of its importance to her. She shows this in her rejection of the purely British history curriculum, wanting one which reflects the world she experiences and is thus interested in. It is also seen in her relationship to the Australian landscape. This aspect of Laura's development is most fully explored in Chapter Nineteen, when Laura spends her holiday on the coast after her period of ostracism at school. The narration lovingly explores the beach environment:

> Whitest, purest sand, hot to the touch as a zinc roof in summer; rocky caves, and sandy caves hung with crumbly stalactites; at low tide, on the reef, lakes and ponds and rivers deep enough to make it unnecessary for you to go near the ever-angry surf at all; seaweeds that ran through the gamut of colours: brown and green, pearl-pink and coral-pink, to vivid scarlet and orange; shells, beginning with tiny grannies and cowries, and ending with the monsters in which the breakers had left their echo; the bones of cuttlefish, light as paper, and shaped like javelins. (*GW* 169)

It is almost as though Richardson cannot drag herself away from this sentence, as she depicts the wild beach lost in sand dunes and ti-tree. These descriptions, so different in tone and structure from the rest of the text, depict an environment of restoration for Laura where 'Sea, sun and air did their healing work' (*GW* 177). In discussing novels of second-wave feminism, Rita Felski observes that 'Two motifs recur persistently in the feminist narrative: nature and the (usually all female) community. Nature is often viewed as an extension of some kind of "feminine" principle' (132). Her (almost) all-female community does not have such a cosy function for

Laura but while Richardson does not romanticise nature she uses it in *The Getting of Wisdom* in a similar way to that of the novelists described by Felski: it has a healing force, and is a place to regroup and reaffirm oneself in the face of an antagonistic social world. Laura moves from the imaginary environment of 'grass as smooth as velvet' in her old world fairy tale to the wildness and immediacy of the Australian coast, in which, for the only time during the text, Laura can experience the 'sheer joy of living' (*GW* 1, 171). Her experience of the Australian landscape is a buffer against the whole imperialistic apparatus of the boarding school, with its demands for conformity, restraint and submission.

Though Richardson is concerned to convey Laura's sense of herself as Australian, she herself needed to look elsewhere for the nurturing of her intellectual growth. One aspect of Richardson's work which continually emerges is her deep intellectual debt to Continental, as opposed to English, literature and ideas. The fact that she lived mainly in Germany from the age of eighteen until she was in her early thirties and that she was involved in the intellectual enthusiasms of her host nation is everywhere apparent in her work. Although the reason she initially went to Germany was to study music, it is clear that Richardson preferred it to England. McLeod records that in England, Ettie, her mother and her sister 'were depressed not only by the climate and the dirt but also by the stuffiness and dreariness of the English' (7). It is obvious that much of Richardson's intellectual formation took place in Germany, and this is apparent in her enthusiasm for Wagner and Nietzsche in particular. Because of the time setting of *The Getting of Wisdom*, it was not possible for Richardson to represent any of the effects of Wagner and his music as she had done in *Maurice Guest*, but the influence of Nietzsche is openly stated. In early editions of *The Getting of Wisdom* several chapters were prefaced with brief quotes from Nietzsche's work, mainly from *Thus Spoke Zarathustra*.[37] Both Wagner and Nietzsche had enormous influence in the Germany of the 1890s, and Richardson was not immune to their effects. McLeod outlines some of Nietzsche's ideas that were particularly prevalent in Richardson's student days: 'Moral subversion and open-mindedness about moral values; the significance of the individual driven by his own will rather than by his duty towards others; the value of embracing and experiencing suffering; the celebration of intense feeling even if it is associated with failure' (24). It is not hard to see aspects of *The Getting of Wisdom* in this summary, particularly in the discussions of truth and morality. Laura can be seen as a Nietszchean hero in regard to her intense feelings and experience of suffering, though her femininity would ultimately preclude her from this role. As noted, Richardson first had to negotiate Nietzsche's misogyny, but this did not stop her from appropriating his thinking, despite its apparent sole application to the male. She was able to use it as she chose, refusing to see females as the underclass that Nietzsche did.

What is striking about Richardson's alignment with aspects of German thought from the period is that she appears to use it in part as a post-colonial strategy. It provides her with an alternative centre to the one which colonised Australia. Admittedly it is but a short step from Britain to Germany, but aligning herself with German thought provided Richardson with a point of resistance, a way of refusing to fall into line with the more confining aspects of English thought, especially its prudery and conservatism. Throughout *The Getting of Wisdom* the British are the keepers of the keys, the patriarchal restrictors of Laura. Obviously the Germans were colonisers too, but they were not the colonisers of Australia. This is quite a negotiation, given a strong German tradition of misogyny, and Britain would seem to have been more advanced in its

---

37 A complete list of these, in German and English, including their sources, is to be found in the appendix to McLeod (244-245). Michael Ackland also discusses the influence of Nietzsche in *Henry Handel Richardson: a life*.

thinking on women at the time than the Continent. However, Richardson was able to make links with Germans who resisted misogynistic thinking, if her membership of the dress reform group is any indication. Because she left Australia before the nationalist upsurgings of the 1890s, Richardson did not participate in the radical nationalist fervour of the era, though it is doubtful whether a sceptical young woman from Melbourne would have found much in common with the very masculinist *Bulletin* school who were primarily centred in Sydney. Regular contacts between Richardson and people in the Australian literary world were not made until after the publication of *The Getting of Wisdom*, so its influence on her was negligible at this stage of her career. Germany then became an intellectual home and alignment with it a positive post-colonial strategy, albeit a Eurocentric one. This is not unlike the way in which those connected with radical nationalism turned to France for their inspiration, as exemplified by both the use of French approaches to landscape painting to build a new sense of Australian nationhood, and by the Francophiles associated with *The Bulletin*.

Through these rather complex negotiations, we see in both Laura and Richardson the beginnings of a sense of nation and resistance, but overall a very ambivalent position in relation to colonialism. In *The Getting of Wisdom*, Henry Handel Richardson examines the public school of 1880s Australia as a prime site for the instillation of patriarchal and imperialistic values. In doing so, she demonstrates how inseparable these two forces are, suggesting that any hegemony that produces hierarchies will use similar methods to maintain itself. If imperialism and patriarchy are so intertwined, it does raise the question of implications for postcolonialism and feminism. Are the connections between the two in fact much more significant than the metaphorical relationship which has been acknowledged in the past? If the British public school, scattered in its various forms across the Empire, 'lay somewhere near the heart of the imperial ethic' (Morris 220), then Richardson's delineation of the processes of power in one small colonial city is in fact an examination of hegemonic strategies in the Empire as a whole. When Laura Rambotham discards her hat, gloves and schoolbag to run away from the college on the final day of school, she is not just, as Bird suggests, discarding the 'trappings of conventional feminine life' (176) but also throwing off the uniform of Empire. However, just as the schoolgirls are shown to have absorbed misogynist values, and taken part in the oppression of one another, so the discourse of colonialism is apparent in Laura's attitude to Australia's history, and in her brief references to the Chinese and Aborigines. *The Getting of Wisdom* demonstrates the tensions of the white middle-class woman in an invader/settler colony. Resistant to both imperialism and patriarchy, she is still caught in their discourses, and indeed cannot speak without being complicit with them. Laura's escape from the school can then also be seen as an attempt to escape the dilemma this creates for the narrative voice.

4.4 Narrative possibilities: *Bildungsroman*, *Künstlerroman* and denouement

Though the presence of a female protagonist in this novel of development results in certain variations in the narrative flow, *The Getting of Wisdom* is still recognisable as a *Bildungsroman*, and even as a *Künstlerroman*. This is because as readers we follow Laura's education and character development in the intense social setting of the school and also because we are privy to the early stages of the practice of her art as a writer of fiction. The tension between Laura's fierce individuality and her social setting, and the compromises and changes which result from this, are typical of the *Bildungsroman* as a genre. One of the areas she is forced to negotiate in her progress as a social being, and as a writer, is the role of truth and its function in society and art, together with the corresponding place of lies and lying. Laura's negotiation of these areas reveals not only the constructed nature of all representation but also the constructed nature of social conventions surrounding truth and untruth, and by implication other commonly held moral values. Allon White suggests that concerns about truth and representation were heightened toward the end of the nineteenth century:

> Lies took on a special significance in a period when it was often felt that neither culture nor individual expression could be entirely sincere. Rationality, social forms, language and objective representation began to seem like fictional constructs, and untruth could not be clearly and explicitly separated from the true and labelled as 'bad'. Falsehood seemed not so much an occasional isolated lapse on the part of an individual but constitutive of representation itself. (62)

Richardson prefaced the chapter which deals with Laura's lying episode with a quotation from Nietzsche's 'Of the Higher Man' from *Thus Spoke Zarathustra*: 'Inability to lie is far from being love of truth ... He who cannot lie does not know what truth is' (McLeod 244). This is precisely what is demonstrated by Laura's companions: it is their conventionality and lack of imagination, rather than their high moral fibre, which leads them to condemn Laura's fabrication. Laura sees that where morality stems from mere convention, it is open to challenge. In such a climate, lies can appear to be just as useful as truth. In her discussion about truth with M.P. and Cupid, Laura shows that she is quite prepared to think outside of the normal bounds of conventionality when she refuses to see truth as an underlying principle, but rather as a social contract: 'I say, M.P., if everybody told stories, and everybody knew everybody else was telling them, then truth wouldn't be any good any more at all, would it? If nobody used it?' (*GW* 183). The girls to whom she tells her fabricated tale actually do not love truth, and Laura has the discernment to see this. She could 'tell the plain truth, state the pedestrian facts — and this she would have been capable of doing with some address' but decides against it (*GW*

145). Stating the pedestrian facts would seem to be the opportunity to take up a naturalist style and method, but this she rejects, opting for the romance plot that her audience craves. She is forced to focus on this aspect too, in deference to them: 'But her public savoured the love-story most, and hence, consulting its taste, as it is the tale-maker's bounden duty to do, Laura was obliged to develop this side of her narrative at the expense of the other' (*GW* 149). Part of the reason that her friends are so susceptible to Laura's fabrications is that her method is so convincing, and 'their slower brains could not conceive the possibility of such extraordinarily detailed lying as that to which Laura now subjected them' (*GW* 149). She is composing a serial fiction, in the manner of Dickens: 'No sooner had she begun practising than she fell to work again on the theme that occupied all her leisure moments, and was threatening to assume the bulk of an early Victorian novel. But she now built at her top-heavy edifice for her own enjoyment' (*GW* 152).

The links between fictional representation and lying are clearly drawn here, and are pursued in Laura's next escapade, which is her foray into the Literary Society. This consists of three pieces which she offers to her young audience, who, claims Greer, 'gave her very good advice and forced her to take it by the most effective means, peer-group pressure' (11). The first piece is based on Sir Walter Scott and definitely cast in the Romantic mould, leaving her hearers unconvinced. This piece is largely a reaction to the shock of reading Ibsen: 'Her young, romantic soul rose in arms against this, its first bluff contact with realism, against such a dispiriting sobriety of outlook' (*GW* 187). Laura is clear in her rejection of Ibsen's style at this point: 'no macaroon-nibblers or rompers with children for her!' (*GW* 189). However, on the failure of her first Romantic piece, she pursues naturalism relentlessly, and records twenty 'distasteful' pages of 'A Day at School' (*GW* 191). When this too is rejected, Laura can only assert 'but it was *true* what I wrote — every word of it' (*GW* 191, emphasis in original). In the third piece, she gets the combination right for her audience, who believe that what she has written is an eyewitness account. She has in fact worked an imagined adventure into a setting she knows very well, and this is the point at which the link between her lying and her written fiction coincide: 'not a word of her narration was true, but every word of it might have been true', making it a perfect realist piece (*GW* 192). This episode reflects an anxiety about representation felt by many *fin-de-siècle* writers, and demonstrates some of the machinery involved in constructing fiction. It also questions social understanding of concepts such as truth and lies. The irony of it is that Laura, who has been ostracised for lying, has now been accepted, for lying on paper:

> Naturally, she was elated and excited by her success; but also a new and odd piece of knowledge had niched itself into her brain. It was this. In your speech, your talk with others, you must be exact to the point of pedantry, and never romance or draw the long-bow; or you would be branded as an abominable liar. Whereas, as soon as you put pen to paper, provided you kept one foot planted on probability, you might lie as you liked: indeed, the more vigorously you lied, the louder would be your hearer's applause. (*GW* 192)

She has, in fact, learnt her fictional craft by lying to her companions, but this is shown to be only conventionally different to the writer's craft. The question of the author's responsibility is another point which is raised by Laura's response to her ostracism after her tale has been discovered: 'She was embittered by their injustice in making her alone responsible, when all she had done was to yield to their craving for romance' (*GW* 177). In an era which had experienced obscenity trials, the issue of the writer giving her audience what they wanted was surely a pertinent one.

In pushing the boundaries regarding morality through questioning the social nature of truth, Laura attacks the conventions which had given rise to the associations between conformity and the role of the heroine in nineteenth-century fiction. It is necessary for her to do so if she is to move beyond them, and also necessary for the narrator, if she is to conceive of a plot which offers possibilities other than those afforded by the marital one. I use the term 'she' of the narrator with some hesitation, as the question of Richardson's pseudonym raises questions about gender and narration.

Another form of lying, which is made acceptable by social contract, is the use of a male pseudonym. It is interesting to note that the girls of the Literary Society, though they are obviously all female, have cast the role of 'author' as a male one. When Laura is to read, 'Cupid, who was chairman, called on "a new author, Rambotham, who it is hoped will prove a valuable acquisition to the Society, to read us his maiden effort"' (*GW* 189). The male role is highlighted by the sexual content of the expression 'maiden effort', and is maintained by Ethel Richardson's choice of Henry Handel as Christian names. Such a practice creates a double drag effect: we are confronted with a woman, writing as a man, writing about the consciousness of a girl. Historically, it is not difficult to see why Richardson wrote her first novel, *Maurice Guest*, under a male name. It was written over a period of eleven years at the time when debate over the 'New Woman' was still raging (McLeod 11). A female author of a tale of sexual obsession could expect to be subjected to both critical and personal voyeurism. There is also the desire to be taken seriously: that is, to be read as a writer rather than as a woman. Regarding her decision to use a male pseudonym, Richardson wrote:

> There had been much talk in the press of that day about the ease with which a woman's work could be distinguished from a man's; and I wanted to try out the truth of the assertion. Well, the laugh was with me. And not only over *Maurice Guest*. When *The Getting of Wisdom* followed, I was congratulated, as a man, on my extraordinary insight into a little girl's mind. (Richardson, *Some Notes* 10)

Although she makes this claim, several of the first reviews, to be found in Richardson's own scrapbooks, show that some reviewers were in no doubt as to the sex of the author, although most were taken in. For example, the reviewer from *The Lady* wrote that 'we feel certain that the author's pseudonym conceals a feminine identity, for no man could have sounded the shallows and the depths of girlish minds as Henry Handel Richardson has done' (*The Lady*, *RP* n.p.). Likewise, the writer in the *The Athenaeum* wrote 'The reviewer assumes the author of this remarkable study of schoolgirl life to be a woman' (*The Athenaeum*, *RP* n.p.), while Desmond B. O'Brien went so far as to assert: 'Nothing will persuade me that a man ever wrote "*The Getting of Wisdom*", by "Henry Handel Richardson"' (n.p.). Despite these early responses, Richardson appears to have kept her identity intact for much of her writing life. This has invited criticism from some quarters, notably from Summers, who sees it as a betrayal of women: 'Richardson played the game by the male rules, denying herself the opportunity to explore her own specifically female experiences and thereby perpetuating the prejudice that women's experiences are unworthy material for a national literary tradition' (Summers, *Damned Whores* 41). I presume Summers is referring to the Mahony trilogy, but these comments, while they may apply to the adoption of a male pseudonym, do not ring true when reading *The Getting of Wisdom* or *The Fortunes of Richard Mahony*. Summers also takes Richardson to task for failing to provide sufficiently liberated role models for women, citing Madeleine in *Maurice Guest* as a poor example (Summers, 'The Self Denied' 8). This criticism is typical of that which came from second-wave feminists during the 1970s regarding earlier women writers. It reflects an inability to see strategies other than rage or utopics as feminist. However, like that of the second-wave feminists, the political drive behind Richardson's irony is clear-sighted and directed against all that stands in the way of female development. Richardson's reasons for using the pseudonym reflect the era during which she began to publish, and have more to do with how she wanted *Maurice Guest* to be read than with a denial of 'women's experiences'.

This is not to say that the use of a male pseudonym is unproblematic, as it is not necessarily a transparent medium through which a woman can write. It carries ideological content, principally because it genders the narrator. This is very obvious in Olive Schreiner's *The Story of an African Farm*, where Lyndall's body is objectified and virtually fetishised by the narrator Ralph Iron. *Maurice Guest* shows the same kind of tendencies, its long descriptions of Louise's face and body tending to involve the reader in the same kind of obsessive gaze as that employed by Maurice himself. Another explanation for this sexualised gaze could be that it is the expression of lesbian narration, rather than the product of the male pseudonym. Lesbianism is an element of *The Getting of Wisdom*, yet nowhere does this seem to be connected with the objectification of female bodies. In fact, such objectification does not occur at all in this text in the way it does in *Maurice Guest*, perhaps demonstrating that in the latter it is a reflection of Maurice's consciousness rather than the narrator's. This would be entirely consistent with Richardson's use of Scandinavian impressionistic techniques, which move in and out of the character's consciousness. Richardson's use of the male pseudonym in *The Getting of Wisdom* does not sexualise the gaze of the narrator, or disavow the experiences of women. Rather, it functions, at least around its publication date, to create a space in which the text could be read without the bias that often came when the author was known to be a woman. A woman's name on a cover seemed to feminise a text, bringing with it the same kinds of prejudices that women themselves experienced. It could also create a distracting lens through which a prurient gaze was directed, a gaze which not only circumscribed the way in which the text could be read, but which also sexualised the author, so that she became a text herself. Richardson, in taking on the given names Henry Handel, sought to avoid this.

While the sex of the author had a profound effect on the way in which her work might be read, the sex of the reader had a profound effect on what she might be expected or allowed to read. Laura's relationship to the Principal's drawing room is mixed. She makes her first visit there to attend a musical evening where the girls, 'Even the totally unfit', were expected to play for their supper of cream-tarts, which 'was not held to square accounts' (*GW* 78). It is here that Laura learns her first hard lesson regarding the conformity required of the boarding school pupil. She quite enjoys the evening, but offends her hosts by not showing enough reserve and her school fellows by breaking a few cardinal rules of school life. She first offends by offering to play for a girl who wanted to be excused from singing the rest of her piece. Not only does Laura fail to take this in, but she draws attention to herself by her obvious ability in sight-reading. To display one's ability is not part of schoolgirl culture. Her final error at the piano is to play a popular piece in stark contrast to the more demure classical ones everyone else has played: 'Thalberg's florid ornaments had a shameless sound' (*GW* 80). She also has the cheek to chat with Mr Strachey, and Richardson has fun with her ignorance of literature, as Laura asks him whether Dante wrote *Faust*. By means of these allusions, the narrator seems to suggest that Laura may in fact be in a kind of hell without quite realising it.

Her ambivalent relationship with the room continues, for this is, in fact, the Stracheys' library. When she becomes one of the few allowed to practice on the grand piano in this room, she suddenly gains illicit access to this library. Despite the possibility that Mrs Gurley could enter at any moment, 'Laura was soon bold enough, on entering, hastily to select a book to read while she played, always on the alert to pop it behind her music, should anyone come into the room' (*GW* 186). Like *Maurice Guest*, Laura reads while practising her scales, as Richardson herself did. In this way, Laura is able to work her way through a very up-to-date literary collection. This scenario perfectly illustrates how Marianne Hirsch sees the female writer in relation to the library as symbol of the literary tradition and of male dominated language: '*A Room of One's Own*, like a number of women's *Künstlerromane* of the twenties, defines the liminal discourse of a female artist who stands both inside and outside of the library, both inside and outside of the structures of tradition, representation, and the symbolic' (Hirsch *The Mother/Daughter Plot* 92). Laura acquaints herself with the major texts of her day, but does so covertly, always in danger of being found out and chastised for inappropriate behaviour. She has no legitimate access to these texts, which were considered unsuitable reading for a young woman, but her desire to engage with them (and the boredom of playing scales) compels her to seek them out. Such a desire can be seen as an indication of the embryo artist in formation, and a strong element of any reading of *The Getting of Wisdom* as a *Künstlerroman*.

The books Laura picks are used by Richardson as literary shorthand for evoking issues of relevance not only to Richardson but to *The Getting of Wisdom* as a whole. In something of a private joke, Laura first embarks on *Faust*. Richardson's husband J.G. Robertson's 'devotion to Goethe and his passion for *Faust*' are well documented, along with his belief that it was central to the European literary tradition (Green 512). Laura reads it 'with a kind of dreary wonder why such a dull thing should be called great' (*GW* 186). William D. Elliott sees the connection between *The Getting of Wisdom* and *Faust* thus: 'Richardson's use of it in shaping *The Getting of Wisdom* is ironic ... since *Faust* poses the very complexities of permanence and transience that form a part of Laura's initiation' (Elliott 73). These are certainly themes that Dorothy Green also emphasises in Richardson. However, another aspect of the relationship to *Faust* is the way Goethe parodies the earlier *Faust* tradition. This reflects the type of parody employed by Richardson, and referred to earlier, in which the whole genre of stereotypical moral tales of school life is subverted into a novel that questions the very morality espoused by the original. Neil M. Flax suggests that 'as a true Romantic parody, *Faust* mocks the simple moralism of its original literary model and openly declares its own aesthetic autonomy; but at the same time it works as a profoundly moral critique of German aesthetic idealism' (Flax 44). In the same way, *The Getting of Wisdom* delineates a certain moral outrage at the inequities and the sheer repression of the school environment, at the same time as using the parodic technique.

Mention of Henrik Ibsen's *A Doll's House* functions to evoke another host of literary associations, the first of which is Scandinavian realism. It is hard to imagine the original impact of this style but Laura finds it shocking. The comments on Ibsen tie into the whole dialectic between idealism and realism which begins with Laura's story at the start of the novel, and continues in her attempts to write convincing fiction. *A Doll's House* is significant, structurally, for its open ending: 'When Nora's slamming of the door in Ibsen's *A Doll's House* (1878) had such a resounding effect upon late nineteenth-century Europe, one reason could be the way in which that action seemed to symbolize the refusal of a new generation to end on a note of closure' (Bjørhovde 176). This is a refusal which Richardson also makes, and she does so in order to expand the possibilities for her heroine. The other concern raised by *A Doll's House* is of course that of feminism. Nora was seen throughout Europe as a precursor of the 'New Woman', one of that dangerous breed who wanted to explore a personhood outside the bounds of motherhood and marriage. As a fictional heroine, her rejection of marriage was not uncommon for the time, but her rejection of the mothering role was made only slightly less shocking by the fact that she considered herself unfit for such an important function. Mention of this text evokes the whole range of debate on the New Woman, directing the reader to see the issues confronting Laura in this light.

Similarly, Longfellow's *Hyperion* is referred to as an antidote to Laura's shock at Ibsen, and 'so much more to her liking' (*GW* 188). *Hyperion* can be seen as an introduction to German Romanticism, as it retells tales from E.T.A. Hoffmann's *Kreisleriana*. In it there are expressions of need which could serve to articulate for Laura vague longings for which there are no apparent fulfilments: 'All these indefinite longings, these yearnings after an unknown somewhat, I have felt and still feel within me; but not yet their fulfilment' (Longfellow 95). When a female character expressed such desires in Victorian fiction, they were generally contained and curtailed, especially in narrative closure. An obvious example of this is Dorothea Brooke, who begins her fictional life as the embodiment of a great longing which is finally narrowed to romantic fulfilment and the abandonment of vocational dreams. Romantic fulfilment is overwhelmingly the only type available to most nineteenth-century realist heroines. For Laura, such desires blow open closure and send her forth, possibly with Longfellow's epigraph in her mind: 'Go forth to meet thy shadowy Future, without fear, and with a manly heart' (Longfellow epigraph). A 'manly heart' may be necessary if she is to avoid succumbing to the restrictions of the romance plot. *Hyperion* thus serves, in Richardson's literary economy, to evoke various unnamed longings associated with aspects of German Romanticism, but they also serve to express Laura's unarticulated desires.

These three texts broadly indicate the fields of literature which Richardson herself found so compelling, and which she posits as the influential pieces for Laura as a developing artist.[38] They represent classical German literature in Goethe, Scandinavian realism in Ibsen, and

---

38 Dorothy Green notes that Richardson 'copied out in bed at night chapter after chapter of Hoffmann's *Kreisleriana*' using Longfellow's version, *Hyperion* (Green 41-42). In her overview of Richardson's literary education, which she describes as 'intellectual reassurance', Green also notes the impact of Ibsen and Goethe, especially in relation to Robertson's exalted view of Goethe.

German Romanticism as represented by Longfellow. Significantly the English canon is conspicuously absent, reflecting Richardson's strategy of finding an intellectual centre beyond Britain's colonising influence. Laura's relationship to this library is an illicit one: the books are owned by the Principal, Mr Strachey, an Englishman. That Laura appropriates some of the contents is made clear, yet she does this under the cloud of sneaking and secrecy, and, with *Hyperion*, under the risk of being found guilty of stealing. Her relationship to the male literary tradition is thus clearly that of outsider, and her status in the library temporary at best, yet her reading *does* help to build in her an understanding of how to construct fiction and of her contemporary literary world. She uses what is to hand to form herself as a potential artist, just as surely as a hero with genuine access to such texts would have done.

The other pervasive literary influence in this text is the Bible. While it does not come in for special examination as a text, its presence is everywhere felt, beginning with the epigraph about wisdom and continuing throughout. There is even a chapter outlining Laura's experiences of faith, some of which read strangely to the more modern ear. However, this examination of Laura's engagement with Christianity, and the ways in which the Bible is used, are integral to the parodic functions of the text. In setting up *The Getting of Wisdom* as an ironic comment on the tales of girls' development that have preceded it, Richardson must give some account of the heroine's faith. Spiritual and moral lessons comprise much of the action of the model girls' texts; in order to parody them Laura must go through a similar process, for in rewriting the model Richardson can comment on the politics of the original. I mentioned earlier that one of the most widely read and influential girls' texts of the nineteenth century was *The Wide, Wide World* by Susan Warner. Almost every aspect of its plot is a lesson in faith. When its heroine, Ellen, encounters difficulties, and they are usually some form of restriction, her path to peace and pleasure is always through tears and submission. She never has a desire fulfilled without first going through the process of self-abnegation before a God who is portrayed as requiring, in a benevolent way, such subservience. Even when others wrong her, and her Aunt is often guilty of this, Ellen still benefits from the experience, becoming more gentle and faith-filled with each devastating experience. Richardson's rejection of such a model of feminine faith could not be more complete. Laura's encounter with 'God' leads her to dispense with a tyrant who would demand such continual testing and most importantly, such submission. The ethic of self-sacrifice which dominated evangelical Christianity of the nineteenth century was also the most singular characteristic of acceptable femininity. In order to create a *Bildungsroman* with a female protagonist, this ethic must be negotiated in some way. Richardson rejects it, and with it the frustrated and finally submissive tears that accompany almost every page of *The Wide, Wide World*.

The account of Laura's experience of faith is treated ironically for the most part. There is no analysis of metaphysical questions such as might be found in Schreiner's work. Rather this episode provides a means of moving beyond restrictive models of Christianity that have helped to maintain patriarchy by providing it with an ideology of submission. Though this episode ultimately rejects the lessons of faith model that had been presented by texts such as *The Wide, Wide World* and the books that followed it, Laura *does* learn from her experience. However, her realisations have more to do with an apprehension of her own aloneness than with improving her moral character and capacity to submit. In her grief at the loss of Evelyn, and in her apprehension about her coming examinations, Laura turns to Christ, whom she sees as 'a young man, kindly of face, and full of tender invitation' (*GW* 217). The narrator does not let this devotion pass without a great deal of irony at Laura's expense, showing that self-interest is Laura's chief motivation. She is described

'Pressing her fingers to her eyeballs till the starry blindness was effected that induces ecstasy', and her prayer is a hotchpotch of biblical language and often inappropriately borrowed snippets of Anglican liturgies: 'I will love Thee and serve Thee, all the days of my life, till death us do ... I mean, only let me pass my examinations, Lord, and there is nothing I will not do for Thee in return' (*GW* 218). Her intent is to strike a bargain, and has little to do with serious traditions of Christian spirituality: 'Laura made a pact with God, in which His aid at the present juncture guaranteed her continued, unswerving allegiance' (*GW* 218). It is only when Laura contemplates her cheating episode and God's role in it that she turns her perceptive attention to the function of religion. Not that her analysis is endorsed fully by the narrator: it is conveyed in the same lightly humorous and ironic tone as the devotion that preceded it. Laura decides that 'She could not go on worshipping a god who was capable of double dealing; who could behave in such a "mean, Jewy fashion"', and she is disappointed because 'she had taken the promises made through His Son, for gospel truth' (*GW* 224). The casual anti-Semitism expressed by Laura would seem to be another joke aimed at her inconsistency and adolescent fickleness. While Richardson may be having fun at Laura's expense here, this episode does allow Laura to think through her dependency, and to realise that she does not want to worship a God who intends to keep her in thrall. If God provided the opportunity for her to cheat as she had thought, then 'it had been a kind of snare on the part of God, to trap her afresh into sin, and thus to prolong her dependence on Him after her crying need was past' (*GW* 223). This raises the problems of evil, human choice and the question of a compassionate God, and shows the limitations of the 'moral lessons' model of faith. However it is not this aspect that is most significant for Laura. The issue of dependency is key, and the reason why this chapter is situated where it is. In rejecting a hierarchical, dominating God, Laura asserts her own valuable selfhood. She will not be dependent. Rather, she will take responsibility for herself. *The Getting of Wisdom* outlines her growth: she begins by craving acceptance and perjuring herself to get it. When this backfires, she tries to conform in other ways, but finds that at heart she cannot. Her emotional dependence on Evelyn is both a satisfaction and a torture, and her deal with God is ultimately something she realises to be beneath her. The next step is to be herself, by herself, as she is in her final action of the text. Though undoubtedly Richardson's use of Nietzsche is done with some amusement, the epigraph to the chapter about Laura's religious episode, taken from *Twilight of the Idols*, is shown to be true in the context of the whole novel: 'What does not kill me makes me stronger' (McLeod 245).

Part of the reward that Ellen, heroine of *The Wide, Wide World*, receives for her submission is marriage to a man who is both her benevolent leader and mentor in faith and life. Her tale of growth ultimately becomes a romance, as most *Bildungsromane* do. We have seen in relation to *Wilhelm Meister* that marriage is the ultimate endorsement accorded the *Bildungsroman* hero at the close of his narrative, and that part of his accommodation to society is to find a suitable life partner, as Wilhelm does in Natalie. However, prior to this, the male protagonist gains emotional and sexual experience through at least one youthful, passionate relationship. In Wilhelm's case his partner in this passion dies repentantly. Buckley's description of the *Bildungsroman* is very definite that such an affair is part of the emotional education of the hero: 'The latter involves at least two love affairs or sexual encounters, one debasing, one exalting, and demands that in this respect and others the hero reappraise his values' (18). For a heroine the narrative possibilities were obviously quite different, as she generally remained pure until her marriage or else died after sexual experience outside of marriage. *The Getting of Wisdom* subverts this sexual/marital plot in two ways: first, by ignoring the classical ending of the *Bildungsroman* and, second, by providing Laura with an experience of passion outside of the romance plot.

Greer claims that 'sexual tension tightens every page of *The Getting of Wisdom*', mentioning not only the girls' obsession with their sexual future but also the mistresses, 'living on the edges of heterosexual fulfilment' with romance fiction to read and plans for escape through marriage (Greer 10). However, there is also the possibility of romantic attachments occurring between the girls. Mention of this latter aspect is made very carefully by Richardson, so as to suggest a real alternative to the falsity required in relating to males. Chinky's devotion to Laura is the first attraction presented to the reader, and mention of it is always directly juxtaposed to Laura's failure with boys. After her lack of success with Bob, Laura seeks out Chinky, who was 'always making up to her', because she knows Chinky will 'cover her silence' and let her forget the incident (*GW* 125). Chinky also provides a foil when Laura is at the height of her misery of embarrassment after failing to hold a boy in conversation at the cricket. It is Chinky who approaches her, touches her 'bare wrist' and says 'What pretty hands you've got, Laura!' (*GW* 134). Laura reacts in a 'repellent way', and continues to be ungracious when Chinky offers her a ring (*GW* 134). The narrator demonstrates the irony of the situation: as Laura bemoans her inability to hold a boy's attention, Chinky offers Laura her devotion. Laura does not return this feeling, but is quite aware of it. She exploits the fact that Chinky is faithful, because Chinky 'garnered the few words Laura vouchsafed her, as gratefully as Lazarus his crumbs; and a mark of confidence, such as this, would sustain her for days' (*GW* 127). It is in fact Chinky's unsolicited offer of a ring that brings her career at school to an end. She is caught stealing to buy it, and removed from the school, which further blackens Laura by implication. Just before this she elicits a promise from Laura that she will wear the ring, prompting her to give Laura 'a hearty kiss', which Laura receives 'ungraciously' (*GW* 150). Chinky is quite clear about where she stands regarding boys: 'Boys are dirty, horrid, conceited creatures', closely reflecting what Laura has thought (*GW* 127). If Chinky is a picture of the lesbian schoolgirl, the portrait is not very flattering. However the juxtaposition of her conversations with Laura and Laura's failure to flirt successfully represents some suggestion of a lesbian alternative. This is more fully explored in Laura's relationship with Evelyn.

It is well after Laura's obvious failures to play the male-pleasing game that this relationship begins. Eva Jarring Corones suggests that it is 'possible to conclude that Laura in the end totally rejects the role-playing necessary with men, by turning from them to a woman' (85). In this affair Laura is once again the victim of her feelings, which tend to hold her up to ridicule: 'the strength of her feelings quite out-ran her capacity for self-control; she was unable to disguise what she felt ... though it made her the laughing-stock of the school' (*GW* 204). Evelyn is the last in a line of possible mother figures for Laura, most of whom have been disappointing. Her relationship with her own mother, though intense, is fraught with misunderstandings. Godmother proved to be only 'good to them all in a brusque, sharp-tongued fashion', while Mrs Gurley, who could have had the same status with regard to Laura as Miss Temple does to Jane Eyre, does not appear to have a nurturing instinct in her body (*GW* 27). Instead she corresponds more closely to Brocklehurst. Most significantly, none of these women really assist Laura in her *Bildung*, but rather they are complicit in the gendering process which threatens to stall Laura's development. Mother does encourage Laura in some ways — she works long hours to provide the money for Laura's schooling — but she wants feminine submissiveness as well as cleverness. Evelyn is different. She 'was the only person who did not either hector her, or feel it a duty to clip and prune at her' (*GW* 197). That this relationship has a mother/daughter flavour is made quite clear. Regarding Evelyn's good nature, 'Laura soon learnt that she could cuddle in under it, and be screened by it, as a lamb is screened by its mother's woolly coat' (*GW* 197). However, both begin to use their power in ways which make the relationship more destructive. Laura becomes completely possessive, even though she dimly realises that this could be repellent: 'Laura knew that it was possible to kill animal-pets by surfeiting them; and, towards the end, a suspicion dawned on her that you might perhaps damage feelings in the same way' (*GW* 211). At the same time, Evelyn does not mind occasionally provoking Laura's jealousy: 'Perhaps, too, she was at heart not averse to Laura's tantrums, or to testing her power in quelling them' (*GW* 207). Tension also comes into the relationship because Evelyn goes out in the company of men, and this is where the reality of the social world comes home to Laura: 'your friend's affection was wholly yours only as long as no man was in question' (*GW* 209). Ties with men are ultimately more important because they lead to marriage, which is *the* economic and social necessity for most women, and Laura is made to experience the compulsory nature of heterosexuality, at least as it relates to Evelyn's life choices.[39] Though the relationship the two girls have is passionate, it is never seen as an alternative to marriage by Evelyn, while Laura is so caught up in the intensity of her feelings that the coming separation is all she can consider. The reality of the school world being what it is, Evelyn leaves and goes back to the country and Laura is left alone. As a final mother figure, she is as unreliable as the others. Not only are her affections under threat from the superior claims of a man but she will be unable to commit to a relationship with Laura, even if she wants to. There is no means whereby they can continue their school connection in the patriarchal world.

This relationship is significant not just because it provides Laura with an alternative to the ritualised game-playing required in relating to boys, but also because of the way in which Richardson has moulded autobiographical material to align this episode with the French literary tradition of schoolgirl lesbian tales. She claims to have treated it more

---

[39] The phrase 'compulsory heterosexuality' is Adrienne Rich's, and her 'Compulsory Heterosexuality and Lesbian Existence' remains a landmark piece in the theorisation of heterosexuality and its preclusions.

lightly than her own experience of such a relationship (Richardson, *Myself When Young* 70). The Nietzschean epigraph that prefaces this chapter reads: 'And do not forget to laugh well!' (McLeod 245). This does not seem to capture the chapter's tone for the reader though, as pain is the dominant element of the episode. Richardson has, however, emphasised the mother/daughter aspects of the relationship, and the one-sidedness of it, which is not how she described her own experience. It is these aspects which reflect what Elaine Marks refers to as the 'Sappho Model' of French lesbian fiction (357). She draws a distinction between texts written by women and men, and states:

> [A]s is usually the case when the author of the text is a woman, it is the younger woman who falls in love ... Whoever plays the aggressive role, the exchanges between the older and the younger woman are reminiscent of a mother-daughter relationship. The mother of the younger woman is either dead or in some explicit way inadequate. (357)

That the end of Evelyn's school life means the end of her intimacy with Laura also links the episode to this French lesbian tradition, where such relationships occur within the bounds of the all-female school: 'Time limits are set by the school calendar whose inexorable end announces the fatal separation' (Marks 357). However, though there are similarities between this episode and the French tradition, there are also marked differences.

In texts such as *Claudine at School* by Collette, which was first published in 1900, the lesbian plots and subplots form the chief action in the narrative. This material is presented to the reader in a form which is more titillating and less challenging than the episode described in *The Getting of Wisdom*, partly because texts like *Claudine* offer less of a challenge to heterosexuality than Richardson's does. It is clear throughout *Claudine* that, though the heroine is attracted to girls, she will ultimately marry and find her sexual fulfilment with a man. This is not the case with Laura, and we are never privy to *her* dreaming the dreams that Claudine shares with the reader: 'I should have liked to dance with someone whom I adored with all my heart. I should have liked that someone there so that I could relieve my tension by telling him everything' (Collette 262). The lesbian material, though it occupies so much of the *Claudine* text, is presented as amusing entertainment rather than heart-rending experience or as a serious challenge to the heterosexism of the romance plot. Even the dominating lesbian schoolmistress is found at the conclusion of the text to be harbouring desire for a local male official. This reaches its conclusion when they are found in bed by the teacher's mother and suffer a public humiliation. Such a representation of lesbianism has more in common with its function in pornography designed for consumption by men; ultimately it serves heterosexuality as it is presented for the male gaze. Though Richardson can be seen to be drawing on this tradition, she reworks the original in order to subvert its politics as she does in other intertextual aspects of the novel. The episode with Evelyn remains a challenge to the heterosexism of the marital plot and provides the means by which Laura can gain an education in passion of the type usually undergone by the *Bildungsroman* hero.

Annis Pratt raises one of the problems the *Bildungsroman* form encounters when it deals with the education of a female protagonist: 'In the *bildungsroman* [sic] proper, with its expectation that the hero is learning to be adult, there is the hidden agenda of gender norms, where "adult" means learning to be dependent, submissive, or "nonadult"' (16). This seems to suggest that to be female is to be unable to participate fully in the *Bildungsroman* narrative. One way in which Richardson negotiates this is in Laura's relationship with Evelyn. In fact Catherine Pratt suggests that 'Laura's relationship with Evelyn, whether doomed or not, is thus the central event in Laura's development' (*Resisting Fiction* 156). There are other significant variations that are forced on the conventions of the form by the feminine. Carol Franklin makes a large claim for *The Getting of Wisdom* when she suggests that 'Richardson has written the first genuine female *Künstlerroman*' ('The Female *Künstlerroman*' 436). This can be disputed on two levels. Firstly it is preceded by *A Daughter of Today*, to cite only one example, and secondly some critics dispute that the novel contains enough elements of the artist in the making to constitute a *Künstlerroman*. Adrian Mitchell for example states that 'Laura's experiences are not all that unusual, not enough really to determine her as an artist in the making' (88). Yet in *The Getting of Wisdom*, Laura is a storyteller from beginning to end. Her 'wisdom' is largely to do with her emerging craft, even though she may not cast herself as 'artist'. McFarlane compares Richardson unfavourably with Joyce:

> Joyce can see the limitations of Stephen Dedalus's achievements but at the same time he clearly values their significance in Stephen's growth. Richardson is too preoccupied with what she sees as the inevitable corruption and disintegration that accompanies [sic] growth for her to give us an adequate sense of excitement that can also be part of the process. (63)

Possibly all this objection signifies is that 'the *Künstlerroman* conventions fashioned by male writers are insufficient' for women's *Künstlerromane* (Gubar 26). When it comes to depicting the development of a female artist, the impact of the gendering process can create a certain grimness of outlook, which McFarlane finds in Richardson. It is a grim process, and one which leaves its mark on the tone of the text.

One early modernist practice which is evident in *The Getting of Wisdom* is the use of an open ending. This change, from the strong narrative and ideological closures of English realism, can, among other things, reflect dissatisfaction with fictional possibilities for heroines in nineteenth-century fiction. As Bjørhovde notes, 'the link between the conventional novel and the conventional female role had seemed both clear and close for a long time' (13). Closure had often been used to maintain the status quo, to order the fictional world according to proper values. Often in women's writing, where the narrative has seemed to offer possibilities that have not been realised in its denouement, the containment thus proffered is somewhat unconvincing. This can be seen as 'the ironic comment of an author at closure' (Du Plessis 7). The next step is obviously to avoid closure altogether, and rather than contain the 'disturbances', to set them loose. Closure in English fiction up to this time had generally brought the weight of moral opinion down on whatever had occurred during the narrative, giving it the 'incurably *fairy-tale-like* quality' that Moretti has observed (213, emphasis in original). This is because such fiction represented the world as ideologically consistent, where breaches of society's codes were punished and those who conformed were rewarded. The heroine who fails to conform *or* repent would not have escaped some kind of retribution in this fiction. Because narrative closure seems to necessitate a conservative ideological closure, the early modernist use of the open ending offers a way of avoiding this regressive impulse. It also signals the move from realism. This allows Richardson to create a heroine who is unlike most heroines who have gone before. McLeod suggests that Richardson departs from the submission required of the characters of Eliot and Hardy: 'By contrast, Richardson's characters are essentially egotistical; they are driven by their own needs and desires' (23). In contrast to previous 'monsters of egoism in English fiction' (McLeod 23), Laura is not condemned for her egoism: in fact, it is shown to be her abiding strength, demonstrating the influence of Nietzsche in such characterisation. This is a departure from Duncan's treatment of her egotistical heroine, who, though portrayed with affection, is nevertheless killed off in the final pages.

In *this* novel's ending, Richardson does to some extent have it both ways. If, as Bjørhovde claims with regard to women writers of this transitional period, '*vacillation* is more typical of their art' (172, emphasis in original), Richardson could be said to vacillate in her approach to narrative closure in this text. She makes a small gesture to closure in her reassurance of the reader with regard to Laura's fate: 'She could not know then that, even for the squarest peg, the right hole may ultimately be found; seeming unfitness prove to be only another aspect of a peculiar and special fitness' (*GW* 230). This passage goes on to describe how Laura will find herself in 'that freer, more spacious world where no practical considerations hamper, and where the creatures that inhabit dance to their tune', presumably the world of fiction, though as readers we cannot be sure (*GW* 230). However, after this glimpse into the future, this gesture to closure, Richardson presents the open ending, in which Laura is 'lost to sight' (*GW* 233), thereby resisting 'the compromise between self-determination and socialization that informs the structure of the European *Bildungsroman*' (Pratt, *Resisting Fiction* 150). Heroines' ends in English realism, with their emphasis on moral judgements handed out in the form of marriages or deaths, have not been so much about possibility as about containment. If there are to be possibilities for Laura, these ends must be discarded. It seems necessary for Laura to reject marriage in order to attain 'these marvellous perhapses' (*GW* 130). Bjørhovde points out that in the late nineteenth century 'other women writers ... emphasized the need to say no to marriage as a precondition for an open ending and an open future for their protagonists' (177). Richardson reflects the narrative patterns of many women writers from the time who saw the plots of *Bildung* and romance as mutually exclusive: 'In nineteenth-century narrative, where women heroes were concerned, quest and love plots were intertwined, simultaneous discourses, but at the resolution of the work, the energies of the *Bildung* were incompatible with the closure in successful courtship or marriage' (Du Plessis 6). Richardson chooses to make room for the *Bildung* plot by discarding the possibility of marriage — Laura is after all too young, apart from being uninterested — and by demonstrating the transitory disappointments of love.

We have an example of more typical nineteenth-century fates in the narratives of Laura's friends, M.P. and Cupid. Though they have great aspirations, neither fulfils them. M.P. asserts 'I shall probably be able to have a school of my own someday', while Cupid 'intended to be a writer' (*GW* 228). They succumb to nineteenth-century ends, and their narratives of *Bildung* are truncated: 'Within six months of leaving school, M.P. married and settled down in her native township; and thereafter she was forced to adjust the rate of her progress to the steps of halting little feet. Cupid went a-governessing, and spent the best years of her life in the obscurity of the bush' (*GW* 229). Governessing and marriage have been the choices for heroines from Jane Austen onwards: Richardson projects them away from her heroine, as they are portrayed as limitations, rather than openings. The removal of limits is utterly necessary to Laura as heroine, if she is indeed to fulfil her promise as artist. She has experienced the pervasiveness of colonial and patriarchal ideology as it is worked out in the cloistered environment of the Ladies' College. Such ideology is all about containment: the removal of the limit of the closed ending is itself a step beyond these ideologies. As Carol Franklin suggests:

> Laura symbolically, and much more artistically makes her run from a cramping restriction on girl and artist on the final page of the novel, leaving the feminized and institutional trappings of gloves, hat, and bag of school books to the 'womanly' Pin, an act summing up her total renunciation of the artificial role which the whole novel has been at pains to explicate. ('The Female *Künstlerroman*' 432-433)

Laura has negotiated the forces of patriarchy and imperialism, and her *Bildung* is as much about surviving these as about developing herself as an artist. '[T]he assertion of selfhood', which Brooks finds to be typical of the female plot, is certainly evident in Laura's plot (39). As heroine, she has to transcend the narratives of the nineteenth century in order to be a potential female artist with an open future. *The Getting of Wisdom* demonstrates that when the *Bildungsroman* has a female protagonist, the impact of the feminine forces the form to change. It also forces a change on the role of heroine, for as this narrative abandons the romance plot, the role of the heroine moves much closer to that active, achieving role which has previously been occupied exclusively by the hero.

5

Conclusion:

From heroine to hero

Olive Schreiner's *The Story of an African Farm*, Sara Jeannette Duncan's *A Daughter of Today* and Henry Handel Richardson's *The Getting of Wisdom* are three examples of *Bildungsromane* in the late nineteenth-century and early twentieth-century *Bildungsromane*. All are written by women writers from British invader/settler colonies, and all deal with the progress of female protagonists. In their negotiations of the *Bildungsroman* form, these writers reflect the frictions arising from various and often conflicting discourses. Such friction results in an ambivalence of voice, which can be seen as a condition of all postcolonial fiction and, indeed, of feminism. Conflicts can also be seen in the narrative ends of these fictions, in that two plots result in the death of the heroine and the other must avoid closure altogether in order to refuse this resolution. The writers reflect their multiple positions in the Empire, many of which result in their own colonisation. They are colonials, removed from and overlooked by the imperial Centre; they are women in an entrenched patriarchy; they are intellectuals and writers in pragmatic emerging cultures in which the arts are feminised and disregarded. They are also members of invading/settling groups, usurping the indigenous occupants of their lands; they are part of the largest empire on earth, and thereby the beneficiaries of the imperial dividend; they are middle-class, educated, mobile and white. As both Othered and Othering, colonised and colonising, these writers produce fictions which reflect these complex subjectivities. Importantly, their positions are not static, making possible that movement in narrative which we see over the period of years in which these fictions were written. Fiona Giles's metaphor of 'enjambment' usefully reflects their position, as it 'implies not only the in-betweenness of the position of the nineteenth-century female migrant ... [but] it also implies *movement* through that space' (16, emphasis in original). While these subjectivities are ambivalent, they are not fixed. These three fictions capture particular moments in the history of Empire, patriarchy, race and narrative in which the possibility of female development can be explored, and the imbrications of patriarchy and the Empire can be exposed.

In *The Story of an African Farm*, Schreiner explores the form in a double male/female *Bildungsroman*. This allows her to contrast the plots available to heroes with those available to heroines. It also allows her to divide her interrogation of certain aspects of the form between the plots of the two protagonists. Accordingly, the belief in vocation, which underpins the whole notion of *Bildung*, comes under scrutiny in Waldo's plot. As an ordering principle in human life it is found to be lacking. The belief in the functions and provisions of a benign universe, expressed so strongly in *Wilhelm Meisters Lehrjahre*, are shown to be the product of a European belief system which fails to stand up to the rigours of life in a racist, unjust and harsh colonial outpost. As part of this belief system, Christianity is questioned and ultimately abandoned. The progress of Lyndall's narrative allows Schreiner to examine the role of gender in the curtailment of narrative possibilities for the white heroine, and also to show the inadequacies of the romance plot as a vehicle for the heroine's development and fulfilment.

Duncan places herself squarely in the midst of 1890s New Woman fiction, with both her title, *A Daughter of Today*, and her subject matter. In doing so she brings to the fore many of the preoccupations of her day, especially associations between art, genius, woman and death. She also demonstrates the conflicts inherent for the heroine in the dual narratives of vocation and romance, narratives which blend so favourably in the classic male *Bildungsroman*. In a truly radical departure from the heroines who had preceded her, we are presented with a female protagonist who is not only egotistically ambitious but determinedly unrepentant. The text also highlights the contradictions inherent in the two categories of 'artist' and 'woman', showing that the discourses surrounding one finally exclude the other in this female *Künstlerroman*. The conflicts arising from these contradictions are resolved in this text by the death of the heroine. Rather than representing a comfortable ideological closure, Elfrida's death raises questions about the dominant discourses which have been brought to bear upon her, especially patriarchal conceptions of the artist. It also reflects the exclusions resulting from the smugness of those occupying the imperial Centre. Contradictions between her own Orientalist position and her aims of feminist self-realisation also contribute to the curtailment of her *Bildung* in death.

Though the atmosphere of *The Getting of Wisdom* is no less stifling than either of the other texts, the fact that the narrative does not close with the death of the heroine is a significant departure. Not only is this an abandonment of narrative and ideological closure, indicating the transitional nature of the whole novel form in the early twentieth century, but it is also a means by which the heroine's aspirations can be given the space in which to grow. Instead of emphasising curtailment, this example of the form finally endorses development. Its parody of earlier fictions serves to critique those nineteenth-century discourses of femininity which typified the feminine as self-sacrificing and restrained. As a heroine, Laura is perceptive, difficult and incapable of conforming to the artificiality of the feminine role assigned to her. Unlike her predecessors, she is not punished for this in the denouement of the plot, but escapes both reader and narrative by running from sight.

One of the most obvious conflicts for the female protagonist of the *Bildungsroman* is that which arises between the plot of *Bildung* and that of romance. For the male hero of the classic *Bildungsroman*, the two were blended in closure with the ideal marriage, expressing both the accommodation of the hero's vocation to society and his romantic fulfilment. Marriage indicated society's endorsement of the hero's aspirations. However, in the female *Bildungsroman*, the romance or marital plot is at loggerheads with the *Bildung* plot and not one of these texts is able to combine the two. In *The Story of an African Farm*, though Lyndall has been able to analyse the shortcomings of marriage as an institution, she is sidetracked by her romantic needs and dies before her *Bildung* plot can really progress. The fact that the notion of vocation has been deconstructed in Waldo's plot deflates it as a narrative possibility for Lyndall as well. In Elfrida Bell's case in *A Daughter of Today*, romance plot and *Bildung* plot at first *appear* to be compatible, though at the point of succumbing to romance, Elfrida's first thought is to abandon her art, indicating the assumption, apparent in almost all late-nineteenth-century fiction, that the two are mutually exclusive for heroines. However, Elfrida's commitment to her art is the most fully realised of the three heroines, and it is the apparent failure of *both* of her plots which leads to her death. Another radical factor in her suicide is the failure of female friendship, which receives more attention in the text than the romance. Even though death provides a very final form of narrative closure and the ultimate truncation of *Bildung*, Elfrida's progress as an artist is confirmed by the posthumous success of her book. Though the text does not reconcile marriage and *Bildung* plots for heroines, it does offer some, if slight, affirmation of the possibility of female vocation. The romance plot is not a real feature of *The Getting of Wisdom* other than in its subversive lesbian form, so it cannot provide the huge obstacle to development that it does in Lyndall's case, and to a lesser extent in Elfrida's. Rather than being a major distraction, it is something of an irrelevance. Laura's development, though cramped by her oppressive environment, is allowed to occur, and we are assured that it continues beyond the confines of the text. Not one of these women writers presents the reader with a positive endorsement of the benefits for the heroine of the romance/marital plot. On the contrary, it is seen as counterproductive for female development, contributing to the death of the heroine and all of her aspirations and dreams. This is in strong contrast to the classic male *Bildungsroman*, in which marriage caps a successful development.

Not one of these writers is prepared to endorse the meritocratic drive of the nineteenth-century *Bildungsroman*. Gender is the greatest factor in this as it so clearly disqualifies the heroine from full *Bildung*. Though these heroines have all the aspirations of their male counterparts, they are discouraged from pursuing them at every turn as gender enculturation is enforced. However, their positions in the Empire have some impact on this as well. Though to some extent they are the beneficiaries of the imperial dividend, especially because of their whiteness, at the same time they are not English, and are either removed or excluded from full participation in the life of the imperial centre, or the life of the emerging nation. Lyndall is the most extreme example of this, and it is in her narrative that the notion of meritocracy comes under the most severe scrutiny. The value systems of Europe are shown to be inappropriate to conditions in a colonial outpost. They are shown, in fact, to be dependent on the superior economic and cultural position of the colonisers, rather than being universally applicable. The technologies by which the Empire is maintained are also examined as they occur on the remote farm, in the colonial boarding school and in the artistic life of the imperial centre, and these technologies are shown to be closely aligned with those of patriarchy. In fact, these two oppressive systems are imbricated closely, as they share the fundamental strategy of Othering.

All three of these pictures of female development depict heroines who share certain characteristics. Though their environments vary greatly, all are conceived as isolated, lonely figures, lacking in mentors or any real external support. There is no benign guild following their progress as there is in Wilhelm Meister's tale. If they are to develop, it will be in spite of the world around them, not because of it. Their positions in the Empire as women are again and again shown to be detrimental to their development. Though Schreiner and Richardson were involved in the women's movement, and Duncan seemed to typify the New Woman in her successful journalistic career, not one of these texts portrays an environment in which the heroines experience sustained female solidarity. Rather, these texts portray the costs and restrictions caused by gender enculturation and the patriarchal and imperialistic structures of the societies they depict. There is also a reluctance or inability on the part of these authors to allow their heroines the same opportunities they themselves had. This is not unusual; George Eliot is an earlier example of the same practice, as her heroines were never allowed her career opportunities or her 'illicit' romantic life. However, it must be said that George Eliot's life was hardly usual for her time, and that in showing women's lives as constantly curtailed and thwarted, Schreiner, Duncan and Richardson were probably depicting the reality of their own lives in part. Certainly not one of them had unambiguous success and romantic fulfilment. However, there is a distance between these authors and their heroines which reflects ambivalence on the author's part.

This distance is shown in various narrative strategies. Duncan and Richardson both employ irony at their heroine's expense which serves to create a space between narrator and protagonist. Because of this, there is some doubt as to whether the actions, thoughts and aspirations of the heroine are endorsed fully by the narrator. In *The Story of an African Farm*, the narrator objectifies the heroine through the fetishisation of her body. Rather than the use of irony, though it is employed with regard to other characters, this objectification creates an almost gendered distance between narrator and heroine. Two of the heroines' plots end in death, and though these deaths need not be seen as punitive, they still bring about the complete curtailment of the heroine's development, thereby creating narratorial distance. These tactics can be read in a number of ways. Irony can be affectionate, even though the joke is on the heroine. Even death can be read as a rescue, where the heroine is taken from impossible circumstances unconducive to further development. It is difficult to read the fetishisation of Lyndall's body as anything other than objectifying and a further example of Othering in practice. However, it could also endear the heroine to the reader, especially as it is her smallness and childlikeness which is emphasised. The fact that two of these authors incorporated their own mothers' names into their heroines' names tends to suggest a large investment on the part of the writers in the fate of their heroines.[40] Alternatively, these distancing strategies could suggest that the authors are not prepared to endorse the feminist aspirations and aims of their heroines. Two of these authors took male pseudonyms. If this involves projecting a male narrating persona, then the expression of some scepticism regarding an unconventional heroine would be consistent with such a projection. Enlisting the sympathy of both publishers and readers could also be the aim of such a strategy. Either way, the distance between author and protagonist reflects that basic ambivalence which is a feature of both postcoloniality and feminism. Unable to escape fully the discourses

---

40 Both Schreiner and Duncan used their mothers' maiden names. The Bell in Elfrida Bell was Duncan's mother's surname, and Schreiner's mother was Rebecca Lyndall (Fowler 217, First and Scott 32).

of patriarchy and colonialism, the colonial woman writer must reflect this condition of ambivalence in her narratives and in the depiction of her heroines. It is not my purpose to make a definitive statement regarding the position of the colonial women writer in relation to her heroine, but her ambivalence regarding this represents one area of discourse analysis which remains to be explored. Another revealing area of research would be to compare these texts with the colonial male *Bildungsroman* to see whether some of the same ambivalences arise.

In their use of the *Bildungsroman* form as a vehicle for the depiction of the growth of a female protagonist, all three authors reveal the form, as it functioned in their time, to be lacking. The marital plot which capped the account of male *Bildung* is seen to undermine female self-realisation. Likewise, the conflict arising from the conventional heroine's role and the protagonist's aspirations as the driving force of narrative are not easily resolved. In two of these narratives they result in the heroine's death; in the other, these conflicts are bypassed by the rejection of narrative closure. The happy resolutions of the classic male *Bildungsroman* are not to be found in these colonial fictions. Rather, the heroines of these fictions chafe at the restrictions of their narratives, as their aspirations are held in check by both the discourses in which they have been conceived and contained and by the conventions of the form. However, the fact that in the most recent of these fictions the heroine is allowed to escape the restrictions of narrative closure is a sign that though its expression is limited, by the twentieth century, female *Bildung* in the British invader/settler colony is becoming a reality in life, as well as in fiction.

Works Cited

Abel, Elizabeth, Marianne Hirsch and Elizabeth Langland. *The Voyage In: Fictions of Female Development*. Hanover, NH: University Press of New England, 1983.

Abrams, M.H. *A Glossary of Literary Terms*. 7th ed. Boston: Heinle & Heinle, 1999.

Ackland, Michael. *Henry Handel Richardson*. Melbourne: Oxford University Press, 1996.

____. *Henry Handel Richardson: a life*. Cambridge: Cambridge University Press, 2004.

Adam, G. Mercer. 'Garth Grafton's Triumph: Literary Success of a Young Canadian Lady'. *The Globe* (28 June 1890): 5.

Ahmad, Aijaz. *In Theory: Classes, Nations, Literatures*. London: Verso, 1992.

Alcott, Louisa May. *Little Women*. 1868. New York: Collier Books, 1962.

Althusser, Louis. *Lenin and Philosophy and Other Essays*. Trans. Ben Brewster. New York: Monthly Review Press, 1971.

Ardis, Ann L. *New Women, New Novels: Feminism and Early Modernism*. New Brunswick, NJ: Rutgers University Press, 1990.

Arkin, Marian. 'A Reading Strategy for Henry Handel Richardson's Fiction'. *World Literature Written in English* 30.2 (1990): 120-130.

Atkinson, Paul. 'The Feminist Physique: Physical Education and the Medicalization of Women's Education'. *From 'Fair Sex' to Feminism: Sport and the Socialization of Women in the Industrial and Post-Industrial Eras.* Ed. J.A. Mangan and Roberta J. Park. London: Frank Cass, 1987. 38-57.

Austen, Jane. *Pride and Prejudice.* 1813. Oxford: Oxford University Press, 1988.

Aveling, Edward. '"A Notable Book": Review of *The Story of an African Farm*'. Progress (September 1883). Reprinted in *Olive Schreiner.* Ed. Cherry Clayton. Johannesburg: McGraw-Hill, 1983. 67-69.

Barreca, Regina. Ed. and intro. *Sex and Death in Victorian Literature.* Bloomington, IN: Indiana University Press, 1990.

Bashkirtseff, Marie. *The Journal of Marie Bashkirtseff.* 1887. Trans. Mathilde Blind. 1890. Ed. and intro. Rozsika Parker and Griselda Pollock. London: Virago, 1985.

Beresford, Bruce. 'Getting "The Getting of Wisdom"'. *Quadrant* 21.10 (1977): 25-27.

Berkman, Joyce Avrech. *Olive Schreiner: Feminism on the Frontier.* St. Albans, VT: Eden, 1979.

Bersani, Leo. *A Future for Astynax: Character and Desire in Fiction.* London: Marion Boyars, 1978.

Bhabha, Homi. 'Difference, Discrimination and the Discourse of Colonialism'. *The Politics of Theory.* Proceedings of the Essex Conference on the Sociology of Literature, July 1982. Colchester, UK: University of Sussex, 1983. 194-211.

____. 'The Other Question ... Homi Bhabha Reconsiders the Stereotype and Colonial Discourse'. *Screen* 24 (1983): 18-36.

Bird, Delys. 'Towards an Aesthetics of Australian Women's Fiction:

My Brilliant Career and *The Getting of Wisdom*'. *Australian Literary Studies* 11.2 (1983): 171-181.

Bjørhovde, Gerd. *Rebellious Structures: Women Writers and the Crisis of the Novel 1880-1900.* Oxford: Norwegian University Press, 1987.

Blake, Kathleen. *Love and the Woman Question in Victorian Literature: The Art of Self-Postponement.* Brighton, UK: The Harvester Press, 1983.

____. 'Olive Schreiner — A Note on Sexist Language and the Feminist Writer'. *Gender and Literary Voice.* Ed. Janet Todd. New York: Holmes and Meier, 1980. 81-86.

Bland, Lucy. 'The Married Woman, The 'New Woman' and the Feminist: Sexual Politics of the 1890s'. *Equal or Different: Women's Politics 1800-1914.* Ed. Jane Rendall. Oxford: Blackwell, 1987. 141-164.

Bonnett, Alistair. *White Identities: Historical and International Perspectives.* Harlow, UK: Pearson Education, 2000.

Boumelha, Penny. *Charlotte Brontë.* London: Harvester Wheatsheaf, 1990.

____. *Thomas Hardy and Women: Sexual Ideology and Narrative Form.* Brighton, UK: Harvester Press, 1982.

Braidotti, Rosa. *Patterns of Dissonance: A Study of Women in Contemporary Philosophy.* Trans. Elizabeth Guild. Cambridge: Polity Press, 1991.

Bristow, Joseph. *Empire Boys: Adventures in a Man's World.* London: Harper Collins Academic, 1991.

Brooks, Peter. *Reading for the Plot: Design and Intention in Narrative.* New York: Alfred A. Knopf, 1984.

Brontë, Charlotte. *Jane Eyre.* 1847. Oxford: Oxford University Press, 1980.

Brontë, Emily. *Wuthering Heights.* 1847. London: Pan, 1968.

Buckley, Jerome. *Season of Youth: The Bildungsroman from Dickens to*

Golding. Cambridge, MA: Harvard University Press, 1974.

Burdett, Carolyn. *Olive Schreiner and the Progress of Feminism: Evolution, Gender, Empire*. Houndmills, UK: Palgrave, 2001.

Butler, Alban. *The Lives of the Fathers, Martyrs and Other Principal Saints*. 1745. Vol. 2. London: Virtue and Company, 1961.

Caird, Mona. 'A Defence of the So-Called "Wild Women"'. *The Nineteenth Century* 31 (1892): 811-829.

Chamber's Encyclopaedia: A Dictionary of Universal Knowledge. London: William and Robert Chambers, 1890.

Chodorow, Nancy J. *Feminism and Psychoanalytic Theory*. New Haven, CT: Yale University Press, 1989.

Chopin, Kate. *The Awakening: and Other Stories*. 1899. Ed. and intro. Barbara H. Solomon. New York: New American Library, 1976.

Clark, Axel. *Henry Handel Richardson: Fiction in the Making*. Brookvale, NSW: Simon & Schuster, 1990.

———. *Finding Herself in Fiction: Henry Handel Richardson 1896-1910*. Melbourne: Australian Scholarly Publishing, 2001.

Cloutier, Pierre. 'The First Exile'. *Canadian Literature* 59 (1974): 30-37.

Collette. *Claudine at School*. 1900. Trans. Antonia White. Harmondsworth, UK: Penguin, 1963.

Connell, R.W. *Masculinities*. St Leonards, NSW: Allen & Unwin, 1995.

Corones, Eva Jarring. *The Portrayal of Women in the Fiction of Henry Handel Richardson*. Lund, Sweden: CWK Gleerup, 1983.

Crenshaw, Kimberlé. 'Mapping the Margins: Intersectionality, Identity Politics, and Violence against Women of Color'. *Stanford Law Review* 43.6 (1991): 1241-1299.

Cronwright-Schreiner, S.C. *The Life of Olive Schreiner*. London: Unwin, 1924.

____. Ed. and intro. *The Letters of Olive Schreiner 1876-1920*. London: T. Fisher Unwin, 1924.

Cross, G.W. '*Trooper Peter Halket*: A Reader's Notes'. *Eastern Province Magazine* (1897). Reprinted in *Olive Schreiner*. Ed. Cherry Clayton. Johannesburg: McGraw-Hill, 1983. 84-87.

Cruse, Amy. *The Victorians and Their Books*. London: George Allen & Unwin, 1935.

Cunningham, Gail. *The New Woman and the Victorian Novel*. London: Macmillan, 1978.

Daymond, Margaret. 'Olive Schreiner, Doris Lessing, Life and Fiction — "on a frontier of the Human Mind"'. *The Flawed Diamond: Essays on Olive Schreiner*. Ed. Itala Vivan. Sydney: Dangaroo, 1991. 171-188.

Dean, Misao. *A Different Point of View: Sara Jeannette Duncan*. Montreal: McGill-Queen's University Press, 1991.

____. 'Introduction'. *A Daughter of Today*. Sara Jeannette Duncan. 1894. Ottawa: The Tecumseh Press, 1988. iv-xxii.

____. 'The Paintbrush and the Scalpel: Sara Jeannette Duncan Representing India'. *Canadian Literature* 132 (1992): 82-93.

____ 'The Process of Definition: Nationality in Sara Jeannette Duncan's Early International Novels'. *Journal of Canadian Studies* 20.2 (1985): 132-149.

De Beauvoir, Simone. *The Second Sex*. 1949. Trans. and ed. H.M. Parshley. London: Jonathan Cape, 1972.

De Staël, Madam. *Corinne ou, L'Italie*. London: Colburn, 1809.

Delamont, Sara. 'The Contradictions in Ladies' Education'. *The Nineteenth-Century Woman: Her Cultural and Physical World*. Ed. Sara Delamont and Lorna Duffin. London: Croom Helm, 1978. 134-163.

De Lauretis, Teresa. *Technologies of Gender: Essays on Theory, Film and Fiction*. Bloomington, IN: Indiana University Press, 1987.

Dickens, Charles. *Great Expectations*. 1860-1861. London: Clarendon Press, 1993.

Donaldson, Laura E. *Decolonizing Feminisms: Race, Gender, and Empire-Building*. London: Routledge, 1993.

Dixon, Ella Hepworth. *The Story of a Modern Woman*. 1894. London: Merlin, 1990.

Dixon, Marion Hepworth. 'Marie Bashkirtseff: A Personal Reminiscence'. *Fortnightly Review* 47 (1890): 276-282.

Duffin, Lorna. 'The Conspicuous Consumptive: Woman as Invalid'. *The Nineteenth-Century Woman: Her Cultural and Physical World*. Ed. Sara Delamont and Lorna Duffin. London: Croom Helm, 1978.

Duncan, Sara Jeannette. *A Daughter of Today*. 1894. Ottawa: The Tecumseh Press, 1988.

____. *An American Girl in London*. London: Chatto & Windus, 1891.

____. *A Social Departure*. London: Chatto & Windus, 1890.

____. *Cousin Cinderella*. London: Methuen, 1908.

____. 'Grandmotherly Repose'. *The Globe* (12 November 1886). *Sara Jeannette Duncan: Selected Journalism*. Ed. Thomas Tausky. Ottawa: The Tecumseh Press, 1978. 32-34.

____. 'Review of *The Bostonians*'. *The Washington Post* (4 April 1886). *Sara Jeannette Duncan: Selected Journalism*. Ed. T.E. Tausky. Ottawa: The Tecumseh Press, 1978. 103-105.

Du Plessis, Rachel Blau. *Writing Beyond the Ending: Narrative Strategies of Twentieth-Century Women Writers.* Bloomington, IN: Indiana University Press, 1985.

Duranti, Riccardo. 'Voices Crying in the Wilderness: Lies and Prophecies'. *The Flawed Diamond: Essays on Olive Schreiner.* Ed. Itala Vivan. Sydney: Dangaroo, 1991. 74-83.

Egerton, George. 'Virgin Soil'. 1894. *Keynotes and Discords.* London: Virago, 1983. 145-162.

Ehrenreich, Barbara and Deidre English. *Complaints and Disorders: The Sexual Politics of Sickness.* New York: The Feminist Press, 1973.

Eliot, George. *Middlemarch: A Study of Provincial Life.* 1872. New York: Signet Classics, 1964.

———. *The Mill on the Floss.* 1860. Harmondsworth, UK: Penguin, 1987.

Elliott, William D. *Henry Handel Richardson: (Ethel Florence Lindesay Richardson).* Boston: Twayne Publishers, 1975.

Ellis, Havelock. 'Notes on Olive Schreiner'. 1884. Reprinted in *Olive Schreiner.* Ed. Cherry Clayton. Johannesburg: McGraw-Hill, 1983. 40-41.

———. *Studies in the Psychology of Sex.* 2nd ed. Vol. 3. Philadelphia: F.A. Davis, 1925.

Emerson, Ralph Waldo. *Complete Works of Ralph Waldo Emerson.* 2 Vols. London: Bell and Daldy, 1873.

———. *Nature: Emerson's Nature — Origin, Growth, Meaning.* 1836. Ed. Merton M. Sealts Jr. and Alfred R. Ferguson. New York: Dodd, Mead and Company, 1969.

———. *Representative Men: Seven Lectures.* Boston: James R. Osgood, 1877.

Esty, Jed. 'The Colonial Bildungsroman: *The Story of an African Farm* and the Ghost of Goethe'. *Victorian Studies* 49.3 (2007): 407-430.

Fehlbaum, Valerie. 'Marion Hepworth Dixon (1856-1936)'. *The Yellow Nineties Online*. Ed. Dennis Denisoff and Lorraine Janzen Kooistra. 2010. <http://1890s.ca/HTML.aspx?s=dixonM_bio.html>, accessed 21 April 2013.

Felski, Rita. *Beyond Feminist Aesthetics: Feminist Literature and Social Change*. Cambridge, MA: Harvard University Press, 1989.

Fiamengo, Janice. 'The death of the New Woman in Sara Jeanette Duncan's *A Daughter of To-Day*.' *Studies in Canadian Literature* 34.1 (2009): 5-21.

____. *The Woman's Page: Journalism and Rhetoric in Early Canada*. Toronto: University of Toronto Press, 2008.

Finot, Jean. *Problems of the Sexes*. Trans. Mary J. Stafford. New York: G.P. Puttman's Sons, 1913.

First, Ruth and Ann Scott. *Olive Schreiner: A Biography*. 1980. London: The Women's Press, 1989.

Fish, Stanley E. 'Interpreting the *Variorum*'. *Critical Inquiry* 2.3 (1976): 465-485.

Flax, Neil M. 'Goethe and Romanticism'. *Approaches to Teaching Goethe's 'Faust'*. Ed. Douglas J. McMillan. New York: MLA, 1987. 40-47.

Fowler, Marian. *Redney: A Life of Sara Jeannette Duncan*. Toronto: Anansi, 1983.

Franklin, Carol. 'The Female *Künstlerroman*: Richardson *versus* Björnson'. *Southerly* 43.4 (1983): 422-436.

____. 'The Resisting Writer: H.H. Richardson's Parody of Gogol'. *Journal of the Australasian Universities Language and Literature Association* 68 (1987): 233-250.

Frierson, William C. *The English Novel in Transition: 1885-1940*. New York: Cooper Square Publishers, 1965.

Gadpaille, Michelle. *'As She Should Be': Codes of Conduct in Early Canadian Women's Writing*. Heidelberg: Universitätsverlag Winter GmbH Heidelberg, 2010.

———. 'Aesthetic Debate in the *Fin-de-Siècle* Novel: A Canadian Perspective'. *Dunjas Festschrift*. University of Maribor. 2008. <http://oddelki.ff.uni-mb.si/filozofija/files/Festschrift/Dunjas_festschrift/gadpaille.pdf>, accessed 21 April 2013.

Gilbert, Sandra M. and Susan Gubar. *No Man's Land: the Place of the Woman Writer in the Twentieth Century. 1: The War of the Words*. New Haven, CT: Yale University Press, 1988.

Giles, Fiona. 'Finding a Shiftingness: Situating the Nineteenth-Century Anglo-Australian Female Subject'. *New Literatures Review* 18 (1989): 10-19.

Gissing, George. *New Grub Street*. 1891. London: Penguin, 1985.

Gladstone, W.E. '*Journal de Marie Bashkirtseff*'. *The Nineteenth Century* (October 1889): 602-607.

Goethe, Johann Wolfgang von. *Wilhelm Meister's Apprenticeship and Travels*. Trans. William Carlyle. 3 Vols. 1824. London: Chapman and Hall, 1874.

Goodman, Charlotte. 'The Lost Brother, The Twin: Women Novelists and The Male-Female Double *Bildungsroman*'. *Novel* 17.1 (1983): 28-43.

Gordon, Marcia Macke. *Absence and Presence in* Wuthering Heights *and* The Story of an African Farm: *Charting the Feminine in Language*. PhD Thesis. Brown University, 1988. Ann Arbor, MI: UMI, 1988.

Grand, Sarah. 'The New Aspect of the Woman Question'. *The North*

American Review 158.448 (1894): 270-276.

Green, Dorothy. *Henry Handel Richardson and Her Fiction.* Sydney: Allen & Unwin, 1986.

Greer, Germaine. 'The Getting of Wisdom'. *Scripsi* 1.3 & 4 (1982): 4-12.

Grenville, Kate. '*From The Getting of Wisdom* to *Illywhacker*: the library and our literary heritage'. *The Australian Library Journal* 38.1 (1989): 55-69.

Gubar, Susan. 'The Birth of the Artist as Heroine: (Re)production, the *Künstlerroman* Tradition, and the Fiction of Katherine Mansfield'. *The Representation of Women in Fiction.* Ed. and intro. Carolyn G. Heilbrun and Margaret R. Higonnet. Baltimore: The John Hopkins University Press, 1983. 19-59.

Haggard, H. Rider. 'About Fiction'. *Contemporary Review.* 51 (1887): 172-180.

____. *King Solomon's Mines.* 1885. London: Penguin, 1994.

Halperin, John. *Egoism and Self-Discovery in the Victorian Novel: Studies in the Ordeal of Knowledge in the Nineteenth Century.* New York: Burt Franklin, 1974.

Hannigan, D.F. 'The Artificiality of English Novels'. *The Westminster Review* 133 (1890): 254-264.

Hardy, Thomas. *Tess of the d'Urbervilles.* 1891. Oxford: Oxford University Press, 1983.

Hardy, Thomas. *The Woodlanders.* 1887. Harmondsworth, UK: Penguin, 1986.

Haynes, R.D. 'Elements of Romanticism in *The Story of an African Farm*'. *English Literature in Transition* 24.2 (1981): 59-79.

Heilmann, Ann. *New Woman Strategies: Sarah Grand, Olive Schreiner, Mona*

Caird. Manchester: Manchester University Press, 2004.

Hemans, Felicia. *Poetical Works.* London: Warne, 1897.

Hirsch, Marianne. 'Spiritual *Bildung*: The Beautiful Soul as Paradigm'. *The Voyage In: Fictions of Female Development.* Ed. Elizabeth Abel, Marianne Hirsch and Elizabeth Langland. Hanover, NH: University Press of New England, 1983. 23-48.

____. *The Mother/Daughter Plot: Narrative, Psychoanalysis, Feminism.* Bloomington, IN: Indiana University Press, 1989.

Horn, Pamela. 'English Elementary Education and the Growth of the Imperial Idea: 1880-1914'. *'Benefits Bestowed'? Education and British Imperialism.* Ed. J.A. Mangan. Manchester: Manchester University Press, 1988. 39-55.

Husband, Thomas F. 'The Story of an African Farm'. *The Westminster Review* 141 (1894): 631-642.

Ibsen, Henrik. *Plays: A League of Youth; A Doll's House; The Lady From the Sea.* Trans. Peter Watts. Harmondsworth, UK: Penguin, 1965.

James, Henry. '*Nana*'. 1880. *Documents of Modern Literary Realism.* Ed. George J. Becker. Princeton: Princeton University Press, 1963. 236-243.

____. *Portrait of a Lady.* 1881. London: The Bodley Head, 1968.

____. 'To Mrs. Everard Cotes'. 1900. *Henry James Letters.* Ed. Leon Edel. Vol. 4: 1895-1916. Cambridge, MA: The Belknap Press of Harvard University Press, 1984. 131-132.

Jones, Dorothy. 'The Post-Colonial Belly Laugh: Appetite and its Suppression'. *Social Semiotics* 2.2 (1992): 21-39.

Konz, Louly Peacock. *Marie Bashkirtseff's Life in Self-Portraits (1858-1884).* Lewiston, NY: Edwin Mellen Press, 2005.

Krige, Uys. 'Olive Schreiner: A New Assessment'. *The Cape Argus* (19 March 1955). Reprinted in *Olive Schreiner*. Ed. Cherry Clayton. Johannesburg: McGraw-Hill, 1983. 76-77.

Labovitz, Esther Kleinbord. *The Myth of the Heroine: The Female Bildungsroman in the Twentieth Century*. New York: Peter Lang, 1986.

Lake, Marilyn. 'The Politics of Respectability: Identifying the Masculinist Context'. *Australian Historical Studies* 22.6 (1986): 116-131.

Ledger, Sally. *The New Woman: Fiction and Feminism at the fin de siècle*. Manchester: Manchester University Press, 1997.

Leighton, Angela. *Victorian Women Poets: Writing Against the Heart*. London: Harvester Wheatsheaf, 1992.

Lenta, Margaret. 'Independence as the Creative Choice in Two South African Fictions'. *Ariel* 17.1 (1986): 35-52.

____. 'Racism, Sexism, and Olive Schreiner's Fiction'. *Theoria* 70 (1987): 15-30.

Lerner, Laurence. 'Olive Schreiner and the Feminists'. *Olive Schreiner*. Ed. Cherry Clayton. Johannesburg: McGraw-Hill, 1983. 181-191.

Levinas, Emmanuel. 'Time and the Other'. *The Levinas Reader*. Ed. Sean Hand. Oxford: Basil Blackwell, 1989. 38-58.

Longfellow, Henry Wadsworth. *Hyperion: A Romance*. London: David Bogue, 1853.

Lytton, Constance, and Jane Warton. *Prisons and Prisoners: Some Personal Experiences*. London: William Heinemann, 1914.

MacColl. '"An Agnostic Novel": Review of *The Story of an African Farm*'. *The Spectator* (13 August 1887). Reprinted in *Olive Schreiner*. Ed.

Cherry Clayton. Johannesburg: McGraw-Hill, 1983. 72-73.

Magarey, Susan, Sue Rowley, Susan Sheridan. *Debutante Nation: Feminism Contests the 1890s*. St. Leonards, NSW: Allen & Unwin, 1993.

MacLulich, T.D. *Between Europe and America: The Canadian Tradition in Fiction*. Toronto: ECW Press, 1988.

McClure, John A. *Kipling and Conrad: The Colonial Fiction*. Cambridge, MA: Harvard University Press, 1981.

McFarlane, Brian. '*The Getting of Wisdom*: Not 'Merry' at All'. *Australian Literary Studies* 8.1 (1977): 51-63.

McLeod, Karen. *Henry Handel Richardson: A Critical Study*. Cambridge: Cambridge University Press, 1985.

Masefield, John. 'A Book of the Day: The Best Novel'. *Daily News* 11 Sep. 1908: n.p. *Richardson Papers* MSS 133 Box 21.

Marks, Elaine. 'Lesbian Intertextuality'. *Homosexualities and French Literature: Cultural Contexts/Critical Texts*. Ed. and intro. George Stambolin and Elaine Marks. Ithaca, NY: Cornell University Press, 1979. 353-377.

Marquard, Jean. 'Hagar's Child'. *Standpunte* 121 (1976): 35-47.

Maudsley, Henry. 'Sex in Mind and in Education'. *Fortnightly Review* 15 (1874): 466-483.

Memmi, Albert. *The Colonizer and the Colonized*. 1956. Trans. Howard Greenfield. London: Souvenir Press, 1974.

Miller, Nancy K. *Subject to Change: Reading Feminist Writing*. New York: Columbia University Press, 1988.

Mills, Sara. *Discourses of Difference: An Analysis of Women's Travel Writing and Colonialism*. 1991. London: Routledge, 1993.

Mitchell, Adrian. 'Fiction'. *The Oxford History of Australian Literature*.

Ed. Leonie Kramer. Melbourne: Oxford University Press, 1981. 27-172.

'Modern English Novels'. *The Westminster Review* 134 (1890): 143-158.

Monsman, Gerald. 'Olive Schreiner: Literature and the Politics of Power'. *Texas Studies in Literature and Language* 30.4 (1988): 583-610.

____. 'Patterns of Narration and Characterization in Schreiner's *The Story of an African Farm*'. *English Literature in Transition 1880-1920* 28.3 (1985): 253-270.

____. 'The Idea of "Story" in Olive Schreiner's *Story of an African Farm*'. *Texas Studies in Literature and Language* 27.3 (1985): 249-269.

'More Fiction'. *The Nation* (21 June 1894): 472-473.

Moreton-Robinson, Aileen. *Talkin' Up to the White Woman: Indigenous Women and Feminism.* St. Lucia, Qld: University of Queensland Press, 2000.

Moretti, Franco. *The Way of the World: The Bildungsroman in European Culture.* London: Verso, 1987.

Morris, James [Jan]. *Pax Brittanica: The Climax of an Empire.* 1968. Harmondsworth, UK: Penguin, 1981.

Mukherjee, Arun P. 'Whose Post-Colonialism and Whose Post-Modernism?' *World Literature Written in English* 30.2 (1990): 1-9.

'New Novels'. *The Athenaeum* (16 June 1894): 770.

Oboe, Annalisa. 'Contrasts and Harmony: The Antithetical Structure in *The Story of an African Farm*'. *The Flawed Diamond: Essays on Olive Schreiner.* Ed. Itala Vivan. Sydney: Dangaroo, 1991. 84-94.

O'Brien, Desmond B. [Review of *The Getting of Wisdom*]. *Truth* (23 November 1910): n.p. *Richardson Papers.* MSS 133 Box 21.

O'Loughlin, Iris. *Differing From the Common Mould.* MA Thesis. Department of Literature, La Trobe University, 1985.

Ouida [Maria Louise Ramé]. 'The New Woman'. *The North American Review* 158.450 (1894): 610-619.

Palmer, Nettie. *Henry Handel Richardson: A Study.* Sydney: Angus & Robertson, 1950.

Parker, Rozsika and Griselda Pollock. 'Introduction'. *The Journal of Marie Bashkirtseff.* Marie Bashkirtseff. Trans. Mathilde Blind. 1890. London: Virago, 1985.

Pater, Walter. *Marius the Epicurean.* 1885. London: Macmillan, 1902.

'Physical Training'. *Englishwoman's Review* (1874): 161-168.

Poe, Edgar Allan. *Essays and Reviews.* New York: The Library of America, 1984.

Pratt, Annis, with Barbara White, Andrea Loewenstein, and Mary Wyer. *Archetypal Patterns in Women's Fiction.* Brighton, UK: The Harvester Press, 1982.

Pratt, Catherine. 'Fictions of Development: Henry Handel Richardson's The Getting of Wisdom'. *Antipodes* 9.1 (1995): 3-9.

____. *Resisting Fiction: the Novels of Henry Handel Richardson.* St Lucia, Qld: University of Queensland Press, 1999.

Pratt, Mary Louise. 'Scratches on the face of the country; or what Mr Barrows saw in the land of the Bushmen'. *Critical Inquiry* 12.1 (1985): 119-143.

Raiskin, Judith. *Unruly Subjects: Nationhood, Home and Colonial Consciousness in Olive Schreiner and Jean Rhys.* PhD Thesis. Stanford University, 1989. Ann Arbor, MI: UMI, 1991.

'Review of *A Daughter of Today,* Sara Jeannette Duncan'. *The Athenaeum*

(2 June 1894): 705.

[Review of *The Getting of Wisdom*]. *The Athenaeum* (24 November 1910): n.p. *Richardson Papers.* MSS 133 Box 21.

[Review of *The Getting of Wisdom*]. *The English Review* (November 1910): n.p. *Richardson Papers.* MSS 133 Box 21.

[Review of *The Getting of Wisdom*]. *The Lady* (8 December 1910): n.p. *Richardson Papers.* MSS 133 Box 21.

[Review of *The Getting of Wisdom*]. *Votes for Women* (18 November 1910): n.p. *Richardson Papers.* MSS 133 Box 21.

[Review of *The Getting of Wisdom*]. *Yorkshire Daily Observer* (11 November 1910): n.p. *Richardson Papers.* MSS 133 Box 21.

[Review of *The Story of an African Farm*]. *The Young Man*, n.d. Reprinted in *Olive Schreiner*. Ed. Cherry Clayton. Johannesburg: McGraw-Hill, 1983. 70-71.

'Reviews'. *The Englishwoman's Review of Social and Industrial Questions.* 124 (1883): 362-364.

'Three Controversial Novels'. *Church Quarterly Review* 29 (1890). Reprinted in *Olive Schreiner*. Ed. Cherry Clayton. Johannesburg: McGraw-Hill, 1983. 74.

Ready, Kathryn. 'Sara Jeannette Duncan's *A Daughter of Today*: Nineteenth-Century Canadian Literary Feminism and the *Fin-de-siècle* Magic-Picture Story.' *Canadian Literature* 173 (2002): 95-112.

Rich, Adrienne. 'Compulsory Heterosexuality and Lesbian Existence'. *Signs* 5.4 (1980): 631-660.

Richardson, Alan and John Bowden. *A New Dictionary of Christian Theology.* London: SCM Press, 1983.

Richardson, Angelique and Chris Willis. Eds. *The New Woman in Fiction and in Fact:* Fin-de-Siècle *Feminisms*. Houndmills, UK: Palgrave, 2001.

Richardson, Henry Handel. *Maurice Guest*. London: Heinemann, 1908.

____. *Myself When Young*. 1948. Melbourne: William Heinemann, 1964.

____. 'Some Notes on My Books'. *Southerly* 23.1 (1963): 8-19.

____. *The Fortunes of Richard Mahony*. 1930. Melbourne: Heinemann, 1946.

____. *The Getting of Wisdom*. 1910. Port Melbourne: Mandarin, 1990.

Richardson, Joanna. 'Romantic Bohemia'. *History Today* 6.7 (1969): 443-467.

Rive, Richard. Ed. *Olive Schreiner Letters*. Vol.1: 1871-1899. Oxford: Oxford University Press, 1988.

Robertson, J.G. 'The Art of Henry Handel Richardson: An Essay in Appreciative Criticism'. *Myself When Young*. Henry Handel Richardson. 1948. Melbourne: William Heinemann, 1964. 153-210.

Roe, Jill. Ed. *My Congenials: Miles Franklin and Friends in Letters*. Vol. I: 1879-1938. Pymble, NSW: Angus & Robertson, 1993.

Roncoroni, O.M. '1895-1903'. *Myself When Young*. Henry Handel Richardson. 1948. Melbourne: William Heinemann, 1964. 136-150.

Rosowski, Susan J. 'The Novel of Awakening'. *The Voyage In: Fictions of Female Development*. Ed. Elizabeth Abel, Marianne Hirsch, and Elizabeth Langland. Hanover, NH: University Press of New England, 1983. 49-68.

Said, Edward W. *Culture and Imperialism*. 1993. London: Vintage, 1994.

____. *Orientalism*. New York: Vintage Books, 1979.

Schaffer, Talia. '"Nothing But Foolscap and Ink": Inventing the

New Woman'. *The New Woman in Fiction and in Fact: Fin-de-Siècle Feminisms.* Ed. Angelique Richardson and Chris Willis. Houndmills, UK: Palgrave, 2001. 39-52.

Schapple, Deborah. 'Artful Tales of Origination in Olive Schreiner's *The Story of an African Farm*'. *Nineteenth-Century Literature* 59.1 (2004): 53-77.

[Sheridan] Higgins, Susan. 'Olive Schreiner: A Free Human Being?' *Refractory Girl* 6 (1974): 18-29.

Schreiner, Olive. *Dreams*. 1890. London: T. Fisher Unwin, 1892.

____. 'The Woman Question'. 1899. *An Olive Schreiner Reader: Writings on Women and South Africa.* Ed. and intro. Carol Barash. London: Pandora, 1987. 63-100.

____. 'The Buddhist Priest's Wife'. 1892. *An Olive Schreiner Reader: Writings on Women and South Africa.* Ed. and intro. Carol Barash. London: Pandora, 1987. 109-121.

____. *The Story of an African Farm*. 1883. London: Penguin, 1986.

____. *Thoughts on South Africa.* London: T. Fisher Unwin, 1923.

Showalter, Elaine. *A Literature of Their Own: British Novelists from Brontë to Lessing.* Princeton: Princeton University Press, 1977.

Slemon, Stephen. 'Unsettling the Empire: Resistance Theory for the Second World'. *World Literature Written in English* 30.2 (1990): 30-41.

Snitow, Ann Barr. 'Mass Market Romance: Pornography for Women is Different'. *Desire: The Politics of Sexuality.* Ed. Ann Snitow, Christine Stansell and Sharon Thompson. London: Virago, 1983. 245-263.

Spencer, Herbert. *Education: Intellectual, Moral and Physical.* 1861.

London: Williams, 1910.

Spivak, Gayatri Chakravorty. 'Three Women's Texts and a Critique of Imperialism'. *Critical Inquiry* 12 (1985): 243-261.

[Stead, W.T.]. '*The Journal of Marie Bashkirtseff*: The Story of a Girl's Life'. *The Review of Reviews* 1 (1890): 539-549.

____. 'The Novel of the Modern Woman'. *The Review of Reviews* 10 (1894): 64-74.

Swales, Martin. *The German* Bildungsroman *from Wieland to Hesse*. Princeton: Princeton University Press, 1978.

Summers, Anne. 'The Self Denied'. *Refractory Girl* 2 (1973): 4-11.

____. *Damned Whores and God's Police: The Colonization of Women in Australia*. Ringwood, Vic.: Penguin, 1975.

Sussman. Herbert L. 'Novel'. *Victorian Britain: An Encyclopedia*. 1988. Ed. Sally Mitchell. London: Routledge, 2012.

Tausky, Thomas. *Sara Jeannette Duncan: Novelist of Empire*. Port Credit, ON: P.D. Meany, 1980.

____. 'The Citizenship of Elfrida Bell'. *Canadian Literature* 63 (1975): 127-128.

The Holy Bible. King James Version. London: Oxford University Press, n.d.

Theobald, Marjorie R. 'The PLC Mystique: Reflections on the Reform of Female Education in Nineteenth-Century Australia'. *Australian Historical Studies* 23.92 (1989): 241-259.

Toth, Emily. 'The Independent Woman and "Free' Love". *The Massachusetts Review* 16.4 (1975): 647-664.

Treagus, Mandy. 'The Body of the Imperial Mother: Women, Exercise and the Future of "the Race" in Britain, 1870-1914'. *Kunapipi* 23.1

(2001): 138-150.

[Treagus] Dyson, Mandy. '"near the heart of the imperial ethic": Imperialism, Patriarchy and the Boarding School in *The Getting of Wisdom*'. *Crossing Lines: Formations in Australian Culture*. Ed. Caroline Guerin, Philip Butterss and Amanda Nettelbeck. Adelaide: ASAL, 1996. 144-148.

———. 'The Feminist as Romantic: Schreiner's Lyndall and the Romance Plot'. *Australasian Victorian Studies Journal* 3.1 (1998): 90-98.

Visel, Robyn. '"We bear the world and we make it": Bessie Head and Olive Schreiner'. *Research in African Literatures* 21.3 (1990): 115-124.

———. *White Eve in the Petrified Garden*. PhD Thesis. University of British Columbia, 1988. Ottawa: National Library of Canada, 1989.

Vivan, Itala. 'The Treatment of Blacks in *The Story of an African Farm*'. *The Flawed Diamond: Essays on Olive Schreiner*. Ed. Itala Vivan. Sydney: Dangaroo, 1991. 95-106.

———. Ed. *The Flawed Diamond: Essays on Olive Schreiner*. Sydney: Dangaroo, 1991.

Walpole, Hugh. '"The Permanent Elements in Olive Schreiner's Fiction": Review of *From Man to Man*'. *The New York Herald Tribune* (1 May 1927). Reprinted in *Olive Schreiner*. Ed. Cherry Clayton. Johannesburg: McGraw-Hill, 1983. 91-93.

Ward, Russel. *The Australian Legend*. Melbourne: Oxford University Press, 1958.

Ware, Vron. *Beyond the Pale: White Women, Racism and History*. London and New York: Verso, 1992.

Warner, Susan. *The Wide, Wide World*. 1850. New York: The Feminist Press, 1987.

Waugh, Patricia. *Feminine Fictions: Revisiting the Postmodern.* London: Routledge, 1989.

Weininger, Otto. *Sex and Character.* Authorised translation from the 6th German edition. London: William Heinemann, 1906.

West, Rebecca. 'So Simple'. *The Freewoman* (3 October 1912): 589-590.

White, Allon. *The Uses of Obscurity: The Fiction of Early Modernism.* London: Routledge & Kegan Paul, 1981.

Wilde, Oscar. *The Picture of Dorian Gray.* 1891. London: Penguin, 1985.

Wilkinson, Jane. 'Nature and Art in Olive Schreiner's *The Story of an African Farm*'. *The Flawed Diamond: Essays on Olive Schreiner.* Ed. Itala Vivan. Sydney: Dangaroo, 1991. 107-120.

Wollstonecraft, Mary. *A Vindication of the Rights of Men. The Works of Mary Wollstonecraft.* a. Ed. Janet Todd and Marilyn Butler. Vol. 5. London: William Pickering, 1989.

____. *A Vindication of the Rights of Women. The Works of Mary Wollstonecraft.* b. Ed. Janet Todd and Marilyn Butler. Vol. 5. London: William Pickering, 1989.

Wood, Joanna. *Judith Moore; or, Fashioning a Pipe.* New York: J. Selwin Tait & Sons, 1898.

Woolf, Virginia. 'Olive Schreiner'. *The New Republic* 42.537 (1925): 103.

Zola, Emile. 'The Experimental Novel'. 1880. *Documents of Modern Literary Realism.* Ed. George J. Becker. Princeton: Princeton University Press, 1963. 162-196.

This book is available as a free fully-searchable ebook from
www.adelaide.edu.au/press